MISSION TO SHANGHAI

THE LIFE OF MEDICAL SERVICE OF DR. JOSIAH C. McCRACKEN

by

Helen McCracken Fulcher

Tiffin Press
New London, New Hampshire

Mission to Shanghai

The Life of Medical Service of
Josiah Calvin McCracken

Cover photograph: Dr. Josiah McCracken with two children in the spring of 1941 when he was also serving as leader of the American Hospital for Refugees in Shanghai. The hospital received substantial support from the American Red Cross; the bags of wheat were used to make matching outfits for the children. The colors on the cover are those of the University of Pennsylvania, his alma mater.

Published by:

Tiffin Press
Post Office Box 1786
New London, NH 03257 U. S. A.
See last page of book for ordering information. SAN: 298-5675

Copyright © 1995 by Helen McCracken Fulcher
First Printing June, 1995

Library of Congress Catalog Card Number 95-60506

1. Publishers Cataloguing in Publication Data
2. Fulcher, Helen McCracken
3. Mission to Shanghai: The Life of Medical Service of Josiah C. McCracken
4. 1, Medical history, China. 2, Biography (J. C. McCracken). 3, China, Shanghai
    I. Title

ISBN 0-9646018-1-8 (hardcover)

Printed in the United States of America on paper with 50% recycled fiber by McNaughton & Gunn, Inc. Saline, Michigan.

DEDICATION

Prepared in loving memory of
her parents
and for
her brothers and sisters
and their children

With grateful appreciation to the
Christian Association
of the
University of Pennsylvania
and its many supporters

TABLE OF CONTENTS

Dr. Josiah C. McCracken (1946)

MEMORIAL

PHILADELPHIA--Dr. Josiah Calvin McCracken, All-America football star, Olympic track champion and a medical missionary in China for 30 years, died yesterday at Rest Haven, Chestnut Hill nursing home. He was 87.

Dr. McCracken played football for the University of Pennsylvania, where he also was captain of the track team. He set a hammer-throw record at Paris in 1900 with the U.S. Olympic team.

He was graduated from the University of Pennsylvania Medical School in 1901 and served his internship at Pennsylvania Hospital.

Medical Missionary

Dr. McCracken married Miss Helen Newpher, of [Cleveland], in 1906. They immediately departed for the Orient as representatives of the Christian Association of the University of Pennsylvania.

The physician helped to establish the Medical School of St. John's University in Shanghai. He was dean of the school from 1914 until 1942, training hundreds of Chinese doctors.

He and his wife were taken into custody by the Japanese in 1942 and repatriated with members of their family aboard the exchange ship Gripsholm. They lived here at 920 Clinton St., Mrs. McCracken died in 1944.

Honored by School

Dr. McCracken returned to Shanghai in 1946 to try to restore normal operations at St. John's Medical School. He served as dean and professor of surgery there until the Communists took over in 1948.

He received an honorary Phi Beta Kappa from his alma mater in 1921. Five years later Penn gave him an honorary doctor of science degree, and in 1938 the Alumni Award of Merit.

Dr. McCracken was named the university's Distinguished Senior Alumnus in 1961.

The New York Times
February 16, 1962
Copyright © 1962 by The New York Times Company. Reprinted by permission.

PREFACE

This book is a chronicle of the life of service of my father, and through him of our family, what became known as the McCrackens of Shanghai. It tells the story of his service in the development of medicine in China as well as raising a family that became dispersed from China to the eastern United States. The story is told largely through family letters and annual reports that he prepared for the Christian Association of the University of Pennsylvania, which sponsored his mission to China for more than forty years.

This family story was prepared first in 1974. In the tradition of the many letters, it was prepared on a typewriter, with an original and several carbon copies to pass around to the family. As such it was difficult to copy and a strain for aging eyes. The task of providing an edition for wider distribution was taken on by my younger sister Martha, whose dream it has been to publish this story, and by her son Michael MacCracken and his wife Sandy. As a first step, Sandy retyped the fading text onto a computer. As a second step, Michael went through the text, better defining chapters, and correcting and reorganizing some of the early family history for which I only had preliminary information. Janet Grevsted helped in improving the organization of the text. Sandy and Michael then further arranged the text for publication.

Much of the story is told by quotes from the letters, extended extracts of which are set off as indented; in that most quotes are extracts from longer materials, indication of omitted text is given only when there are internal deletions. Idioms and the grammar of the letters remain largely as they were, except for minor corrections to improve readability. Chinese city names have also been left as they were at that time to be consistent with the letters as quoted; thus Guangzhou remains Canton and Beijing remains Peking or Peiping; because English transliterations changed over time, there are sometimes varying spellings in the text. Ethnic references also remain as written, referring generally to the situations created by individuals; my parents were loving of all they met.

In recognition of the wider audience of this version, my use of "Mother" and "Daddy" has been changed to "Helen" and "Joe" except in quoting their letters, although this does make some of the stories seem a bit less vivid and personal to me. Where helpful for clarity, I have distinguished my brother Joe and me from my parents names by insertion of "Jr." Photographs have also been collected and added to help better connect the story and its characters to their time. A list of graduates has been compiled based on records from my father; it is included as an appendix.

Even though more than four decades separate us from the conclusion of the period in China, the multiple threads of this chronicle stretch to the present. The role of foreign doctors in advancing medicine in China, the story of a family maintaining connections across the world, the challenges faced and overcome by my sister Mary in becoming a medical doctor in a man's world, and more.

For allowing the retelling of this history, I am thus very grateful to my family, to Martha, to Michael and Sandy MacCracken, and to the many family friends who contributed materials to make the telling of this family portrait possible. To publish this book, they formed Tiffin Press and volunteered many hours in final preparation of the text, finding photographs, and checking on details. While we have tried to check carefully on the accuracy of names and spelling, this has been difficult and we apologize for any errors in the reporting.

The family is grateful for the assistance in gathering materials and photographs provided by Kaiyi Chen, archivist at the University of Pennsylvania Archives and Record Center, and Martha Lund Smalley, curator of the Day Missions Library and Special Collections at the Divinity School Library of Yale University (see Notes on page 275). Both of these locations have archives of speeches and annual letters quoted in this book. The family is especially grateful also to the Christian Association of the University of Pennsylvania for their long-term interest in medicine in China. Encouragement for and assistance in preparation of the materials in this book have been provided by Cham-ber Huang and Jen-Hung Chao, both graduates of the Medical School at St. John's, to whom the family expresses its gratitude. Quotations from *The New York Times, The Plain Dealer* (of Cleveland), *The Philadelphia (Morning) Inquirer*, the *Old Penn Weekly Review*, the *Pennsylvania Gazette* (alumni magazine of the University of Pennsylvania), the *Blue Cross Quarterly*, and *Quest for Gold* by Bill Mallon and Ian Buchanan are gratefully acknowledged; quotations from other publications no longer being published are also recognized.

Helen McCracken Fulcher
January, 1995

Note: Helen McCracken Fulcher died February 3, 1995 at the age of 87, just as the final stage of preparing this manuscript for publication was being completed.

Helen McCracken Fulcher (May 1991)

Isaac Lawrence McCracken and Ellen Watson Stewart McCracken,
parents of Josiah Calvin McCracken

CHAPTER ONE

GROWING UP IN KANSAS
1874-1896

Josiah Calvin McCracken, who would ultimately help in the development of medicine in China, was born March 30, 1874 halfway around the world in Lincoln County, Tennessee. He was the seventh child and fifth son of Isaac Lawrence McCracken and Ellen Watson Stewart. In addition, medicine was not a tradition in his family; their background was instead educational and religious. Joe's father was the son of Samuel Wilson McCracken, a well-educated professor and minister. Samuel was in turn the son of John McCracken, who was born in north central Pennsylvania in 1776[1] and became a farmer near Butler County, Ohio. Out of this middle-American background, however, came an Olympic athlete who would go on to serve and lead a medical school in China.

Joe's trip toward China started in 1882 when Kansas was opened up for homesteading. The McCrackens, with little Daisy about 4, Joe 8, Gilbert 11, Lee 13, Charley 16, Myrta 19, with oldest sister Alla and her husband and the Ramsey family into which she had married, drove their wagons from Tennessee to the middle of Kansas. Joe was just old enough to remember his legs dangling off the wagon and the beautiful horses he saw when they stopped at Memphis to cross the Mississippi.

After only two years, the family moved again, this time to Ness County, Kansas where Isaac claimed a mile square of land: one pre-emption quarter, one timber quarter where he had to plant out at least ten acres to trees, a school quarter, and a deeded quarter. The family lived in a sod house. They raised cattle and Joe helped herd them. He rode two miles horseback to go to school and it was here that he went through the fifth grade. There was one teacher for every subject; some years there were only three months of school, sometimes four or five. The teacher was not much older than the students and played all the games with them, including kissing games, popular in those days.

Seventy-five years later Joe would recall for his children:

> If I can remember correctly I joined the United Presbyterian church when I was about 8 years old in a church built of sod in the corner of a lot donated by father. Your grandmother wrote relatives and friends in Ohio asking for donations to help put down a floor in the church. That was a pretty long time ago but I am glad that I got an early start. I hope and pray that my grandchildren will wish to do the same under much better circumstances.

1

In later years Joe also remembered driving across the prairies to the "literary society," one of the few entertainments they had at that time, and racing the horses home. In the winter they used sleds, in the summer carriages. He also remembered taking Sunday afternoon walks with a girlfriend and picking up "buffalo chips" for fuel. The first money he ever earned was carrying sorghum to the crushers, at fifty cents a day.

In January of 1891 Joe went to Sterling, to attend Cooper College. Based on excerpts from old records provided by Sterling College, Cooper College seems to have started about 1887. In these times Cooper College also served as a preparatory school, because many of the western counties in Kansas did not have high schools. When he arrived in Sterling he had wound around his neck yards of knitted comforter and he and a friend, Fred Weed, carried his trunk between them to the boarding house to save the cost, twenty-five cents, of having it delivered. Joe's father had given him a colt the year before, which he had trained and also taught to lie down and roll over; it was the sale of this horse which gave young Joe the money to attend Cooper.

College expenses then bear little relation to those of today: Joe paid fifty cents a week for his room, and a dollar a week to the boarding house owner for his food. The first six months his expenses were $107. He was constantly engaged in efforts to raise funds for his education. One summer he sold photograph albums throughout the surrounding country. In the summers of 1895 and 1896 he was "advance agent" for the Cooper College Quartette, and rode his bicycle through Kansas and Colorado setting up bookings for the musicians in small towns.

Sterling College was an outgrowth of Cooper College; Joe was there as the transformation took place. The first "Commencement Week" for Sterling College became a reality with the senior class of 1891-92. Joe is listed as participating with four other students in the first Annual Field Day, June 4, 1892.

In the summer of 1893, the family moved to Sterling. Joe continued at Cooper while Gib, the next older brother, went to Michigan to a telegraph school. In these early years, Joe wanted to be a teacher. After two years Joe received a certificate to teach school and in 1893, 1894, and 1895 he taught at Triumph, a country school nearby. He continued to attend Cooper, and by 1895 he was hired to teach at the Stone School; its year was eight months of schooling. He had to teach everything from "A B C to Algebra."

Joe's versatility in sports was early evident and the developing athletic program at the college provided many opportunities for wide participation: the 16-pound shot put, the 16-pound hammer throw, 100 yard dash, hurdles, and other events. In the spring of 1893, Joe and two others were sent to Lawrence to compete in the State Intercollegiate Track Meet at Kansas University. They came in second, scoring 34 points against 63 made by Kansas University's team of twenty contestants. By 1896, he held the state record for the hammer throw of 92 feet, 8 inches. Early that year he met Wylie Woodroof, an athlete from Penn, and, when shown how to make an extra turn in throwing the hammer, Joe threw it 125 feet in practice.

In 1893 he and one or two friends went to the World's Fair in Chicago. Here he saw a football game, played at night between the New York and Chicago Athletic teams. Having seen one game, Joe now became the coach at Cooper, and the next fall their team went to Kansas University and played the second team there. Both track and football would soon open new doors for him.

Joe McCracken's character was shaped by these "pioneering experiences" of the McCracken family. From their homesteading of the West, he learned of the physical labor involved in maintaining a family, the financial lessons relative to earning and managing money for his education, and the opportunities provided by a small Christian college. But most important was the religious influence of his family and the church. He had developed a simple deep faith in Jesus Christ and the power of God in one's life, which would soon respond to the challenges of the Young Men's Christian Association (Y.M.C.A.) and the Student Volunteer Movement, leading to his career of service in promoting Christian medical education in China.

Joe and brother Gib McCracken (about 1877)

*Joe McCracken in a family picture from about 1892.
Sitting(left to right) are Ellen Stewart McCracken (Joe's mother), Charles,
Isaac Lawrence McCracken (Joe's father), and Lee; standing (left to right) are
Alla, Joe, Gib, and Daisy. Brother Frank had died as a child; sister Myrta is not pictured.*

CHAPTER TWO

TRAINING AT THE
UNIVERSITY OF PENNSYLVANIA
1896-1901

Joe was invited to attend the University of Pennsylvania because of his athletic abilities. This was first suggested by George F. W. Benn, a friend of his who was taking postgraduate work at Penn. Then late in the summer of 1896, Wylie Woodroof (whose advice had improved his hammer throw) and his brother, who were both guards on the University of Pennsylvania football team, approached Joe about going to the University to enter in the fall of 1896.

So, at the age of twenty-two, Joe stepped off the train in Philadelphia, put his trunk on his back and, with five dollars, started his long affiliation with the University of Pennsylvania. Not knowing just what course he wished to pursue, he initially enrolled in the Wharton School of Finance. He switched to Medical School the next year.

Joe excelled in all he did. His leadership is reflected in his record as president of his class for four years, as president of the Houston Club, as president of the Y.M.C.A. for three years, and by "his universal popularity with his professors and the governing body of the University." His friend Dr. John Gardiner, in a letter for inclusion in the celebration of Joe's 65th birthday booklet, described his character:

> He has changed very little since his college days. He has that frank, generous, western approach supplemented by a gentleness of appreciation that makes him such a lovable character. Joe can always see the kindly, amusing side of any serious problem without diminishing its importance. He has the gift of drawing people to him which enables him to wield a very great influence. Such are my thoughts of him when he was, I like to think, my greatest friend in college.

During these years in Philadelphia Joe and another friend, William Remington, who later became an Episcopalian Bishop, started a club for boys which became the University House, sponsored by the Christian Association. They were walking over the South Street Bridge and noticed some neighborhood boys re-enacting scenes from the Spanish-American War in the middle of the street. Realizing that there was no place other than the street for these children to play, these two set out to remedy the situation. The December 1947 *Christian Association Advocate* contains the account of a rented house set up to serve as a temporary recreational center until University House was opened in 1906, with Andrew Carnegie contributing to the building fund.

Joe continued to hold summer jobs to raise funds. During the summer of 1897 he was park guard for college at Wayside Park and the next summer captain of the park guard; by 1899 he had a patient to take care of.

According to Dr. Wharton, a long-time coach at Penn:

> McCracken came from Kansas, a big raw-boned westerner. He was six feet two inches tall, weighed 180 pounds, and was one of the finest physical specimens at the University at that time. He was agile, active and quick, and was one of the remarkable football players of that year, considered by the experts as being on a par with the great Truxton Hare, a four year All-American. He was equally prominent on the offense and defense.

Joe was on the varsity football team all four years at Penn, playing for two years as guard and then two years as fullback. In those days, the position of guard was special in Penn's football playbook, for there was a "guards-back" formation in which the guards lined up in the backfield. From this formation, the guards served as lead blockers in what became a devastating charge (this line-up was subsequently outlawed, although pulling guards remain an aspect of many plays). During the four years Joe played (1897-1900), the Penn team was successively 15-0, 12-1, 8-3-2, and 12-1, often running up big scores against what are now very strong teams (e.g., 24-0, 50-0, 47-0, and 17-6 against Penn State); only Harvard had a winning edge over Penn during these years. For his contributions, Joe was named an All-American along with two classmates: the legendary T. Truxton Hare (also a guard) and Peter Overfield (a center)[1].

Joe's religious upbringing was evident even with the football team. He regarded the Sabbath as the Lord's Day and he refused to participate in any sports on that day and he would not even return from any sport activities on Sunday. He waited to return on Monday in every case but one, when he was injured and the team refused to leave him behind.

Joe was equally successful in track. In 1897 he finished second in the hammer throw and third in the shot put in the intercollegiate championships. The following two years he won both events, setting intercollegiate records, and in 1900 was second in both events. Records indicate he broke the world's record in the sixteen pound hammer throw in 1898, throwing 153 feet, 2 inches.

His all-round ability led to his selection as a member of the United States Olympic Team that participated in the international games in Paris in 1900. He represented the New York Athletic Club, stopping

6

first in England for preliminary sporting events. At the Olympics, he placed second in the shot put and third in the hammer throw[2]. He might have bettered some of his throws but for the fact that he and other teammates would not participate on Sunday.

Joe graduated from the University of Pennsylvania in June of 1901, reportedly one of the most popular persons ever to graduate. As he received his diploma "the whole audience rose to their feet and loudly applauded, an ovation never before given in the history of the University."

Joe in his football uniform at the University of Pennsylvania
(taken about 1900)

Joe (seated, center) and the University of Pennsylvania track team (about 1899)

CHAPTER THREE

STARTING TWO LIFETIME PARTNERSHIPS
1901-1906

In the five years following his graduation, Joe made the choices that carried him through his life. It was during this period that he met and married Helen and that he chose medicine as his career.

Helen Newpher, who was to become Joe's wife and partner through the many years in China, was born in Cleveland, Ohio, October 17, 1877. She was the daughter of Francis Newpher and Carrie Briggs. Carrie Briggs[1] was born on November 11, 1855 in Medina, Ohio and married her husband there on January 14, 1875. Little is known of him[2]; he was ten years older than his wife Carrie and was an iron worker; the older buildings in downtown Cleveland are witness to the type of work that he did.

Just as Joe was molded by his early life and family, so were Helen's character and personality influenced by the fact that at one time her father was alcoholic and her parents' broke up. The details are not recorded, but in one of Joe's letters he mentioned that Helen lost her lovely home and way of life as a consequence. After nineteen years and with Joe's help, she resumed correspondence with her father when they were home on furlough in 1921. Francis visited the family in Atlantic City from the Civil War Veterans Home in Ohio and sent gifts to his grandchildren until his death in 1929.

Helen was named for her mother's sister, Miss Helen Briggs. A career woman of the late nineteenth century, she was a music teacher at Lake Erie College from 1884 to 1898 and also gave private lessons[3]. She is surely the person who developed Helen Newpher's love of music and taught her to play the piano.

Helen was close to her mother, Carrie, and, in March of 1921, visited her in Montreal, where she had been living for some years. She must have been a capable, independent person, for she maintained herself at a time when it was not usual for women to support themselves.

Helen's brother, Charles Newpher, became a very successful businessman and his family was later helpful to those of Joe's daughters who attended Lake Erie College nearby. Elsie, Helen's unmarried sister, had a settlement house job in a business taken over by the government in World War I, and then continued to work for the government in Washington, D.C. until her death.

Helen attended the Hathaway Brown School in Cleveland from October 1891 to June 1895, when she received her high school diploma. Mrs. Sophia Taylor[4], who later provided generous support for Joe and Helen when they were in China, paid her tuition at this private school. Helen also played the piano to help with expenses. Although she received honors and book awards, Helen apparently had a difficult time with the authorities. For example, she is reported to have tried to wear her pleated gym bloomers pushed up above her knees by their elastic leg bands; she also remodeled her jumper so she had short sleeves and a low collar. Her independent streak made her one of the best "tight-wire walkers" in the school.

After graduation, Helen attended the Cleveland Kindergarten Training School, an affiliate of the Chicago Kindergarten College. There she earned the first year certificate in 1896-97. While she was earning the second year certificate, she was also co-director of the Haymarket Kindergarten from January to June, 1897. The next year she became full-time Director at Haymarket.

At the age of twenty-one she was hired by the Laurel Institute in Cleveland to teach kindergarten, doing so from October 1898 to June 1899. A later letter from Helen describes how she temporarily lost her job at the end of that year; however, she was then able to continue at Laurel Institute, teaching the first three grades in 1899-1900, the first four grades in 1900-01, and the third, fourth, and fifth grades in 1901-02. Of this time, she wrote:

> I had a few experiences myself losing a job. At the end of my first year at Laurel, Miss Prentiss told me that she had gotten someone with a well known name to be a drawing card for her kindergarten. I had my mother and the rent on my hands and how I felt! The kindergarten children's parents made such a fuss about my being dismissed that Miss Prentiss took me on the next week as head of the Primary Department for which I had had no training and certainly no more name than as the kindergarten teacher, but it satisfied the mothers whose children were leaving kindergarten. And it gave me a job.

Helen had another anxious time three years later when the school went bankrupt. She found then that she could not get another teaching job without some training. Helen did not have a cent. While she lived with Mrs. Taylor, her clothes were provided by Mrs. Taylor; Helen's entire salary and the $900 Mrs. Taylor had paid Helen for her Steinway piano had all gone for the support of her mother, brother, and sister. Mrs. Taylor came to the rescue again later and at age 24 Helen entered the Teachers College of Columbia University in New York in the fall of 1902.

Joe also was headed for New York. Following his graduation, Joe spent the summer in Atlantic City at the Children's Sea Shore House, a summer home for poor children. During 1902, Joe participated in the founding of Camp Tecumseh on Lake Winnepesaukee near Center

Harbor, New Hampshire. In a letter of February 29, 1952, Joe de-scribed this event:

> This evening I am an invited guest to the celebration of the 50th anniversary of the beginning of Camp Tecumseh. I think you may remember that Alex Grant, George Orton and I--three members of the 1900 Olympic Team--decided we would start a camp for the sons of well to do people. I have a picture taken in 1903 of the house on the old poor farm we bought on which to begin the Camp. I went up in the Spring of 1902 and put a roof on the house, put on a veranda, built in a very large fireplace and removed the four or five iron cages from the cellar. The old building is still there but many others have been since built. The dinner is to be at the downtown Princeton Club and I am told that over six hundred invitations to alumni--anyone who [has] ever been a boy at the camp--have been sent out.

In the fall of 1901, Joe went to Columbia University as the Y.M.C.A. secretary. Columbia was building Earle Hall, its Y building, and Dr. Mott urged him to go there for one year to get the work started. This he did, but as the building was not finished until spring, he agreed to stay one more winter, the years 1902-03. He was deter-mined to go back to medicine. During these two years in New York, he also worked in the out-patient department at St. Luke's Hospital and substituted in Philadelphia at the Pennsylvania Hospital, which he later entered in October of 1903. He remained there as intern for two years.

It was at Columbia that Joe and Helen met. In a 1959 letter to his brothers and sisters Joe recalled, "Helen was a lucky pick-up I made in 1902 at Columbia." But Helen's account in a letter to her youngest daughter gives the exact date of their meeting as March 7, 1903:

> Since you asked me in your last letter about where and when Daddy and I met, I shall tell you about our first spring in New York. When I entered Teachers College in 1902, I was told, "New York is not like Cleveland. No one knows you and no one cares what you do. If you are asked to go out to din-ner with a man, go along and have a good time." In Cleveland at that time, no girl I knew ever went out to dinner with a man; there was no nice place to go.
>
> But I arrived in New York one night and went out the next, with the uncle of Dr. Hutchins of the University of Chicago, whom I had known for several years. I began that week and went two or three times a week from then on with every man I met. Sometimes we went to hotels, and after dinner to the

theater, and sometimes to places whose names I cannot remember, and once or twice to "Rathskellars", for in those
days if any small eating place was in a basement, and called a
"Rathskellar," it seemed to be popular.

After Christmas I was so tired of the food at the dormitory
that I had a permit to eat outside for a week. (Unless one had a
permit from the school doctor one had to eat at Whittier Hall.)
My friend, Lilian Rule, and I went to a boarding house kept
by a Miss Smith, at 457 West 123rd Street, and that very first
night I sat at the table with Daddy and he walked up the hill
with me. That was March 7, 1903.

After that, of course, as we both ate at the same time, I saw
him quite frequently. When my week was up I did not go back
to eating at Whittier but kept on at the boarding house. Nothing would have induced me to go back where I belonged.

We did not have very much time left that spring but we did
go about to various things like church, and walks, and very re-
spectable affairs.

However, Helen also continued to go to the dances she enjoyed so
much. Later in her letter she admitted, "But he did impress me from
time to time; such as the day he casually mentioned reading his Bible.
I had not known many men who would have owned to it if they had
ever done it."

In June 1903, when the school year ended, Helen went to Coney
Island in charge of the children in the Association for Improving the
Conditions of the Poor home called Sea Breeze, a three-month summer job. Joe visited her there, and they went to the beach for a swim.
As they got to the beach, Helen said something about the tide, and Joe
said "What difference does that make?" He jumped in and swam
right against the tide, pulling Helen along. Helen would later note, " I
believe that he has been doing that all his life, going against the cus-
tomary way people have, just liking problems and hard things, instead
of following the crowd."

When their summer jobs ended, they each decided to go west to
visit their families. Helen took the train from New York at eight in the
morning and Joe got on in Philadelphia at ten, and they had the day
trip through the mountains of Pennsylvania together. Helen stopped
in Pittsburgh, while Joe continued on to Kansas.

In September 1903 Joe entered the Pennsylvania Hospital, at
which he had been substituting, and Helen returned to Columbia.
They corresponded and saw each other when Joe came to New York
on his way to referee football games. In addition to her studies, Helen
worked four hours a day in a doctor's office and returned to work at
Sea Breeze in the summer. Their lives continued this way for two

years as Joe's medical skills developed and her dedication to him increased.

In November, 1905 when Joe finished his internship at the Pennsylvania Hospital, the Christian Association asked him to go to China. He was not anxious to do so, but the Association wanted him to take a "look-see" to determine whether China needed doctors or not. While in New York City that winter, Helen was teaching in the Horace Mann School, teaching at the Hartley (settlement) House three times a week, and finishing her course work at Columbia. Joe came to New York and he and Helen had a precious Sunday together across on the Palisades. When it was ended, they had decided that Joe should go out and see what China was like, come back in six months and they would be married in the fall.

In an interview for an article in the *Blue Cross Quarterly* of December, 1944, Joe recalled that preliminary fact-finding trip extending from January to August 1906 and how it convinced him that China would be his workshop:

> When I compared the number of excellent doctors serving Philadelphia with the handful in the whole country of China and saw the desperate need of medical education, I made up my mind that I could do more there than here....There were only 600 modern doctors in all China. The old Chinese doctors had never been to school, knew nothing of the causes of disease and read their prescriptions out of two thousand year old books. Patients were never examined directly. Every doctor had dolls--miniature men and women. The patient pointed on the doll to the area in which his pain was located....
>
> Teaching then was vastly more complicated than similar work in Europe or Asia; before 1901, no science was taught in Chinese; medical students had to learn not only medicine but chemistry, biology, physics, and other "pre-medical" sciences. In addition, the Chinese language had neither words nor characters to express basic medical terms; the Chinese student was forced to learn the English language before he could study medicine.

In 1800 the Chinese Empire had extended from the Great Wall to the borders of Vietnam and Burma and from the Pacific Ocean to the Tibetan and Mongolian marshes with a string of dependencies acknowledging Chinese suzerainty: Tibet, Sinkiang, Outer and Inner Mongolia, a larger Manchuria, Burma, Korea, Vietnam and the Loochoo Islands. The Manchurian Dynasty was fighting to keep out the "barbarians", but it was a constantly losing battle with the greatest losses dating from 1841 onwards. "Unequal Treaties" were being forced on China by foreign nations, so that in addition to Canton, other ports were opened for trade and missionary work. The "Open Door" policy of the United States was intended to ensure that U.S. interests were provided for as other nations moved into power. "Extraterritorial rights" were extended, with nations developing "spheres of influence" and cutting off Mongolia, Korea and Vietnam for their own control, and forcing freer trade within China itself. The weakening Empress and Manchu government could do little as the provincial governments became more independent, their leadership either anxious to or forced to deal with foreigners.

This "gunboat" diplomacy was very humiliating to the Chinese people. Their resistance included secret organizations, including those which participated in activities leading to the Boxer Rebellion in 1900. Despite its feeble efforts to modernize and to resist foreign domination, there was little willingness to consider the Manchu dynasty a suitable government. Young men volunteered to go to Japan and to Russia for educational and political training in military and revolutionary tactics; the development of regional warlords broke up the central governmental activities.

It is into this context that western doctors came. An Englishman named Robert Morrison arrived in Canton in 1807 and stayed. He first sought protection with the American Consul because the East India Company did not allow any Englishman to remain in Canton except to conduct trade. Under great difficulty, for it was forbidden that a Chinese teach his language to a "barbarian," Morrison had translated the Bible into Chinese and later published a dictionary as well as other material.

In 1830, Elijah Bridgeman came to Canton as a representative of the American Board of Missions; he became the first American missionary. Through Bridgeman's encouragement of other mission efforts, Dr. Brown, a Yale graduate, and his wife, arrived in 1841, the first appointment for purely educational purposes. Dr. Bridgeman was the vice-president of the first medical society in Canton in 1838 and Dr. Peter Parker established the first mission hospital about this time. Thus Canton was the first trading center for foreigners in, what might be called, "modern times."

Through Joe's visit, he recognized that, while Canton was the oldest locale for American contributions in missionary and education activities, there was still an opportunity for expansion. In his 1911 report, he wrote that Canton was the "commercial, literary and official metropolis of South China, with an immediate population of over a million and in the province with over thirty million, whose knowledge of medicine, hygiene and sanitation is practically nil and whose tremendous medical needs are being met by less than twenty modern trained western physicians." It was also a center of revolutionary activities, leading eventually to the overthrow of the Empress and the

Manchu Dynasty in 1911 and the establishment of the Republic of China in 1912.

In August of 1906 Joe returned to New York and quickly went to Long Island for a reunion with Helen. That summer she was working at Miller's Place, Long Island, in a summer home belonging to the New York Working Girls' Club. She was serving as the official chaperone and organizer, responsible for putting on dances and parties in the barn, which had been made over into a ballroom.

Joe also met with several of his friends to discuss his decision about China. He recalled these events in the *Twentieth Annual Report of Pennsylvania in China*, published in 1925:

> When George Wharton Pepper, Samuel F. Houston, Charles Frazier and I met in Houston Hall in the Fall of 1905 and guaranteed the first fifteen hundred dollars necessary to start this work, they hoped to accomplish several things: (1) to get me out of the country; (2) to establish in China somewhere a Pennsylvania work; (3) to make this work distinctly Christian; (4) to specialize in medical education; (5) to do something to help Pennsylvania undergraduates and alumni to understand and appreciate this great country; (6) to give China a living example of Christian love in operation.

Joe accepted their urgings and the challenge, and made plans to go to China.

On the day after Labor Day Helen went to Cleveland and had just a week at home in which to get ready for their wedding on September 12, 1906. Helen remembered:

> About thirty-five people were at the wedding and we were very informal. We all got together in the dining room and visited until the minister said it was time for the ceremony. Our minister was Rev. Stearly of Emanuel Church, since then Bishop of New Jersey. We had salad, ice cream and cake and coffee and then Daddy and I left for the station. I wore a grey suit and white embroidered blouse and a black velvet hat, a little toque, with a white feather, a small ostrich feather, quite good-looking!

They went to Buffalo that night and the next day took the train to Eaglesmere where they spent ten days at Cresmont Inn. Then back to Philadelphia where they lived in the Settlement House, which was just being finished. Their quarters included a sitting room, bedroom and bathroom. They cooked breakfast in a chafing dish, with an alcohol percolator for the coffee, and ate the other meals with the gang. It was

15

a wonderful winter for them. Joe refereed games all fall and Helen went everywhere with him.

Their lives changed forever a few months later. They left Philadelphia the first of February and sailed for China on the 11th of March, 1907.

Helen Newpher in her wedding dress in 1906

CHAPTER FOUR

FIVE YEARS IN CANTON
1907-1912

The McCrackens first five years in China were spent in Canton (now Quangzhou), where Joe was associated with the Canton Christian College and the development of a medical school. It was here that Joe's sense of mission took shape, first as an instructor in medicine and then as leader of the medical school.

Upon arrival in Canton in 1907, their first responsibility was to learn to read and speak Chinese, a process that typically took a few years. Over this period they became able to read *The Bible* and *Pilgrim's Progress*. Morning prayers were conducted in Chinese because the servants were included.

Although still relatively new to China, Joe prepared the 1910-11 report in his capacity as "President of the University Medical School as well as Clinical Instructor in Surgery and Instructor in Embryology and Anatomy." In this report, published by the Christian Association of the University of Pennsylvania in September of 1911, he summarized the first five years as "a period of slow, constant growth spent mostly in preparing foundations." Joe described the complicated procedures he had to go through in order to write the deeds and purchase small plots of land so that they would become the property of the University Medical School and could be placed under the protection of the United States:

> Another peculiar privilege of a missionary is his legal right to buy property anywhere in any part of China. How perplexing are the problems arising from such purchases only the missionary and the [American] Consul will ever know. During my first term in China it fell to my lot to make over four hundred real estate purchases netting the large amount of fourteen acres. It took me five years to make the purchases and the Consulate three years of time and the best diplomacy of several Consuls to get the deeds stamped by the Chinese government.

A mat-shed hospital was opened in 1909 and new staff members were added each year. The dispensary served about 17,000 cases in its first five years. A medical class of five students was started in February of 1910.

Plans were underway for building a permanent hospital (the western wing was completed and opened in 1912 and still serves as part of Sun Yat-Sen University). Joe was proud of a postgraduate course for

13 physicians representing eight missions which had been given during the two weeks of the Chinese New Year--the start of what he foresaw as "continuing education." That first report spoke of the Director of Religious Education (a Chinese doctor-preacher whose work was supported by Helen's friend, Mrs. Taylor, for several years). He also mentioned the Bible classes led by volunteers from the staff, medical students, nurses, and a druggist, as well as the blind old lady Bible teacher who received her rice and five cents a day. His letter also listed the eleven Protestant missionary organizations which had voted to unite in supporting (with funds and additional staff) the medical education work then being done only by the Christian Association of the University of Pennsylvania.

The budget for the school was approximately $11,000 for 1911-12. Joe's support was listed: $1500 for salary, $100 vacation allowance, $275 for annual appropriation for traveling expenses for the furlough planned for 1912-13, $25 for a language teacher, $200 for life insurance, and $400 for house rent.

A year later, the 1911-12 report indicated that progress continued despite a temporary cessation of the medical education because, under the new Republic, some of the students had passed competitive exams and had been chosen to be sent abroad for medical education on government fellowships. In addition, several had dropped out due to illness. A training school for nurses had been established and hospital personnel had been augmented by the addition of a Superintendent of Nurses and a Hospital Matron. The medical staff was also providing medical services to some four hundred students, staff, and employees of the Canton Christian College, to which the Medical School was attached.

It was also a busy five years for Joe and Helen personally. Three children were born: Helen (hereafter Helen Jr.) on January 29, 1908, Margaret on May 2, 1909, and Mary Elizabeth on February 2, 1911. They first used a rented house. Later, Joe supervised the building of a bungalow which had no running water, electricity, or central heating--not too unusual for those years.

They also acquired a stone house on Cheung Chou Island (or Dumbell Island, as Joe called it), which was a summer resort. The summer months away from the heat of Canton were essential to their health, and also were pleasurable because of the social activities and ocean bathing. Joe got there as often as he could and was able to pay for it by taking in boarders.

A 1951 note from Joe to Helen Jr. recalled those days:

> In 1911 a cousin of Dr. Cadbury's visited us on Dumbell Island west of Hong Kong and put on her bathing suit in our home, consisting of low-cut collar, short sleeves and skirt just below her knees and no stockings. She walked to the beach in

that awful outfit and shocked all the missionaries; and when she swam she put her chest out of the water as far as possible. What a gal, and a Quaker too!

Although busy with three pregnancies and the nursing of the three children, Helen also was involved in her own community activities. She taught a Chinese blind girl to play the organ and read music using the raised signs for the blind. Even before Dr. Liu was employed as Director of Religious Education, Helen was helping his daughter personally: She wrote home:

> She is a sweet girl, probably the only girl in this part of China who has had education enough to go to America and enter college classes. There is almost no education for girls in south China; the few schools are poor and there are no teachers who have any preparation for their work. They are like the teachers at Dr. Swan's new school, who read a book on surgery to the class and do not even know enough to read the medical terms. It sounds well to say that, since there was an edict issued by the Empress Dowager about universal education, schools are springing up all over China but it does not mean anything much for there are no teachers. We think there is enough hope in [Ah] Hin for us to invest some of our money in her.

Servants were essential, but were always to be a challenge to Helen. Servants expected to have their "squeeze," or profit, over and above their wages. This was a way of life, lending a contest-like atmosphere to what might otherwise be labeled stealing. Through the years Helen had to keep her cupboards locked and dole out what was immediately needed. A family story tells of them using forty pounds of sugar the first month they were married!

Frustrated as Helen would get with the servants, she also became very fond of them and took an interest in and helped their families. The story of the laundry woman who suddenly refused to go with them to the summer resort provides an example:

> A Yung, my good friend, has returned; with the opening of school the desire to have her boy "read the books" brought her pride now. She is such a good woman that I rejoice as over the return of the prodigal. I was so afraid that she would see how glad I was that I turned my back while I talked to her and she was so afraid that I would see how glad she was that she leaned over and talked to Helen [Jr.]. She is a splendid woman and she can iron everything from Joe's collars down. I tell Joe we shall never part again, she and I. She is

19

now to take Helen [Jr.] when I want to play tennis or go somewhere; I have played three times this week and am renewing my youth.

In September of 1909, soon after Margaret was born, Helen wrote Mrs. Taylor not "to take her complaints about boarders seriously. I am too happy to let even a thing like that trouble me but if you do not mind I like to talk things out to you and then forget that they trouble me at all." Her main complaint was the lack of privacy. The college and medical school were so crowded for faculty living space and food service that it was necessary for them to share the bungalow. Joe also had to have his office and conduct his secretarial work there, which meant keeping the children reasonably quiet and under control. In her own words:

But to look forward all of our lives to having someone in with us, makes me just sick and if it is not all of our lives it will be so long that I hate to contemplate it. I suppose all of these missionaries that have other people in with them have faced this same question and had to decide to make the best of it in the same way; but it is a dreadful thing. Joe and I are never alone; he is so busy all day long that I ought not to talk to him and interrupt him. And we have a late dinner and by the time I have seen the buyer and done my ordering it is about time for bed; at least for me it just seems as though I never see him at all.

On the other hand it is almost like a duty to make a home for either a single man or woman who are forlorn enough to be out here alone. Looked at in this way it becomes part of one's life as a missionary and we have so much that there is not much else to give up. Only I have to shut my teeth hard sometimes and keep this thought inside or I would not even be polite. Being polite to our boarders and being a Christian before our servants are the two things that will turn my hair gray. We have five [servants] now and with every one added it takes a little more patience. I have one for the boarders, a cook, boy, laundress, and a coolie to carry water. We got along for two years with two and now have five. Such is the result of custom. If we had an amah [a Chinese nanny] we would be right in style but I have not succumbed to that yet.

Five Years in Canton (1907-1912)

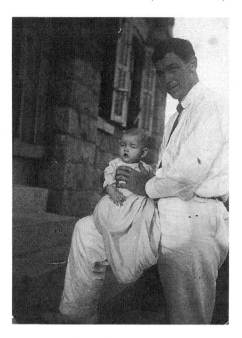

Joe holding daughter Margaret McCracken (fall, 1909)

Mary Elizabeth McCracken (September, 1911)

21

*The University Medical School staff in Canton in April 1911.
Front row (from left) Po Wa (the cook), Dr. Howard, Dr. Josiah
McCracken, and Mr. Leung (the druggist). Back row: Dr. Cadbury,
Miss Macher, Dr. Liu (director of religious education),
Mr. Hoh (the teacher), A. Kai (a nurse), Saam Koo (Bible woman),
Lai Chan (a nurse), Taan Mok (a nurse), and A Yuk (a nurse).*

The first graduating class of the University Medical School (1911).

CHAPTER FIVE

THE FIRST FURLOUGH
1912-1913

After five years in China, Joe and Helen returned to the United States for their furlough year. They sailed in March, 1912 on the boat *Mongolia* with Helen, Jr. four years old, Margaret almost three, and Mary, thirteen months.. Once in the U.S., they took the opportunity to visit relatives and friends, traveling east across the country to show off their three daughters, to tell of all their experiences, and to settle down in a home in the suburbs of Philadelphia.

Amidst all of their excitement, tragedy struck in September when Margaret and Mary came down with polio. Margaret's case was light and she soon returned to normal. But Mary was almost completely paralyzed, except for her lungs. Both her parents worked tirelessly with her, and Helen's training in physical education was invaluable. Helen kept notes of her slow recovery, keeping track of progress-- when she could be propped up by pillows, of her re-learning to move around on the floor, of dates she got braces for her back and legs, etc. The remarkable progress she made was due to their persistent efforts to secure available medical treatment, their following through on exercises, and the stimulation of her development to make her life as normal as possible.

A bright spot for the family was the birth of their first son, Josiah Calvin McCracken, Jr. (hereafter, Joe, Jr.) on December 20, 1912 in Philadelphia, Pennsylvania. Years later Helen remembered the year of Joe Jr.'s birth:

> Tomorrow is Joe's twenty-fifth birthday. That year we had a wonderful Christmas in America, four little children, and everybody trying to make up to us for Mary's illness. But not knowing how badly off Mary was, and having my first son, nothing bothered me. That first year I was sure Mary would return to normal as Margy did.

Joe was kept very busy professionally that year, too. He focused most on seeking ways of interpreting the needs of the Chinese for medical services and education, and working closely with the leaders at the Christian Association to raise money and make plans for his next stint in China. He traveled a great deal, not only for speaking engagements, but also to pursue his study of advanced surgery, hospital administration, newer programs in medical education, and the latest discoveries in treatment of tropical diseases. His comments reflected his optimism about the new government's leaders, some of whom were Christians, the liberal policies towards economic development by foreign investment, the government's fight against opium, and the efforts to establish a Public Health Administration with emphasis on treating leprosy and stamping out tuberculosis.

Soon after their arrival in Philadelphia, there was a major official event. It was a complimentary dinner given by the Provost and the Trustees of the University of Pennsylvania on May 20, 1912 at the Bellevue-Stratford Hotel in honor of Joe and John R. Mott. Dr. Mott was described as "the greatest authority on student life in the world and leader of the American Intercollegiate Christian Association, the Student Volunteer Movement for Foreign Missions and the World's Student Christian Federation." He had just returned from a tour of British and continental universities. Joe always credited Dr. Mott with "having as much to do with my deciding to go to China as anyone."

Joe's address was entitled "The Work of the Medical School in China," and was published in the *Old Penn Weekly Review*.

THE WORK OF THE MEDICAL SCHOOL IN CHINA

China is, and is going to be, the center of attraction for ages to come. Around her will center the political and commercial interest of the Orient, and henceforth when reckoning the history of nations, she must be taken into account.

Some six years ago the Christian Association of the University of Pennsylvania sent a representative to China to study the conditions there, and acting on his report, decided to establish in that great Empire a medical school, a medical school where the Chinese could be taught medicine in their own language. For two reasons Canton was chosen as the location for this school: First, because of the need of medical education in Canton; and second, because of the relationship that this school would have with the Canton Christian College, which is the largest and most influential college in South China. Canton is the largest non-Christian city in the world. Canton is the center of Southern China with all its activities. It has two million inhabitants crowded in one-fifth of the space of Philadelphia. It is a city as well advanced as any other native city in China, and yet the health conditions there are such as make us sorry indeed for those who must live there every day of their lives.

There are no streets in Canton wide enough for a vehicle to go through, except one main street which has been built since our arrival there. There are, therefore, no wagons in Canton. Men and women are the beasts and the vehicles of burdens. There is no sewer system. The water runs out of the houses and seeps down through the cracks between the stones

24

in the sidewalk, and beneath there is a ditch which carries the water away, when it is not clogged up, which is quite frequent.

Then, to show you their idea of sanitation, some three years ago the city water works were put in, and, being the easiest thing, therefore the most natural thing to do, they placed the water pipes in the dirt and filth found in their ditch below the sidewalk. There are no health ordinances or health boards to torment the people. There are no sanitary regulations. No one knows, and no one considers it his business to know, what the death rate per thousand is or what per cent of the population dies before one year of age--the foreigners do know death rates to be very high and the infant mortality appalling.

And yet there is much about Canton and about China to encourage us. There has grown up in the last two or three years a desire on the part of the young men of China for an opportunity to study "Western Medicine," as they call it. There was a body of students last year, probably between two and three hundred, who are attempting to study medicine in Canton. Medical schools are organized there nearly every year and as rapidly disorganize. But few of those who organize these schools have ever had a regular course in medicine, but they get together, organize a medical school, rent a small room and begin to turn out doctors with degrees! You can imagine the rest.

The objectives of our medical school are several. I think you will see that they cover a very broad field, and every object is to meet a very definite need. The objectives are to give thorough instruction in medicine and surgery to the Chinese in the English and Cantonese languages, and therefore

A. To provide to mission hospitals well-trained physicians.

B. To train the Chinese for positions as teachers in these and other medical schools.

C. To assist in providing this empire or this republic now with a Christian medical profession.

D. To take an active share in the investigations of the causes and preventions and treatments of diseases peculiar to China, and to encourage scientific investigators of other countries to make use of the school's laboratories and hospitals for this purpose.

E. To insure and make provision for post-graduate study.

F. To extend--and it is all summed up in this--to extend the knowledge of Jesus Christ to all who come within the sphere of the influence of the school.

There is not a hospital in all China, I dare say, but what would welcome a native trained physician and an extra one, two or three. In China a physician who is put in charge of the hospital, is the only trained man in the hospital. The first thing he must do is to choose from those who know nothing about medicine and from these train his helpers. These helpers prove after a while to be very useful men, considering the opportunity they have. You may be surprised at our chemist, a man who has been with us since the work was first begun. All that he knows is what he has picked up, and what we have shown him, and yet he fills our English prescriptions very well, although he cannot speak English. He knows the alphabet, and he can take our prescriptions and read from them the names of the drugs and find the bottles labeled with the same names, and fill our prescriptions quite accurately. It takes all of a man's time educating his help. What we hope to do is to put there a school which will turn out trained men who will go into these different hospitals which are so much in need of trained assistants.

Why is it we wish to train teachers and translators? How is China ever to have a medical profession of her own, and schools of her own, if she does not have teachers and translators? Absolutely impossible. Therefore, we hope to put a sufficient number of men there to educate men who will go out as teachers of medicine and men who will be translators of medical books and magazines.

Our third objective is to provide this great republic with a Christian medical profession. There is at the present time about one trained doctor for five hundred thousand people in Canton, comparable to three doctors for all of Philadelphia. In all China, at the present time, there is about one well-trained doctor to 1,000,000. In order to have one doctor for every two thousand of its inhabitants, two hundred thousand doctors are needed. Think of it! How can that country ever progress any distance without a medical profession? The government so far has felt no interest in the welfare of her own people. No one can imagine the conditions of the people in Canton at the present time. Yet we know that we see smallpox in all of its stages on people walking around the streets. We know that we see lepers, some six or eight thousand, coming in and out of the city gates. We know that there is no provision for segregation of the plague-stricken. There is no regulation which tries to protect the well people from the sick.

Then, our fourth reason is "to take an active share in the investigation of the causes and the prevention and treatment of diseases peculiar to China, and encourage scientific investigators of other countries to make use of the schools, laboratories and hospitals for that purpose." There is no greater field in the world for investigation along scientific medical lines than China. There are many unknown and unnamed diseases there. Years of research will be needed before we can intelligently treat these diseases, and if we can but put these laboratories there, and supply them with sufficient apparatus, of the proper kind, men are going to be attracted there and the unknown is to be found out. If we can but give them the start, the Chinese will be able to do splendid research work for themselves.

Then the next objective is "to insure and make provision for post-graduate study." All of the graduates of the present medical schools, at least, are going to be woefully weak in laboratory work, because there are no laboratories to speak of connected with any of the existing medical schools. For that reason we would like to be able to offer these men provision for further study along laboratory lines. We all become more or less dusty in our laboratory work after working in the field for a number of years, so we wish to also offer post-graduate courses for mission doctors.

The last objective, and the fact is all of the work tends to promote this object, and that is to spread the knowledge of Jesus Christ to all coming within the influence of the school. The medical conditions of China are very, very bad indeed, but the conditions which exist because of the lack of knowledge of the Great Physician who gave His life for the Orient as well as for the Occident are still worse.

But it is very encouraging to know that the new officials of China some three or four weeks before we left had up for discussion the question of destroying all the idols of Canton, because they believed they increased superstition and superstition prevented progress. We are greatly encouraged because of the changes for the better we are seeing every day in China.

If we are to do the greatest good for China, and especially for the medical profession, we must give it men of character. There is greater need for medical men of character in China than in any other country. In this country a man is prevented from doing his worst by laws and regulations, but in China there are no laws and there are no regulations, so that a man may practice in any way and do anything he pleases. So, then, to give the Chinese a medical education and not at the same time give him character is to do a very questionable thing for China. Of course, we intended to take into our colleges Christian students and non-Christian students, but while they are there we hope to be able to have such influence over them that they will go out men of character. A medical man without character in China becomes a dangerous man.

What has been done towards carrying out these objectives? Not much, but we believe that a very good start has been made.

In the first place, eight acres of land have been bought as a campus. A staff of four physicians, one secretary, one superintendent of nurses, one hospital matron and one evangelist are already giving their lives to this work. For the most part they have a working knowledge of the Chinese language, which is the most difficult in the world to master. In the dispensary nearly twenty thousand patients have been treated, and in the hospital about four hundred. There has been one wing completed of a two hundred and twenty-five bed hospital. A medical class has been taught up to the third year of medicine. There has been a course in graduate work.

A school of nursing has been begun, and now has six pupils; last year alone some one hundred and fifty pupils were in regular Bible classes. Most of these students were students taught by our evangelist, and were students of the Canton Christian College.

Sunday services and village preaching have been carried on during the five years. Thousands and thousands of people have heard the gospel for the first time. A number have joined the Chinese mission churches. We have had tracts on religious, social and medical subjects translated into the native tongue and spread broadcast. All this has been done that we may develop character.

At present this is the only medical college in South China under Christian control where men may study medicine. The Canton Christian College is [a] large non-denominational college of about two hundred and fifty students, with a property worth $200,000 located on the adjoining campus. The two are working together and developing there a large Christian institution. The mission doctors of South China, through the South China Branch of the Medical Association, have joined with the mission boards to make this college the one college in South China supported by the Christian people of all lands.

If I could I would like to make a great telescope, big enough so that all Americans could look through it and see the exact conditions that exist in China at the present time. If I could do that, I would be willing to spend the rest of my life building that one telescope, because I confidently feel that if the people of America could see the actual conditions in Canton and in China that hundreds and thousands of lives would be saved. Yet, that is impossible, and we must be willing to spend our lives, and we do spend them, in trying in the ordinary way to make known the needs of that worthy people.

During the furlough Joe also further pursued his plans for a union medical school, the vision he had worked on for five years. But apparently such a project required too much cooperation between too many agencies to be implemented.

Also while on furlough Joe served as trainer (or medical advisor) for the University of Pennsylvania football team in the fall of 1912 due to the illness of Mike Murphy, the famed trainer. But medicine and China were his first interests.

On March 26, 1913, an appointment was made for President Wilson to meet with a group of missionaries, including Joe, at the White House. In this interview the missionaries requested speedy recognition of the Republic of China and expanded efforts towards opening new channels of communication and trade between the two nations.

During the furlough year in the United States and in the following year (1913-1914) in Canton, it gradually became evident that it would be best for Joe to go to Shanghai. A letter written by Dr. Paul J. Todd in 1939 described the situation:

> I met you when you commenced your first service in Canton 33 years ago and for the following eight years we were closely associated in our work. During that time I do not remember that we ever differed in our opinions as to our policy on methods in regard to carrying on Medical Education or Hospital Work. We spent many hours in conversation on the above subjects and in conference with the South China Branch of the China Medical Missionary Association and it was to my great regret that it was impossible to work out a scheme that was satisfactory to all who were vitally concerned in the South China Medical Educational Work and that you finally felt it best to go to Shanghai. I believe it was just as great a disappointment to you as any of us that you had to give up Canton.

The Christian Association's explanation of the change in plans is found in the Pennsylvania Chapel Service Bulletin of May 24, 1914, when the offering was to be for the work of Dr. McCracken in China:

> The Foreign Missionary Department of the Christian Association has adopted the plan of having representatives of the University of Pennsylvania in various foreign mission fields working under Church or special mission society auspices. The medical work which was established in Canton has been

turned over to the Canton Christian College, to become its medical department.

Hereafter the medical work of the Association in China will be attached to the famous educational institution in Shanghai known as "St. John's University." Dr. J. C McCracken, '01 M, is taking up work there this spring, and the Association is planning to take charge of the medical department of St. John's University--which will be known as the University of Pennsylvania Medical School in China. Two classes in medicine will be conducted in this school, beginning with the next fall term.

Joe and Helen's first four children in 1915
(Helen Jr., Margaret, Mary Elizabeth, and Joe)

CHAPTER SIX

THE FIRST YEARS IN SHANGHAI
1914-1920

When they returned to China from his leave, Joe settled the family at Mokansan, a mountain resort near Shanghai. He began work at the Medical School and at St. Luke's Hospital while simultaneously working to get a new family house at 8 Darroch Road completed and furnished. Unfortunately, in spite of all of the time spent learning to read and speak the Chinese language, he was no longer able to communicate in Chinese because the dialect in Shanghai was so different; he thus became forced to depend upon an interpreter.

Both St. John's University and St. Luke's Hospital were supported by the Episcopal Church. At its beginning, the school included high school preparation; gradually college courses were added and the school was recognized as having University status in 1905, granting the B. A. degree. The medical department began under Dr. Henry W. Boone with a dispensary at St. Luke's Hospital as early as 1866[1]. Various reorganizations in the training of medical students led to four students in 1908 receiving medical certificates. These certificates permitted them to attend graduate schools in the United States, without further exams, as third and fourth year students at the University of Pennsylvania.

A history written by Mary Lamberton indicates that the medical school had many problems when Dr. McCracken joined the staff in 1914: "It was like a poor relative clinging to the skirts of her wealthier sister who does not have the face to shake herself free however much she would like to do so."

For about five years, there was also a small medical school in Shanghai sponsored by Harvard. During this period the Rockefeller Foundation was also talking and surveying the situation and considering a large union medical school; however, they withdrew to concentrate on establishing a medical school in Peking. But the Foundation did contribute money to help develop a Science Department at St. John's. This indirectly assisted the Medical School, in that it strengthened the training of pre-medical students.

The 1914-1915 Report of the President of St. John's University is quoted here to provide a little of the setting in which Joe started:

> All departments of mission work in a country like China are sure to be affected by the political situation, and hence it is appropriate to refer to the effects of the war [World War I] on China. At the outbreak there was considerable commercial depression and there was some fear lest the number of students

31

would decline for financial reasons. This, however, did not prove to be the case to any appreciable extent.

More serious than the setback to commerce was the breakup of the balance of power in the Far East. For many years the Great Powers have acted as a restraint upon one another. Although China was weak, her integrity was preserved, owing to the fact that the policy of equal advantages for all hindered one nation from becoming too aggressive. Occupied by the war in Europe, many of the western nations have been unable to pay much attention to China. This has given Japan the opportunity for which she has long been seeking, of carrying out her programme of becoming the dominant power in Asia. Her seizure of Kiachow put her in an advantageous position and she immediately made demands upon China which appear to threaten seriously the sovereignty and integrity of the country. These demands met with strong opposition on the part of China. Fortunately war was avoided, and a modus vivendi was arranged. The future, however, is full of uncertainty and China is in a critical situation.

President Yuan Shi-Kai has succeeded in obtaining a firm hold on the country and has suppressed all attempts at revolution. The first attempt at establishing a republican form of Government has proved a failure, and a policy of centralization has taken its place. Whether a more representative form of government will be gradually evolved, or whether a monarchy will be established, it would be difficult to say. Amid much that is dark there are certain hopeful features. The national consciousness is growing, men of new spirit are gaining an influence, and the need of moral reform is being realized.

This report continues describing the situation of the medical school:

> Since the amalgamation of our Medical School with the Pennsylvania Medical School this department has become more efficient. Beginning next term there will be three classes under instruction at the same time. The strength of the Faculty has been increased and the outlook for the future is full of encouragement.

In 1916 Joe was accepted into the Fellowship of the American College of Surgeons, having applied originally in May of 1914. The application shows that he served an internship at the Children's Sea Shore House in Atlantic City for three months in 1901 and the Pennsylvania Hospital from October 1903 to October 1905. While in New York from 1901-1903, he had been a member of the staff of St.

32

Luke's Hospital as Assistant Surgeon Clinical. He was listed as Surgeon of the University Medical School in Canton, China from 1907-1914, and was also surgeon at the David Gregg Hospital for Women as well as the Kung I Hospital in Canton. He also was Dean of the University Medical School in Canton from 1912-1914 and was a member of the China Medical Missionary Association and the South China Medical Association.

Joe's 1916 letter to supporters featured a dramatic drawing by Dr. E. S. Tyau depicting a child called Medical Work in China wrestling to combat the problems caused by the Giant called Disease. In it Joe is listed as the Dean of the "Pennsylvania Medical School being the Medical Department of St. John's University, along with twelve other faculty members." Speaking of the ten years of Christian Association medical work, he reported to his supporters that it was now connected with "St. John's University, the foremost university in China. Her graduates are found in high places, not only in this country but also in the diplomatic circles of many nations." The letter continues:

> This year we have seventeen students, four of whom will graduate in the Spring. These will be the first students of Oriental extraction to receive a Pennsylvania degree. If you could only know how hard it is to get the Chinese students far enough along in English to study medicine, and how hard it is to keep them from accepting the thousand and one opportunities for making money, and persuade them to begin a five year course in medicine you would appreciate how proud we are to have this class of four ready to graduate. All our clinical teaching is done in St. Luke's Hospital, which is owned by the American Church Mission and is located in the centre of Shanghai. Its one hundred and forty beds are kept full all of the time. Much of our surgery is emergency work, due to accidents. You must realize that Shanghai has tram-cars, cotton mills, silk filatures, and automobiles by the thousand; this rapid introduction of motor power and machinery among a people who a few years ago had never heard a steam whistle, plays havoc with many of them. Some of the poor fellows cannot realize that an automobile can and does go faster than a water buffalo, nor do they seem to understand fully that if they step in front of a rapidly going street car they will probably get the worst of the impact.
>
> The Chinese themselves know nothing about the proper care of accident cases. The native doctor believes he can stick an old rusty, dirty, six-inch needle deep into the body in a hundred different places with good result to the patient. Such practice goes on right here in Shanghai; in fact, anything goes here. A coolie who has slept one night in a hospital may

practice medicine if he wishes. It takes money by the barrel to establish such a school, in China as well as anywhere else. There is now a move on foot to combine our school with two others in this part of China in order that we may secure more backing and more money and consequently greater effectiveness in teaching. George Woodruff used to say "Keep your eye on the ball;" just so, we want you to keep your eye on this work here in China for we need you, your interest and your prayers, to help Pennsylvania do her share in bringing a knowledge of the Great Physician to these hundreds of millions of people.

The 1917 letter was dated February 22nd, although it had of course been written much earlier, just as the 1916 letter was dated January 1 to arrive as a New Year's Greeting. It is quoted only briefly:

You may be busy and I hope you are, but I want you to take five minutes and study the pictures on the back of this sheet. You will then know something more about the conditions in China and what Pennsylvania is doing to change those conditions. Far better if you could visit the Orient and see for yourself as did one of the members of the University faculty three or four years ago. Before the visit he was not at all in sympathy with foreign missions or even the Christian religion. He had often made fun of me for going to China to "waste" my life among such people. Nevertheless after a three days' visit with me he said, "Joe, I did not know what kind of work you were doing out here. It is a very good work," after which he sat down and wrote a codicil to his will leaving a sum of money to help support the work.

Descriptions of family life during this period have been assembled from letters from Helen to her friend Mrs. Taylor. The six years from 1914 to 1920 were crucial years for Joe and Helen as their family grew to become the "McCrackens of Shanghai." Joe was forty and Helen thirty-seven as the tour in Shanghai began. Helen, Jr. was six and started second grade at the Shanghai American School; Margaret, fifteen months younger, entered first grade; Mary turned four in February of 1915 and Joe, Jr., two in December of 1914. They would have three more children, including twins during this period in Shanghai. During these years Helen's first concern was caring for Mary and encouraging her to develop to the best of her physical and mental capabilities.

The daily work done with Mary was in addition to the regular homemaking activities, their social life, and Helen's own community activities. Helen's long affiliation with the Chinese Y.W.C.A. started with her appointment to the National Committee in the early fall of 1915 as well as to the chairmanship of the Physical Education Department's committee. The Y.W.C.A. was particularly concerned with providing physical education training to young women, both Christians and non-Christians, so they could be teachers in the mission or government sponsored schools. This Training School accepted students from all parts of the country. The Y.W.C.A. in Shanghai was the first in China and efforts were being made to set up Associations in other major cities. Helen's letters through the years reveal both the inspiration and pleasure she received from working with the American and Chinese staff members.

Despite all their efforts to assist Mary, she was in need of more orthopedic consultation. Dr. Abraham Flexner was consulted in October, 1915. Through him contacts were made and reports sent to Dr. Lovett in Boston. In April of 1916, Joe took Mary to Boston for consultations and a new type of operation intended to free the hip joint and reduce the pull which tended to make her back crooked. Helen remained in Shanghai which, though very hot, seemed the best place for the family. The family went to the Hongkew park frequently for walks, picnics, and concerts. Occasionally friends with cars would take them for rides or Helen would rent a carriage. Her letters to Mrs. Taylor reflect her concern for Mary and Joe, who were so far away, and her high anticipation, because of her pregnancy, for their return August 27th. Ruth Stewart was born September 24, 1916, and then Helen was able to resume her special work with Mary.

Helen and Joe scrimped and saved to finance the family. Mrs. Taylor had sent clothes with Joe for the children and the new baby, and had included, as she said "a regulation suit" for Helen. In her thank you letter, Helen told Mrs. Taylor, "I finally decided to pass on the regulation suit. It seemed selfish to keep it....When I have five children, do you think I shall feel young enough and gay enough to wear a sailor suit? I am afraid just now I am beginning to feel my years."

Her friends kept her supplied with old clothes and Helen was constantly sewing and remodeling them for herself and the children. She made all the underwaists, panties, pajamas, slips. Later she began to use a Chinese tailor to help her. Helen did not think it fair to have too many clothes; when she received new ones, she passed on what could still be used. Because at some point Mrs. Taylor had promised to shoe the children, many of the letters included drawings of their feet.

Mrs. Taylor also offered to buy them an electric car. There were letters, including one from Joe, discussing the offer and what it would mean to the family, the cost of sending one out or buying locally, the upkeep and comparisons with a 1917 Ford. The letters also provide a glimpse of Joe's travels by street car, rickshaw, and his bicycle. Some of the medical students were at the University, which was six miles from home (an hour's trip by street car and almost as long by bike); another class was taught at the Red Cross Hospital five miles away and another at St. Luke's, which was two miles away. He also had ten families on his private patients list at this time.

The 1916 letters contain the first mention of Helen's interest in "The Door of Hope." A group of dedicated women had developed and maintained a home and an industrial center for abandoned baby girls and women. Helen went to make a contribution as repayment because she had asked Mrs. Taylor for special laced shoes for Mary to wear on Sunday, which was Mary's holiday from exercises and braces, as well as rubbers for all the children. Down through the years Helen's letters tell of her contributions and how they came as an answer to the prayers of the women directors--food for the next meal, bedding, etc.

In one letter she wrote:

> The Door of Hope is one of the special interests I have in Shanghai though I am not sure that I always approve of "faith missions"; it seems to me that sometimes the workers do not get all that they need to eat!...
>
> Little Joe evidently believes in faith without works; he wanted Mary to play with him yesterday but it was time for her work (exercises). He said, "Mary no need learn walk. Jesus make her walk, she no need work, Mama." He prays for her every night and knows she is getting stronger and can do more things so I suppose he thought prayer was all that was necessary. I have tried to teach him to say in his prayer, "Help Mary learn to walk" and he has refused all summer to say anything but "Make Mary walk." He says "My way no b'long proper way."

In the late fall of 1916 Mary began to go to school in a long wagon brought from the States, and she stayed for increasingly longer periods of time. This meant Helen, though sometimes amah substituted, took her in the morning, returned home; went over at recess to help her move about and go to the bathroom, returned home; got her home for lunch and then back for the afternoon session and again went for her at the end of the school day. The Shanghai American School was a private school located two or three blocks from the family home. It had a boarding department for the upper grades and high school students from mission families in the interior of China, plus the day students of missionary and business families in Shanghai. Helen and Joe paid tuition for three children at this time.

In February of 1917 Joe was off to a three-week medical conference in Canton. World War I was affecting many plans for expansion of their work, both the sending of new missionaries and the replacing of those leaving. St. John's decided to start a new medical class in the fall of 1917. Helen wrote:

It gives Joe work for several more years to come. Other doctors at St. Luke's are off from work frequently for illness or leaving. Daddy keeps plodding along with all kinds of extras--fourteen families and some old maids and a lucrative medical work for a Chinese firm. He turns all this extra money over and it is divided between the hospital and the medical school. But he is the only doctor who does anything outside. The rest turn it down and have time for their wives and families....He is also president of the University Club and on two or three other committees that it seems to me are always meeting.

They had decided not to accept a car from Mrs. Taylor, who instead deposited a considerable sum in their American bank, part of which was to be used in rental of cars for special trips. Helen felt, "Unless Joe's private practice increased so it was necessary for him to have one [car], and everyone knew it was a business thing, I think it too much for us. It is a temptation but not a necessity." A car became a necessity within a year.

In the summer of 1917, the American Song Service was started, which evolved to become the Shanghai Community Church. Although first begun to interest the young men, it soon expanded to include all. The family had been attending a British Union Church. There were many who longed for an American service and its familiar hymns. Helen wrote, "We hope now that someday we will have an American church here in Shanghai; there are 1300 Americans in the Settlement and we could easily have a church of our own."

A letter of May, 1917 from Helen to Mrs. Taylor offered interesting insights:

And do you ever remember that I am nearly forty years old? It has been a long time that you have been an influencing factor in my life; the children were asking me the other day about when I learned to sew; I told them how we had the Lend-A-Hand Band and you taught me not to sew backhanded. Only I am sure when you were not looking I probably turned my work around. I did not tell them that!

Music was important in the family's life. They all sang together, and as time passed Helen taught all the children to play the piano. She wrote to tell Mrs. Taylor that she was playing as accompanist for the soloists at the church and for the American Song Service. She also mentioned going out to church services run by the Navy Y.M.C.A.

secretary for three little gunboats and one small cruiser in the harbor with about 100 sailors and five officers.

When the United States entered World War I, the American women in Shanghai discontinued their assistance to the English and started their own war projects. Helen wrote of flying the flag outside every day now instead of keeping it in the vestibule for special occasions.

In the summer of 1917, they vacationed in Unzen, a mountain resort near Nagasaki, Japan. Here they rented a Japanese style bungalow belonging to a mission group. In Japan they could use gold and go more cheaply, as well as get Joe away from vacationers in China, whom he would be expected to help with medical problems.

Unfortunately, in late October Mary had to have another operation because the contraction was returning to her right hip. Dr. Morse from Chengtu, who had been working under Dr. Lovett in Boston, was able to come down and perform the operation.

With the start of the fall term, Joe agreed to be the physician (faculty member) for the boarding students at the Shanghai American School; he ended up being the longest serving faculty member in the history of the school. His income for this service helped with tuition costs, and enabled Joe to purchase a 1917 Ford. Helen wrote:

> I always hate to have him take outside patients; Joe makes as much as our salary in outside work and that is divided between St. Luke's and the Medical School. Yet when I know how people need a good doctor I feel selfish not to encourage him in it. People need the kind of man Joe is; he says half of them do not need medicine as much as they need sympathy and advice.

During most of these years, the family lived in their house at 8 Darroch Road. To Helen's regret it was the last of the four double houses on the block and backed on the Chinese section and had a vacant lot on one side. She always spoke of how distressed she was that her children were exposed to the ugliness and poverty of Chinese life from their bedroom windows. The house had a front porch and enclosed side vestibule for the bikes, Mary's walking bars and wheelchair, flag pole, etc. There was a large living room and a dining room: there was also a kitchen and a long pantry with the closet at one end in which Helen kept her groceries and which could be unlocked to give out food.

Off the back porch was a laundry room and across the small concrete yard a cookroom for the servants, a bath for the servants, and a coal storage room. Upstairs was a long, screened-in porch that was used for a sleeping porch. There was a bedroom for Joe and Helen, one for the children and an office for Joe as well as the bathroom. The hot water system never did work; hot water for baths was bought from the hot water shop out the back door in the Chinese section and carried by a coolie with two wooden buckets on a bamboo pole over his shoulder. The water was then poured into a huge tub. The three young children took their baths together.

There was no central heat--only a coal stove in the living room. An upstairs back hall separated from the front of the house gave room for ironing and provided access to the stairway leading to the third floor, which had two bedrooms, later used by Margaret, Helen, Jr. and by the amah. Above the kitchen and washroom were two bedrooms for the servants.

The servants included a cook, a "boy" who cleaned and served meals, an amah who could assume some responsibility for the children in the absence of their parents, a second amah who was strong enough to carry Mary, a washwoman and a chauffeur who did not live in the house. For many years they had an amah who was somewhat like a Southern mammy; she could talk pidgin English enough to answer the phone, do mending and be really helpful. In her spare time she made the cloth uppers of her shoes with lovely embroidered flowers and then had the leather sole attached. Her feet had once been bound but then unbound. The second amah was her daughter-in-law from the country, who had unbound feet and was able to carry Mary.

Outside, part of the yard was fenced in for the laundry with a fence twice as high as normal, but still attempts would be made to use long sticks to steal the clothes. The front and side yards had space for the sandbox, swings, seesaw, croquet, and other games. There was a mat-shed building put up in one corner for Joe's car. With stealing so prevalent and a scarcity of garages, it was necessary for Joe to have a chauffeur. They had the same one for many years and he, like one amah, became part of the family. Later this man taught himself enough so that he started the first taxi service in Shanghai.

The year 1918 was especially busy with the war work added. In March Joe was made Chairman of the Junior Red Cross; his second cousin Henry Noble MacCracken was chairman in America[2]. As the War Relief Association workrooms were changed into branches of the Red Cross organization, the tempo of the work increased. The men were looking for production and began to employ Chinese tailors to do much of the actual work, using funds from wealthy foreigners who would give money but not labor. Helen helped with supervision. She felt that American women were slackers, because less than 100 out of 500 would come to the workrooms. She also enjoyed meeting a different group of women. In addition to her family sewing, she was sewing for the Women's Exchange. For the first time she wrote of making cereal out of local wheat and earning money that way. Wheat, turned into cereal with her coffee grinder, became one of her best projects for raising money for her own charity projects.

Helen continued to work regularly with Mary, trying to help her in every way possible to prepare her for her return to the States for high school, which would not be until 1924. Margaret and Helen, Jr. began carrying her around as soon as they were strong enough. Even more important, Mary was given every opportunity to develop as normally as possible. Helen referred in a letter about this time to a boy of Mary's age whose family had simply not followed through with the recommendations for exercise, proper training in using crutches, and encouragement of his intellectual abilities, and how sorry she felt for the boy's resulting undeveloped potential.

In June of 1918, Helen wrote happily about the purchase of the little house in Unzen for $900 gold:

> Joe ought to get away....This winter his income from out- side practice has averaged $550 a month; this is divided be- tween the hospital and the medical school. I must own that it sometimes is a temptation to me to urge him to go into private practice for himself. There is only one American firm here, and Joe turns down more work all the time. It would be a satis- faction to know that one could lay aside a little for such a family as ours. But I tell Joe that they have more promise of good education and training than I had at their age. They are very fortunate in this choice of a father. He himself would hate to give up his missionary purpose.

In this same letter she says:

> Ruth is the funniest, loveliest baby we have had yet; she is into mischief all the time and amah says it takes two women to look after her. But she also says "Missy, this baby more clever any baby."

In June, Helen was also matron of honor (and they paid for the wedding) for the young Chinese girl, Ah Hin, whom they had helped to go to Wooster College from Canton in 1910. Ah Hin had gone from there to Wellesley and graduate school at Columbia before re- turning to teach at Canton Christian College and becoming Mrs. C. F. Wang. The combination of the wedding and a Fourth of July picnic for 70 in their yard, intended for those who could not afford the cost of the official American celebration, forced Helen to bed for the sec- ond time in the year. She wrote, "It is the hardest thing I have ever done to stay in bed; I [would] much rather work."

After going to Unzen in 1918 with plans for a six week vacation, Joe had to return after just two weeks--doctors were needed for the Red Cross in Vladivostok in Siberia and Dr. Tucker chose to go. Fortunately, Helen had the amah and washwoman from Shanghai with her:

> I wouldn't have come a step if I had known that I must stay without him and have him go back as one. St. Luke's is fullest in the summer and Joe already had those 100 surgical beds full from June 20th when Dr. Tucker left for his vacation until the very day we left (July 23rd) but we feel it would be foolish to take the children home when it is so hot there and so wonderfully cold here. We have passage for the 5th of September.

Plans, however, were changed. With Dr. Tucker gone, the furlough was postponed to 1919, and then when Dr. Tucker returned from Siberia he took furlough, delaying the McCracken family's furlough until the summer of 1920.

In the fall, she described Joe's continuing health campaign, explaining that he was now requiring a physical examination before employment. Even so, friends and prospective servants were not very cooperative, she added, giving examples of syphilis, infectious parasites, and T.B. passed on to employing families.

Joe was also campaigning for better health maintenance practices for foreigners and their servants. Early in 1920, the newspaper published a long article, "How to Maintain Health in China." The article discussed the increasing efforts of countries to emphasize pre-natal and pre-school care of children. Joe stressed the Mission Board's responsibility for health care of its scarce number of missionaries. He called for more careful examination of applicants for the mission field, provision by the Boards of preventive health measures and sanitary living conditions (including at least enough funds for screens and modern plumbing). The details of the article make one more aware of the constant efforts that had to be made by mission doctors to protect the lives of their families.

In his campaigning, Joe pointed out that it was not enough to install a filter for water and to boil it frequently in the summer, but it was also necessary that the filter be cared for:

> We found our cook scrubbing ours with the brush he uses impartially on the floor, the veranda and the sink....I do not believe our servants have been any better or any worse than the average Chinese of their class yet we have found them doing the most revolting things: washing themselves in the kitchen dipper; carrying dishtowels around their necks; breathing into the drinking glasses to give them an extra polish, etc.

He then discussed the fact that many clean-appearing servants are "cesspools of diseases." He explained that two years earlier the doctors at St. Luke's had planned an examining unit at the Hospital where any household could send its servants for a thorough examination:

What is called the Safety First Club was formed and a few families offered membership. The examinations already may convince the staff more than ever of the real service such a department will be. Facilities are now available so that the general public, business firms as well as private families, may join this club by making a contribution to St. Luke's Hospital.

The same article touched on what is now called mental health:

Another cause for removal from the [mission] field is nerves. Little may be known about this subject but volumes might be written. Enough is known, however, to show us that of all the fine mechanisms found in the body none is so sensitive as the nervous system and none so much influenced by the habits of thought of the individual....We have at our home cut out of our conversation the adjective nervous and the noun nerve. There is nothing more dangerous to health than an atmosphere which is permeated with the thoughts of nerves and nervous breakdown. Far fewer missionaries would be lost to the work should there be an organization which would fully eradicate from the family talk as well as the tea table gossip all references to nerves and nervous manifestations and diseases of all kinds.

After other comments regarding the importance of exercise, he closed the article with:

And I do believe that whoever is wasteful of his gift of health is misusing mission funds as truly as though he were squandering actual money. Illness or accidents may overtake us, but let us not be guilty of shortening needlessly our length of service [in] the field.

In addition to playing at Sunday School and church services, Helen was doing much more for soloists and singers at various club activities. She expressed her appreciation for sacred music sent out for use by herself and friends.

Helen was delighted to extend her concern for physical education through the Y.W.C.A. to a new field: Because of the illness of the first and second grade teacher, she substituted during the fall months, and she managed to put 20 minutes of gym into the classroom schedule! Because of her good servants, she managed to teach despite the fact that four of the five children and all the servants had bouts with flu and she was extremely hesitant to leave little Ruthie.

For Armistice Day, Joe arranged entertainment for his Junior Red Cross Auxiliary at the school, with speakers, songs, and movies. Helen wrote that it was Helen Jr.'s and Margaret's first evening out; "I took them out of bed to go, knowing that they would never get over it if they went to sleep when the rest of their classmates were going. But I let Mary and Joe [Jr.] sleep, much to their disgust."

There were many big celebrations in Shanghai to celebrate the Armistice and the end of World War I. Wearing new Jack Tar Tog sailor dresses which had just arrived from Mrs. Taylor, the McCrackens marched with the thousand English, French and American School children from the Race Course to the Bund and then around on Foochow Road to the new drill hall, where the program included speeches, national songs, a cowboy exhibit, moving pictures, and candy for all. Helen wrote:

> We had never let our children do such things and they were overwhelmed at having permission to go. As Daddy was caught up in an emergency operation, I took Joe [Jr.] and Mary in the car and some of the men carried Mary in so she could be with the rest at the hall.
>
> Everyone is anxious to have the Chinese thoroughly understand that the Allies won, for the Chinese have a tendency towards admiration for Germany. The newspapers printed a cartoon of the Kaiser and under it an explanation and asked households to give it to their servants. There have been thousands of posters put up all over China so that there would be no mistake about who is the victor.

A 1919 letter from Joe reported:

> The Spanish Grip, as you folks call it, has been in this town for the past month and I have been kept busy as a bee. About one-half of the American School Children and faculty have been down with it. So far no fatalities. Last Thursday Mary came home from school with it and the rest of the children were in bed by Saturday and I should have been, but a labor case appeared at the Hospital, so that I did not get to bed until five the next morning. I had another operation at nine, and got to bed Sunday about eleven. Felt better the next day and am quite all right today. The children are all over the worst of it we think. Up country the Chinese are dying off by

the hundreds with it. All the spare doctors have gone to Siberia, so that there is not much help for the poor Chinese.

I have just checked up my year in private practice, November 1st to October 31st, and I find that I have been able to turn over to:

University, for Medical School	$2,500.00
To St. Luke's Hospital	2,400.00
To Medical School Library	556.00
To Ford Sinking Fund	205.60
To Underwood Typewriter	138.75
TOTAL	$5,600.35

besides paying expenses of John Henry [the name given Joe's Ford motor car] and other operating expenses . Unless we get more help at St. Luke's I must cut somewhere, but it is hard to do.

In February of 1919, Helen started taking Mary to the Red Cross Hospital for electrical treatments three times a week; these treatments continued through the spring. It was seven miles to the hospital. Mary had to be brought home from school early to rest before going; the treatments lasted about an hour and a half. Usually Helen went with her to undress and dress her, because they did not like to have the children ride in the car alone with Chinese servants; there were too many accidents. By this time Margaret and Helen, Jr. could share in pulling Mary to school in the wagon or pushing her wheelchair; she sometimes walked part of the way with her crutches. An older student was also employed to carry her up to her classrooms if members of the family could not.

As the treatments continued they seemed to improve her circulation. Helen frequently mentioned the problems of Mary's hands and feet being cold in winters, of warming them up by rubbing and hot water bottles. Mary was growing so fast that her braces had to be lengthened and Helen had to sew new waists monthly to cover the steel of Mary's back brace which cut through the strongest cloth Helen could find.

In May of 1919, Joe went as medical advisor with a team of Chinese athletes who were to compete in a Far Eastern Athletic Meet in Manila. Helen missed him but was glad he could have a complete change of pace, because it would be too much to try to go to Unzen for the summer, and there would be no one to cover the work at St. Luke's.

The summer of 1919 was a happy one; the children could enjoy the yard more because a large Japanese-owned house had been built in the vacant lot next door and this shaded the yard and helped create a breeze. The girls dressed Kewpie dolls, made paper doll families cut from Montgomery Ward catalogues and covered the living room floor with houses furnished with the furniture advertisements. There were other children on the street and friends not too far away--ten cents a mile was the charge for a ride in a rickshaw.

The Rockefeller Board people came to visit in August, and Joe would not have missed that for anything. He spent nearly a week of his spare time showing them here and there and talking over plans for the future. Although they had a six million dollar plant [in Peking], they had only six students entered for the fall term. Joe had seven coming into the Pennsylvania school, plus eleven or twelve in the third year, and some seniors.

Helen's letter of September 8, 1919 to Mrs. Taylor provided another important reason why they stayed in Shanghai for the summer:

> I have not written about this baby to anyone for two or three reasons, until just recently. For several months I was not well and I hate to write long distance letters and speak of not being well for fear people will think I am worse off than I am. It has been a new experience to me to have to be thoughtful of what I did. And when I wrote to you about Ruth, you sent me an outfit almost sufficient for two babies and I was afraid to tell you for fear you might think I expected you to outfit another, and you have already done so much for us, that I just felt I could not let you do that again.
>
> For some time I was not sure whether this baby would surely arrive safely but there seems to be no reason now why it should not. I shall be glad when I am home again and equal to everything that comes along. The children can scarcely wait; they talk about it all the time and the questions that I have answered in the last few months have been most interesting and often puzzling. It is hard to say on the spur of the moment what one would want to say; and to keep my answers complete and satisfying.

On October 1, 1919, Helen wrote to share with Mrs. Taylor the news of the twins who were born September 27 at the Victoria Nursing Home:

> Most people think it is quite shocking to have six girls and hesitate to congratulate us. But they have not seen the babies yet. They are the most perfect little things; one weighs 5 lbs. 11 oz. and one 5 lbs. and 12 oz. and so far we have not found a way of telling them apart. We depend entirely upon a blue ribbon....The older by fifteen minutes is named Elsie. The second one is not yet named; the children have the privilege of choosing....It is such fun for us all....The children are wild with delight. They can scarcely wait until the two weeks Joe

45

thinks safest are up and we are all home together. I feel now better than in months. My heart which was upset for all those months calmed down two weeks ago and is now going at its normal, slow steady pace. All the other disturbances too are things of the past.

The second twin was soon named Martha Constance.

In December of 1919 Mary broke her leg, but continued to attend school despite her cast.

Helen's letters to Mrs. Taylor included more descriptions of her activities with Chinese friends, "I always think every time I have Chinese guests that I will never waste my time entertaining or calling on foreigners. The Chinese I know are so much more interesting." Shanghai was the center for the increasing number of Chinese who had been educated abroad in the same colleges and universities as the Americans. Social intermingling increased as the international organizations came into being--the Rotary, the Varsity Club, and others. As the Song Service moved to become a Community Church, it frequently drew the Chinese couples who had met in the States, because they could not understand each other's home Chinese dialects and so turned to a church using English rather than to membership in a Chinese church.

As the time drew close for them to use the reservations on the boat to go back to the States, Helen expressed her concern for the 1920-1921 trip:

> The more Joe and I hear of conditions at home and the more we contemplate life at home with seven children to look after, the less we wish to go. It does not sound very loyal to one's relations nor very patriotic, but it seems like a dreadful undertaking to move our family twelve thousand miles for a furlough....Three times in the past year the Trans-Pacific steamers have raised their schedule of prices. It would cost our association between three and four thousand dollars to get us to San Francisco and back. With Ned Wood tearing his hair to get enough to keep us here at the present rate of exchange, and with all the money needed here for various important things, it seems to me very useless to spend that much to take a family home that does not really care to go.

Nonetheless, by March of 1920 the decision had been made to use their reservations and sail July 31st, 1920. In May Helen wrote she was dreading the visit to Kansas because seven years ago on their way out to China she had never been so hot in all her life, even in Canton, but she knew that Joe must see his family and friends.

The First Years in Shanghai (1914-1920)

We are going to wait and see if we can stand a week in Kansas. Isn't it funny--millions of people in America would think it funny to prefer Shanghai or Canton! Shanghai is lovely in the summer. We have fans and ice and wonderful markets full of fresh fruit and vegetables, and parks and always cool breezes at night.

Later in the same letter she was concerned as to whether everyone will be well enough to sail:

If they keep well we shall be all right. With meningitis cropping out here and there all over the city, scarlet fever crowding the isolation hospital and measles and whooping cough showing themselves in our neighborhood, I shall be thankful if we get started with an unbroken circle....Our front yard is controlled by the Municipal Council but our back yard is on the Chinese territory and what goes on there cannot be controlled by the foreign police and the Chinese police will do nothing about a small matter like sanitation. I went out each morning last summer and got it cleaned up and put lime all over the road. We really had fewer flies than ever before as one result of my private campaign.

In his book *My Twenty-Five Years in China*, J. B. Powell, who was a friend of the family, provided a vivid description of what it was like in the years after his arrival there in 1917:

For years the International Settlement Administration had no sewage disposal system or modern plumbing. We had, in our bathrooms the sanitary devices known as "commodes" consisting of a square wooden box with a hole in the top and an earthen chamber pot. Our house boy was responsible for keeping them emptied and in some fashion this was collected and sold for fertilizer. In fact, the International Settlement received a large revenue from the sale to the contractors who in turn made it a profitable business to supply the farmers and gardeners of the surrounding countryside. Later, when we took our famous family houseboat trip, we were caught in a group of such boats moving up the canal to sell their product, which the farmers stored in large earthen pots.

Mr. Powell stated that the term "stink pots of Asia," which appeared in Marco Polo's description of his travels in Cathay more than six centuries ago, came from this practice.

The gate to St. John's University, presented by the class of 1913. Just beyond the gatehouse is the university infirmary, which provided a clinic for villagers.

The Cooper Memorial Gymnasium at St. John's University.

CHAPTER SEVEN

THE SECOND FURLOUGH
1920-1921

It was quite a trip across the ocean and the country with seven children, including the twins who were about eleven months old and Mary who had to be carried. There was a huge wicker basket that held the second-hand collapsible twin baby buggy. This basket was placed on the ship's deck and served as a playpen.

From Sterling, Kansas, Helen commented, "Kansas has had a wonderful August. I expected to do with heat and now hope to get out of the State before we freeze." They stayed there for two weeks, visiting with relatives and friends--six of the seven brothers and sisters with their wives or husbands, children, and grandchildren; renewing old friendships and speaking engagements for Joe; stopping over in Urbana, Ohio, to see Joe's uncle who was 85, then Helen's brother and sister in Cleveland.

After finding a suitable house and settling the family into it, Joe's first responsibility was to take Mary to Boston for a check-up, and new back and leg braces. He then began his work with the Christian Association and the various mission boards as well as fund raising. These activities took him away from home often and Helen was fortunate that one of his sister's, Myrta, came and stayed with her until late March. Mryta's presence did make it possible for Helen to go to some special meetings with Joe, to attend and enjoy a two day meeting of the National Y.M.C.A.-China Section in New York, and to take a trip to Montreal to visit her mother.

While they were in the States, Joe was made an honorary member of the Phi Beta Kappa. He was chosen as one of the most representative men the University has turned out who was doing worthwhile things. He spoke at their annual dinner and then was given this honor.

Joe's annual solicitation for funds was dated December 15, 1920:

> It is a real pleasure to get back to one's own native land and meet old friends, make new ones and again get in touch with the latest in our medical profession....Our Medical School in Shanghai is graduating Chinese doctors, well qualified to practice scientific medicine, but the number of graduates is small. We are now bending every effort to reorganize the School on broader lines, with greater support, so that our staff may be increased, and larger classes admitted annually. Heretofore, because of a limited faculty, we have been able to take in a new class only every other year.

What greater blessings can we of America give to China than those which will surely flow from a high grade Medical School, conducted under Christian surroundings? Suppose the University Medical School, with its faculty, could be transplanted into the midst of that needy land--what a leaven to the whole nation it would be! I'd rather spend the next fifteen or twenty years of my life strengthening the foundations of such a coming Medical School in China, than any other thing I know of in this land or any other land....

America is rapidly becoming the medical center of the world. Let us not permit medical influence to stagnate here, but in the unselfish spirit of our profession, let us see to it that its blessings flow freely and rapidly on to that great new republic where it is still true that millions of sick men, women and children are failing to receive intelligent treatment of any kind.

The request for funds included the following:

Dr. McCracken plans to return to Shanghai next summer, where he will continue his hospital and medical educational work, in association with Dr. Tyau and Dr. Morris (University of Pennsylvania graduates) and their colleagues. He also takes an active interest in the Junior Red Cross and other similar activities.

While St. John's University sends forth collegiate and medical graduates of good standing, many of them desire further preparation before finally entering their professions. That accounts for the presence in our own University of four St. John's men studying in our graduate medical school and thirteen collegiates in other departments. So is the good spirit of our University being spread among the Chinese people through these future leaders of their nation's life. St. John's University has 256 students, including 23 in the School of Medicine, who, with 229 in the Middle School, make a grand total of 485 students, with a faculty of 45, of whom 18 are Chinese.

To show the disinterested goodwill of the doctors who went out from this country, whatever fees they receive from private practice they turn in towards the deficit of the hospital and medical school. It is hardly necessary to say that their compensation does not admit of any adequate provision for the future "rainy" day. The Chinese support is increasing as the value of the school and hospital is being more broadly recognized. To McCracken, who will soon return to China for another term of years, the consciousness of strong and faithful backing from year to year by his friends at home will be a great encouragement....Last year two hundred and ninety-two contributors provided his budget and he felt a legitimate satisfaction at this evidence of their approval of his efforts.

The furlough was also quite a challenge for the family. Helen had great difficulty arranging for Mary to attend school until finally a druggist nearby permitted one of his employees to carry her in and out as necessary. In December Joe Jr. ran out in front of a truck while playing on the way home at noon. Helen, Jr. rode with him to the hospital. Joe was visiting in New York for a few days, and luckily Helen knew where he was having lunch. She managed to get him on the phone, persuaded the temporary maid to remain with the small children, and then ran out into the street and asked the first person with a car to take her to the hospital. Joe Jr. had a concussion but made an almost miraculous recovery.

In January and February they all had diphtheria and the house was under strict quarantine. As soon as the quarantine was lifted, and after careful consideration, Helen made the heart-wrenching decision to take Mary to the Watson Home for Crippled Children outside Pittsburgh for operations and residential care under Dr. David Silvers. She stayed about a week with her before leaving alone to return to the family. In reporting on the removal of casts from Mary's back and legs and of his plans for muscle training, Dr. Silvers concluded, " I hardly feel able to yet give you any definite opinion as to the possibilities. She is, of course, very severely affected and we must fight for all we can get but I am hoping that we will see a very considerable improvement in the next month or so."

In April of 1921, the family moved to Ventnor, a suburb of Atlantic City, New Jersey, to take one of the houses rented to missionaries on furlough. This entailed changes in schools for three children, but despite the higher standards in the new school system, they made their grades. May and June were extremely difficult months, for the twins and Ruth were very sick with whooping cough. Myrta had returned home and Helen carried most of the responsibility alone. However, during late June, Helen's father and then her mother came for a visit.

Quite suddenly, Joe got word that their ship reservations had to be changed to a sailing either in July or a much later one which would mean the children would not be in Shanghai in time to start school in September. The decision also had to be made as to whether to take Mary or leave her at the Watson Home. On June 23rd, they took a train trip to San Francisco, with Mary being put on the train at Pittsburgh. A letter to Mrs. Taylor written on shipboard just before reaching Shanghai told of a lovely, relaxing trip and Helen's pride in the children, who were well-behaved and popular with everyone.

The McCracken family in 1920.
From left: Helen, Martha, Helen Jr., Joe Jr., Ruth (in front),
Margaret, Mary Elizabeth, Joe, and Elsie.

The twins: Elsie and Martha (1921)

CHAPTER EIGHT

SHANGHAI AGAIN
1921-1926

The period between their return and the next furlough in 1926 were busy years for Joe. His November 18, 1921 letter to his friends reads:

> It was fine to have had a year in America with an opportunity to see relatives, friends, classmates, leaders in my profession and a host of others interested in hearing about our work in China. A rare privilege it was to be able to visit the large surgical clinics of America and meet personally the men who are putting America in the front along surgical and medical lines....
>
> Since our return much of my time has been taken up with promotion work. Soon after we arrived I was sent to Peking to meet with the Council on Medical Education, of which I am chairman. This Council approved of a larger union medical educational work in East China, an area including about 100,000,000 inhabitants. At present our medical school is the only mission medical school in that district. I am now trying to get the five Christian universities and colleges in East China to unite with our school to form a union medical school which shall be not only the medical department of St. John's University but also the medical department of each uniting institution....
>
> We have more students than we have ever had before-- thirty-three, and with increased facilities that number would soon be several times larger.

Helen returned to her membership on the Board of the National Committee of the Y.W.C.A. and chairmanship of the Physical Education Committee, the school of which was one of the most outstanding missionary projects. In a letter to Mrs. Taylor, she wrote: "Dorothy Canfield Fisher says a woman should keep up some interest outside of her home while her children are small so that she will not be lost when they grow up and leave her; I have decided to take an interest in this one thing."

Joe was a leader in the establishment of a community soup kitchen for White Russian refugees. He wrote his supporters:

We served nearly sixty thousand meals with the one thousand dollars granted us by the American Red Cross. Our funds have given out, and we are turning the work over to a local committee who are feeding six hundred a day. Winter is coming on, and these people are in a terrible plight, and I see but little hope in the situation....

There is some satisfaction in giving what is wanted. Here is what the Russians think about the Community Soup Kitchen which for fourteen weeks has been quietly handing out the bowls of soup and the half loaves of bread with the cups of sugared tea. [This letter was published in the *China Press*, June 10, 1923.]

McCracken, Esq.
Sir:

The horrors of Bolshevism forced us to leave our country; in arriving here as outcasts we hoped to find some work which could give us means of existence; very soon, helas, we saw that without any assistance, no job could be obtained, no help could be received! GOD SENT HELP.

Our position and especially that of our children and wives became the most awful. And just then God sent us a help; at 106 North Szechwan Road a soup kitchen has been established where we and our families could receive a free dinner or at a minimum cost. But we became much happier when we saw the kindness and the cordiality with which we were met when coming to have our meal. Nobody looked at us as at beggars, these people saw in us men who wished to work, even for a loaf of bread, and they do all that is possible to let us earn our living honorably. Many of us have received employment or temporary work; many others a roof and clothing. We do not know what organization keeps this kitchen; we only know that it is kept by a U.S.A. community, and that you seem to be at the head of the organization. That is why we address our thanks to you, Sir, and we beg you kindly to remit them to the U.S.A. organization, ladies and gentlemen responsible for such a useful, clever and hearty work.

Assuring you that we shall never forget what the U.S.A. citizens of Shanghai have done for us, we remain, Sir,

> Yours gratefully,
> (Signed by fourteen Russians, each
> signature for every thirty customers
> of the Community Kitchen)

Shanghai Again (1921-1926)

Excerpts of letters to Mrs. Taylor indicate that Helen was having difficulty getting good servants:

> I have had no cook again for a month, my good one refusing to stay unless I took his wife, who is four feet tall, small-footed, and almost blind from trachoma. I have never had such a winter, nor such going-ons in the kitchen department, "squeezing," eating our food, inefficiency, and continual annoyance. I am expecting to go to the hospital any day now for another baby, and am leaving my poor family to the mercy of what poor servants we have. When I come home I shall send the whole crowd off and begin again with a fresh supply from another part of the country. This crowd will not have anyone who is not from their province and I think I have tried all of their poor relations in some capacity or another.

The McCracken children were not immune from the usual diseases of childhood. Helen's letter of February 9, 1922 reported:

> An epidemic of German measles is sweeping through the school and it arrived in our family two weeks ago. Margy began, it being her seventh contagious disease!!! Helen [Jr.] and Joe [Jr.] followed. So we have been in quarantine and I have lessons each morning. Margy went back in 8 days, Helen [Jr.] goes back tomorrow and Joe [Jr.] Monday. Mary had it four years ago and so has been going all the time.

And on May 3rd she added:

> After avoiding the "real measles" for two months, at last Martha came down with it. She was quite sick for a few days but got through without pneumonia and no "running ear," both of which have been prevalent in this epidemic. Elsie came down in two weeks and she was quite sick but is all right. Ruth has not yet but has had to stay at home.

Helen was also constantly sewing; for instance, a letter mentions fourteen pairs of bloomers cut out and ready to be put together and the prospect of making winter night clothes suitable for an unheated house.

> I have just made my first shirts. They were not for big Joe but for little Joe. He plays with two boys of thirteen who wear shirts "with tails" instead of blouses. So I borrowed a pattern and made him three. Then I found that soft collars out here cost fifty cents each so I made him five out of an old pique

55

skirt. He said, "When I went to America I wore babyish coats like my trousers. Then I began to wear suits with belts to the trousers and blouses. The last winter I began to wear soft collars like Daddy's. And now I am old enough to have shirts with tails." Thus we see progression in the life of a boy.

Amidst all her activities, Helen again became pregnant upon their return to China. From a letter on June 9, 1922 following the birth a month earlier:

I came back from the hospital on the tenth day and have been busy ever since, so busy it is hard to realize that I did stop for that long. The baby, Stewart, is growing like a weed. He weighed ten pounds and a quarter the day he was four weeks old. He is such a tall baby, with long legs and long forearms and husky little shoulders. I believe he will be like his father....

Yesterday school closed and now the children are to have three months vacation. I am planning to spend time reading to them history and biography and geography. We made a plunge last week and bought quite a number of books, taking your Christmas gift, mother's[1] and some that father sent the children not long ago. One of the books is Van Loon's "History of Mankind." Have you seen it? The children are quite fascinated with it. We have been reading two or three chapters a day.

Helen enjoyed Van Loon's diagram illustrating the age of the world compared to the age of man and this apparently made a great impression on Joe Jr. At Sunday School he spoke of it when the teacher was giving the *Genesis* story of creation in six days and his classmates became quite interested in their friend's story. In a few days Helen had a letter from the teacher who said he could not have such a heretic in his class influencing the other students.

In a July 10, 1922 letter:

My old amah, the one who was with Mrs. Brockman fourteen years, has to go home and take care of her daughter-in-law who is to have a baby in a week or so. She sat and talked it over with me the other day, the tears rolling down her face, because she did not want to leave the twins. She has been taking lessons in caring for a little baby by watching me look out for Stewart. She is a dear old thing, an awful slacker but reliable in many ways....I expect I shall take her back when she is able to leave.

Shanghai Again (1921-1926)

On January 25, 1923 Helen wrote, "Our children have all been well this winter; it is the first time for several years that at this time of year we have not been in quarantine." The letter also includes a humorous story illustrating her trials and tribulations:

> After losing things out of the yard and house for eight years we at last have caught a thief. I do not know when I enjoyed anything so much. The yard where we hang our clothes is enclosed and there is a padlock on the door. One day I asked amah to go out and get something and when she went out I heard a loud "walla-walla." I looked out and saw two empty lines which had been full but a moment before. I ran down to see what it was that had been taken and to know the worst and saw Margy coming in with an armful of clothes into the front yard. She and Helen were coming from school and had met a man with an armful of clothes. Margy said, "These look like our clothes." The man turned and started to walk rapidly in the other direction and she called to Helen [Jr.] and the young teacher with Helen [Jr.] made after him. The thief dropped the wet clothes in the middle of the street and began to run but the teacher held on to him. We took him to the nearby station and they said, "Where are the clothes?" so I had to come back and take the whole lot of wet clothes over to the station but I did it gladly. They asked me if I were willing to appear in the Mixed Court and I said, "Delighted," so the next day we went down clothes and all and testified. He had been convicted of stealing ten times before; a warrant was out for him and had been for year, and he had been banished from the Settlement before so he has a year of prison and banishment again after that.

A May 8, 1923 letter to Mrs. Watson of the Watson Home in Sewickley, Pennsylvania solicited support for a church building project:

> I wanted to tell you how dear to Joe's heart his church project is. You know I do not think there is any one else like Joe. He works so hard over things utterly outside his regular work, running a soup kitchen under the Red Cross for the Russian refugees, and keeping track of its helpers, its tickets and its supplies. Then he is on this Red Cross Committee. And he is on this church committee and Chairman of its Board of Trustees. Last Spring when the annual meeting took place, the congregation voted for the members of the governing board; the names receiving the most votes were to be Trustees. To my great surprise and to Joe's amazement when the list was read,

Joe's name led all the rest. And now we are one and all so anxious for this church; to have some place for the children to go to Sunday School and for this Sunday congregation to meet....You do so much for us that I felt at first that I did not want him to ask you to take an interest in this. But he feels and has persuaded me to think that this is not for ourselves though, of course, our whole family will enjoy this church home....

Last week we had a rare treat. On Wednesday morning as Joe was hurrying off to an operation, he found a letter of introduction to Jane Addams in the mail. He went down that afternoon to call on her and asked her to come for dinner the next evening. We filled out the table which seats twelve and asked others to come in the evening.... The next day I had the pleasure of taking her out to our Physical Education Training School and then to the local Y.W.C.A.....Helen [Jr.] and Margy stayed up for dinner when she was here. And Mary and Joe had ridden down to get her and bring her out....I had read to them the story of her life the night before so that they could know who she is and what she has done....

In January of 1924 Helen wrote:

It is Sunday morning and seven of my children are away at Sunday School. That is the one hour in the week when the house is rather empty and the only disturber of the peace is Stewart. He is just beginning to walk alone. That is rather slow for he is nineteen months old, but he can creep like lightning and hasn't time to walk. When it comes to the business of his life, he gets there crawling, as quickly as possible. He is such a precious and such a pet. Margy is his favorite of all the children and she is always willing to do anything for him.

Joe, Jr. is playing soccer on the "midget" team that takes in the boys under twelve. Joe likes all kinds of sports. The other day one of the Y women, whose boy is in Joe's class asked him why William did not make the team, why he did not play better football.

"Well," said Joe, "He is just a little afraid to go into the game. He doesn't go after the ball. He is afraid he will get hurt."

"Don't you ever think about getting hurt?" she asked him.

"Oh, no." he replied, "When you play football you never think about getting hurt, you just think about the ball. Why you never know whether you are hurt or not until the game is over."

58

She told me this after Joe was here for luncheon, and then I knew that he would probably follow in his father's footsteps. He isn't as tall as he would like to be and takes it quite seriously, goes to bed early, opens wide his windows and measures himself almost every week. But he is larger than the average eleven year old and is growing quite normally.

In March, 1924, another appeal for funds was sent out along with a list in which Joe compiled his major interests:

(1) Dean of our Medical School. Now that we have a very capable secretary in the hospital, Miss Anne Lamberton, this position does not require a great deal of time.

(2) Professor of Surgery and surgeon at St. Luke's Hospital. This year I am on call for all emergency abdominal work and for part of the more serious accident cases. This is of course my major responsibility. St. Luke's was founded in 1866 and is owned and controlled by the Protestant Episcopal Church. Our students do the last three years of their work in St. Luke's Hospital which has one hundred beds for surgery and fifty beds for medicine. In connection with the hospital there is a Training School for Nurses in which we have fifty Chinese boys enrolled as pupil nurses, supervised and taught by two American nurses. In addition to these two there is one other foreign nurse who acts as matron of the hospital....there are also six graduate Chinese nurses--men--in charge of various departments.

(3) Leader of a voluntary Bible class in the medical school. I am trying to show them that the Christian religion is more than attending church and saying prayers. There are represented in this class Episcopalians, Presbyterians, Methodists, Roman Catholics, Seventh Day Adventists and non-Christians. A Christian physician in this country may become not only a great preserver of health but also a living example of the influence of Christ, the Great Physician, on the lives of those who follow him.

(4) Physician to the American School which means the care of their faculty of twenty-one teachers and over one hundred boarding students.

(5) Honorary member of the Medical Advisory Committee of the Y.M.C.A. and the Presbyterian and Methodist Missions.

(6) Consultant and surgeon to a number of missionary families in and out of Shanghai.

(7) Vice-president of the American Association in China, which has a membership of three or four hundred. It is the oldest American organization in the Orient.

(8) Pennsylvania representative on the Executive Committee of the American University Club.

(9) Chairman of the Board of Governors of the Community Church which has a membership of four hundred and fifty and an annual budget of $16,000.

He included a listing of Medical School Support for 1924-25:

Board of Missions of the Protestant Episcopal Church	M$46,000
Christian Association, Univ. of Pa.	8,000
St. Luke's Hospital	13,120
St. Elizabeth's Hospital	2,400
St. John's University	7,700
Volunteer services of physicians	12,100
TOTAL	M$89,390

To this sum, he added other sources such as salaries of the nurses from the Episcopal Board of Missions, M$28,000, St. Luke's Hospital other sources of M$83,497 and St. Elizabeth's Hospital other sources of M$45,158--thus making the total expenditures for the past year of M$246,045 for these three institutions, with over one hundred and fifty thousand dollars coming from local resources. At this time one dollar Mex (as the Chinese dollar was called) equaled a little over fifty cents gold, American money.

A few weeks later she wrote:

I have had no amah for just a year tomorrow. In no other way could I cut down living expenses so successfully and we all like it much better. Occasionally I have to give up something because the girls cannot be at home at the time, and sometimes they think it nice to have someone to help with the babies' baths but on the whole it is good for them and for me to do these things and much better for the small children. The twins nearly dress themselves, only stockings over union suits are too hard as yet, and I know of no other four year olds who are not dependent on amahs. And I save fifteen dollars a month in wages which is quite worthwhile.

We have not sent the twins to kindergarten for it would cost twenty dollars a month and with five in school we felt we could not add that much to our budget....The chauffeur we have had five years lives downstairs in the basement now with his wife and they are quite an addition. I dreaded having more people around but Al Do is one of those rare servants that steady the whole lot of them and he can do many odd jobs that do not come under his work. He looks after everything and keeps the rest of the servants faithful....Helen will be sixteen in two days. She does not behave in a very grown-up manner as some of the school girls do; she has not yet the "boy craze" and she enjoys hide-and-seek, hockey and tennis and such things in a wholesome way.

From a letter in March, 1924 Helen wrote:

Elsie and Martha are here plying me with questions. They are crazy to learn their letters and make them. I think I shall have to teach them to read. I taught Ruth when she was four and she is a very good reader now. They have been giving intelligence tests at the school and because Joe is a member of the faculty we have heard about our children's marks. Ruth passed the highest tests of any seven year old and was third in a room which has some nine year old children in it. Margy is highest in the sophomore class irrespective of their ages and she is almost the youngest in the class. Helen [Jr.] was quite a little above the average but not remarkable. She gets better marks than Margy because she works so much harder and is steadier about everything. We have not heard of the rest.

McCracken family home at 8 Darroch Road in Shanghai.
They lived here from 1913 to 1923.

The McCracken family home in Shanghai at 5 Avenue Petain.
They lived there from 1923 until selling the home in 1939.

CHAPTER NINE

NEW HOMES FOR THE FAMILY AND MARY

As they returned to China for their third term of service, the Christian Association had not yet decided about purchasing property and building a home for the family. Their rented home was up for sale, with the rent being increased in the meantime. By August 1922 Helen could write:

> Joe and I are deep in house plans. We cannot have all we might want but I think we are going to have more than we have had before and much more than I ever dreamed of having in China. For we are going to have what Ruth calls "American poons," namely flush toilets.
>
> We went out to see our land the other day. They are taking the graves up and leveling the ground and putting the boundary stones in. We hope a year from now to be in the house that has a little more room for such a large family.

In her letter of December 10, 1922, Helen wrote:

> Our house is begun! The foundations are in and they begin the brick work tomorrow. It will be a comfort to have a little more room. When anyone is sick and has to be isolated or kept quiet, we have not a place to use. The new house is not going to have such large rooms as this one but more of them. Our children need to be scattered and not all have to dress in the same place. Now the ones sleeping on the veranda all dress with the ones sleeping inside and five children and two amahs in it all at once are a daily trial. One amah helps Mary and one the twins. I have a new wash amah, as big nearly as Joe, who cares for Mary.

Work on the new house progressed slowly. Joe had a difficult time with the Chinese contractor, then tried to use the Russian refugees:

> I have had to use Russian Refugee carpenters for part of the work to finish our house. I have had fourteen working for five weeks, and it will take another three or four weeks before the house is finished. They are doing excellent work, and the house will have a much better finish than it would have had under the original set of Chinese carpenters. They are men who work fully eight hours a day, board themselves, sleep on boards in a shed with practically no bedding, all for less than fifty cents gold per day. And they are happy to have the op-

63

portunity to work, for thousands of their associates have nothing to do and nothing to eat except the soup kitchen fare.

But they, too, began to slow down and he had to find another Chinese contractor. He did most of the supervision himself.

Helen's letter in September of 1923 told of what she was looking forward to:

> I do not know what the servants will think. They are to have a flush toilet. I do not know how that will affect my own family to say nothing of the servants, but for nine years I have had to keep their outside toilet clean and free from smells and now that load will be taken off my mind. Joe says I will have another for they will doubtless clog the drains but I tell him that is pessimism.
>
> The servants are to have a Soochow bathtub and a place to cook their stuff outside our kitchen. Such luxuries for a poor woman! The whole basement for them sounds very spacious. But there is a laundry and a furnace room and a coal room and a place for all the wagons and vehicles that now clutter up our front vestibule and dining room....
>
> I hope our house looks comfortable as well as like an "establishment." It is larger than our other one but there are ten of us; someone the other day saw our dining room table and was so surprised at its size. But when he was told that ten were seated there at least twice a day, he did not think it so large. It is not an extravagant household; we have nothing very expensive inside of the house and we use very few servants according to Shanghai standards.
>
> There are some things about it that I am sure will add years to our lives. The fact that we have hot water, for instance. No one who has not tried to bathe eight children and buy water for baths as we used to do, knows what it means: the dirty coolies coming into the house, the danger from the big buckets of boiling water, the delay waiting from one bath to the next and the risk of having any old coolie come into one's private bathroom.

The new house was a great boon to Helen in other ways, too:

> Sometimes after breakfast I feel as though there were something that I should be doing; then I realize that it is the back alley that I am missing. Our Japanese neighbors dumped their garbage in our alley rather than in the municipal receptacle; the servants' toilet was there and as fast as we bought a lock, the lock was stolen. Every passing coolie used the room

not the receptacle. I used to go out day after day and clean up the alley and the toilet and put around fresh lime and Jeyes fluid and try to keep down the flies. Servants do not do those things and mine always looked on while I worked. Now our servants have a decent bathroom with a flush toilet.

There are just dozens of things about this house that mean the same kind of saving to me, of energy, time and temper. We had one room before where in the winter, the studying, the practicing on the piano, the little children's games and any guest all had to be at the same time. No other place was warm enough. Now the children can go to their rooms and study away from interruption, the children can play somewhere else and we all can have a little privacy. For years Joe has lost sleep because he heard the children at night and always got up to save my getting up. But that is my job and I can always sleep in the daytime if I lose sleep at night. Now he sleeps on the third floor and goes through night after night without hearing anything, even the telephone.

We had to have "up and down" stairs because with the amount of money allowed us, we had to build up and not out. I thought I would hate a high house but now I like it very much. We have a lavatory on the first floor and Mary can use that. And she does not need then to go up and down as often as she did before.

Mary's condition failed to improve. In July of 1922 Helen worried:

Mary's back is not so straight as it was a year ago. It troubles me terribly. She is so well, so happy and much stronger than ever before, but the lateral curve is increasing....Joe hates to tell her that he cannot carry her but she is all he can do; we are going to try having a little chair with poles for the servants to get her up and down stairs here in the house, and have one at school next year.

On January 5, 1923 Helen wrote Mrs. Taylor:

Mary has a new cast but it was not a success. I thought this week that I could never live through the next four years without sending Mary back to Dr. Silver. Her back is getting so much of a curve. But if she can never be much straighter she will develop normally in other ways here with her school and her home and contact with other people which she would not get isolated as they do isolate them at the Watson Home.

A few weeks later she added, "Mary has had four casts in the last four weeks...I am afraid that out here casts are not going to help."

Mary's condition continued to weigh heavily on the family. Helen wrote:

> Mary's back is not any better. I am quite convinced that Mary ought to go home. I am so anxious for her to have expert advice that I would be willing that Joe should take her again and leave us out here as he did before. [The local doctor] had the training but lacks experience, for children out here with such deformities are not taken care of so that they live to get to a hospital, or if they live they are not brought into a hospital. And he does not have the equipment to do for her what could be done at home. Joe is not ready yet to have her go home. He thinks that in sending her back to China Dr. Silvers thought ahead and knew that she would not improve much, and that he felt her normal development along other lines was more important....It troubles me dreadfully; but just now there seems to be nothing that I can do but to wait until we have some inspiration that will be convincing to either Joe or me.
>
> We measured Mary this morning and she is five feet tall, as tall as I am without my shoes. We began this last week to try massage and some Swedish exercises to see if this masseuse can devise anything more than I can to straighten that spine.

Then in April she wrote:

> We have decided to get Mary home this summer....I have written to Dr. Silvers to see if she can be re-admitted. She herself wishes to go. She has for some time had the idea that if she had stayed at the Home she would have been walking by now. I cannot bear to have her think that we have left undone anything that we thought would help her no matter how hard it seems.
>
> The question of how to get her there will have to be settled later. I want very much to take her, for I feel that it is enough to ship a child off for two years until our furlough without going along to see what the doctors think about her. I do not see how I could wait for the mail. Joe thinks it hardly fair to the rest of the children to spend our savings on such a luxury, and a great risk to leave them here with Helen [Jr.] and Margy in charge for two months. He thinks we should not ask the Association for extra trips which are luxuries and not necessities.
>
> But he has gone so far as to engage a second class passage for Mary and me on the Empress sailing in June, hoping how-

ever that we can find someone who would take her for us. He cannot get away just now. It is not an easy matter to find someone who will take a child that has to be carried everywhere she goes, who will wish to go straight through and not do a little side stopping on the way. But having gone this far I am willing to let the rest of the decision wait until nearer the time of her going. She will be ready for high school but she is only thirteen and if she does not progress so fast at the home, has plenty of time. She is such a sport about things; just now when all the girls are interested in hockey and basketball and the outcome of the boys' games, Mary leads them all in enthusiasm. At the games she is the official timekeeper and cheers and yells for her teams. Joe hates to take her away from all this school life, so do I. But I see her day after day, never on her feet, never any better; it makes me long to try something else....

I am busy sewing up the family for the summer on a chance that I may have to leave them. I have just made six dresses with bloomers for the twins, and four underwaists for them, and two petticoats for the older girls.

Helen did take Mary on June 16, 1924 across the ocean and the country to the Watson Home. Except for a day's visit with Mrs. Taylor, she stayed at Watson Home with Mary and was grateful that she was not charged for her expenses there. Mary was forced to lie on her back as part of the efforts to determine what her condition was in regard to her spine and hips. There was always something a visiting mother could do for the forty children, such as playing the piano, reading aloud, teaching games and songs. She reported to Mrs. Taylor:

Dr. Silver took it quite for granted that I realized the extent of the destruction in the spinal cord--that she had little to hope for beyond moving a little on crutches and braces. I have tried to face it for two years but never acknowledge it. I must say that my talk with him took away the last props to my hopes....It was hard to leave her. She is not a child who says much--nor would she allow herself to break down--so we were quite cheerful and smiling at the end. But it took me several days to get over it--and starting off alone on the ship I felt very forlorn.

Joe wrote of Helen's return on August 15th:

Helen got in right on time as she always does and found seven lively children and one anxious husband on the dock to meet her. It was a gala day for the McCrackens. How glad we all were to see her and what a wonderful mother she is anyway. The longer we live together the more I wonder at her capabilities and love her.

In a letter on August 23, Joe continued:

We all for the first time since Helen's return went to the church picnic in our car. With the car chock full and baskets tied on the foot boards we are one of the sights of Shanghai.

Imagine a 1921 Ford with the chauffeur, Helen, Jr. and Margaret with the twins on their laps in the front seat while Joe, Helen, Mary, Joe Jr., Ruth and Stewart were in the back!

It is difficult to imagine what anguish it caused Joe and Helen to place their thirteen-year old crippled daughter at Watson Home in 1924 and to prepare to send a very young seventeen and a half year old daughter to college in 1925--sending them so far away at a time when it took about a month for a letter to be delivered and another month for the answer to get back. Helen comforted herself that she was not a British mother who had to part with her sons at the age of seven or eight so they could get the proper educational sequence in order to attend the universities.

CHAPTER TEN

HELEN, JR. LEAVES THE NEST

As the school year of 1924-1925 opened, Joe was fifty, Helen forty-seven, Helen, Jr. a senior in high school and Margaret a junior. Joe, Jr. was in seventh grade, Ruth in fourth, the twins were not quite five, unable to enter school until February, and Stewart was two years old. At Watson Home Mary was doing both eighth grade and first year high school work.

In December, Helen wrote Mrs. Taylor:

> This has been one of those weeks that upsets all one's plans and calculations and has made me tremble at the thought of what might happen to our precious family circle. Stewart has dysentery of the most severe type. He began Saturday and this is Friday. He is better but so weak and sick and drowsy. He is the "light of our eyes" from the biggest to the least of us--and to have him laid low has even made the twins anxious for fear he would "go to be God's baby...."
>
> Helen, Jr. has been very busy writing an "oration." The Masons give each year a prize for the girls and one for the boys in the Senior Class--for the best oration on some subject about America. They have to have it in by the holidays and delivered before the High School and a special Committee in January. Helen's subject is "American Influence on Education in China." I have been reading her books and helping her outline her work and after she wrote it, I did the first copy on the typewriter. I think she has done very well and certainly when she gets home and as long as she lives she ought to remember and be able to use the knowledge she has gained about those early missionaries.

But Helen was horrified when her daughter came home and reported that the teacher said it would be a good idea to put into the oration quotations from the Bible, for then people would believe one was saying something true and important.

The letter continues:

> She played in a school recital yesterday and I was quite proud of my first child. Tonight she has gone to McTyeire School to a "Student International Fellowship" dinner. She joined this and likes the meeting of Chinese, Japanese and other nationals' students....

It keeps one's brains active to help four children with school work. This week besides Helen's oration, Margy was writing 1000 words on the "Molecular Theory." Joe [Jr.] had to write an original story of 500 words and be coached in "interest problems" and have explained to him Dicken's "Christmas Carol," and Ruth long division and geography. Every night there is something.

Helen enjoyed undertaking special projects to raise money for her personal charities. In her January, 1925, letter she described her wheat grinding project.

Did I tell you that I was grinding wheat for the church? Each member of the Women's Auxiliary is to earn ten dollars. I ground American wheat and made cereal and made thirteen dollars. Now I am using Chinese wheat. It is much dirtier but very cheap. I bought 27 pounds for a dollar Mex. Counting dirt and poor measure I will get about six dollars worth of stuff finished. I sell four pounds for a dollar. If people would rather pay me that price than go and buy it at a rice shop and have their cooks prepare it, I am willing to go on and fix it for them, but it seems like a high price. I would not do it myself. I have orders to thirty-two pounds and the sound of the coffee mill is continually in the air. I told my cook about it and he has been quite helpful about doing it: we wash the wheat, dry it in the oven, browning it a little and then grind it in the coffee mill. It is much like George Erdman's "wheat-hearts." I only wish I had a bushel or more of American wheat and I would go into business....

I got my first capital by selling a platter. When I was at home I had three given me and as I had bought a set of dishes in 1912 and in 1920 I had nine altogether. Mrs. Ruth wanted one and insisted that she would not let me give it to her. So when she paid me I told her that would be the start of my first ten dollars. We all have a great deal of fun over this business and much rivalry over methods.

The highlight of the spring of 1925 was a houseboat trip for five days. It was hardly a true vacation, for everything had to be taken-- mattresses, bedding, food, dishes, boiled water, fuel for the lamps and stove for heating as well as two little "funglos" or Chinese stoves. The boat was rowed and towed along the canals to the Shanghai Hills about thirty miles away. For four days the family could walk the tow paths, take side trips through villages and tramp over the hills. On the fifth day they were towed home by a steam launch.

Helen, Jr. Leaves the Nest

As the time drew near, Helen began to be concerned about an appropriate college for her namesake. They had entertained Dr. Wooley, President of Mt. Holyoke and were hoping that Helen, Jr. could pass the college boards in June. But she did not--though there were others who managed to do so. So in August of 1925 Helen, Jr.--a young, unsophisticated seventeen and a half year old girl--set off for the States expecting to be accepted at Lake Erie College in Painesville, Ohio, where she would be near Cleveland, Helen's brother's family, and Mrs. Taylor.

Helen's concern about the poor teachers Joe, Jr. and some of the others had made her determined to push her own efforts to see that each child was helped at home. Charles Boynton, the principal, did the best he could, but most of the teachers were young college graduates out to see the Orient and had little experience. In the summer of 1925, Ruth, who wanted to earn money, was given the job of "playing school" with Stewart and the twins every day:

> Ruth has it quite well organized already. She is a born organizer. Then she practices herself to keep up her music. Ruth has already had piano lessons for two years. The rest were just beginning at her age. She can swim, dive, swim under water, roll in, do anything she pleases. She is what I call a bright child....I storm at the school, to Joe, and to you, but after all we are glad to have it and keep our children and some way somehow they will get through, if not at a big Eastern college, somewhere....
>
> We had quite a scare over Martha last week and she is in bed though quite all right now. She had an acute attack of asthmatic bronchitis and was quite sick for twenty-four hours. I have never seen anyone bronche as she did. We are always having some excitement and with Martha we are always afraid of her kidneys beside anything else that may be troublesome. I wrote you did I not that the twins and Stewart had their tonsils out a month ago? After a day or so I told Elsie that Martha was much better, and asked if she was not glad. She said, "Of course she would get better. Didn't we ask God every little while to make her better and of course then He would." She is such a sweet youngster.

October, 1925, to Mrs. Taylor:

> Little Joe has been having "Hongkong foot" which is some form of skin infection and he has been and will for a time still be wearing old shoes cut along the side. We were quite concerned over a week ago. The infection went up to his thigh and there was swelling there and he had a fever. As a

71

boy in school had just died of blood poisoning after a scratched mosquito bite I was so worried that I could scarcely think all that day. But he pulled through another time. He is always having narrow escapes of one kind or another....

We are so interested in the mails these days. [Jr.] is having many new experiences and she is very good about writing all about them. I expect she is making a good many mistakes but I trust that she will come through all right. She is meeting a good many things at once, finances, independence about study and choice of work, and other decisions which are new to her. Margy is a little better equipped to start off alone than Helen. And perhaps I am so impressed by Helen's dependence that I am making Margy more independent. Perhaps I shall learn too by experience and how to make it easier for my next daughter to leave home.

It was difficult the first few months for Helen, Jr. to adjust to college life, although by Christmas she had begun to find her place and enjoy some activities. She frequently went to visit Mary at the Watson Home and was sharing the social life of one of Mary's teachers. Reports of this led her mother to come to the conclusion that Lake Erie College was much too worldly and Helen, Jr. should be at Wooster.

In a letter to Helen, Jr. in November, 1925, Helen wrote:

I am wondering about these new friends and about "blind dates." It isn't so absolutely necessary is it to have a boy at a party there, that you have to resort to strangers! And if you do such a thing yourself don't take the responsibility for anyone else, and ask a "blind date" to bring any more with him. I want you to meet boys but there is no such rush. Do it in the regular way. I trust you, my dear, absolutely but you haven't been in America long and must not follow "strange gods" until you know a little more about the accepted way of doing things....

Remember, dear, that you are representing your Daddy and Mother and your home training in all you do and someone is judging us by what you do. I do not know [your friend] but if I were to judge by your descriptions of her subjects of conversation and by her assistance in this case I would prefer you to accept no more of her invitations.

Dear, we seem so far away and this is just the kind of thing we could talk over so much more easily. Maybe it is all right. It just doesn't sound so to my old fashioned ears. The reason I want to warn you is because I made many careless mistakes myself, going around with people for whom I cared nothing and of whom I did not approve but looking for a good time. I went to New York and lost my head a little. So don't lose yours....

There is a little responsibility about being the first born and the first to do things like going off to America alone. And believe me, dear, there is a responsibility about being the mother of the first.

Fortunately for her mother's peace of mind, college rules were strict--students were to be in their own room at 10 and lights out at 11, chaperones, etc. Helen did extract a promise from her daughter that she would not marry until she had completed college.

In October, Joe wrote to Helen, Jr.:

We do so much enjoy your letters; we can hardly wait until the mail is delivered. We like to know all about what you are doing from day to day; what people say and what you think and what you spend, etc. I know from my own experience that the first year in college you are having many new questions to solve and some of them are not easy. They were not for me even though I was much older than you are. Your training has been much better than mine and your devotion to a high purpose in life I am sure will help you very much when deciding what things you will do and what things you will not do. We cannot do everything we might like to do but we, if we are to get one, must choose out the better things and leave the less important things alone. I am sure that you will be leader in the better things in college as well as in your books.

I think you got home economically. I was glad to send in such a report to Mr. Wood. We have to keep reminding ourselves that what you spend and what we spend is raised by self-sacrifice on the part of a great many people who contribute to our work in China. Some of these people, I know, do not have as many comforts as we enjoy so I do not feel like spending money too freely on my own pleasures. Then too your mother and I have felt that we should save whenever and wherever we could in order to be a little surer of being able to put through college this big family. Should we because of war or sickness have to give up our work here or if the Christian Association should go broke it might become very hard for us to offer the younger children a college opportunity. Under those conditions such responsibilities might fall on the older children who may have already received their college training.

As you know, the Christian Association has offered, if necessary, to give twelve hundred dollars for twelve months. This amount is to cover everything that we spend on you and you spend on yourself and on others. It will be necessary for you to watch your outlay very closely if you [are to] get through the twelve months on that amount and have as many clothes as you had the first of September....

I have gotten a little book in which I will keep the accounts you send me each month. I began with your September balance. I hope that we can keep somewhere near each other. I had already sent you a check for $100 before I got your letter. Of course where we ask you to buy for us or for Mary these accounts should be kept separate and settled by separate check.

We want you to have an opportunity for getting the best education possible and get as much of it as you want but we cannot promise definitely any allowance after you are twenty-one for according to the present arrangements that is as long as the Christian Association is responsible for our children. If you do your first four years well other opportunities should, I am sure, open up, should you wish to continue.

Helen's response to Mrs. Taylor's initial criticism of the college includes:

I want her [Helen, Jr.] to be happy, to have "youth;" good times unclouded as my years at her age were by any such troubles. I want her to play hockey and out of door games and be faithful to her work indoors, and keep that little sweet dignity that she has, and keep free a little longer from the "boy craze"....Joe and I are much pleased about her music. We did want her to go on with it but felt we could not afford it. [Mrs. Taylor paid for lessons.] We have to save some of our money for the next seven and cannot give it all to the first one, though Helen has much more music in her than Margy. Ruth is the most promising of all of the first five. Elsie and Martha are beginning to want to pick things out on the piano and I am trying to give them a little of reading of music, learning the notes and their places, already. I began with Ruth when she was six and she reads music now like a fourteen year old, so her teacher says.

Joe wrote again late in January reminding Helen, Jr. she was just eighteen:

You are young, you are going through many new experiences; you are studying new books, and at best [this] is a trying time for most young people. Some lose out entirely and throw everything up and begin to say and do things they would never have let themselves do before going to college.

The thing which saved me during my college days was my active connection with Christian work in the University. I do not believe any boy or girl is strong enough to go to college, refuse to take part in the religious life of the institution and come out with as high ideals as he or she entered college. It can't be done.

If a fellow on the other hand will decide to tie up and actively promote the best things in college and will stand out for what he knows to be right and "keeps himself unspotted from the world" doubts and misgivings will not seriously affect his life. Stick by your Bible study and prayer and try to persuade others to do likewise and when you get through your college course one of your happiest recollections will be the help you have given the other fellow. Some girls in your dormitory evidently have not been brought up as you have and do not think, talk, or act as you do. It is not easy under those conditions to live just the sort of life you want to live but I am sure if you do live an honest, sincere life before them they will respect you for it and you will be helpful to them even though you do not try to discuss theology with them. Keep us posted fully on all you think, experience and want to do and we will help you decide what can be done another year.

By late February, Joe was scolding her about her financial records:

Evidently you are not keeping your accounts very carefully and in a businesslike way. When you put under one item--books, stamps, theme paper, hairpins, shines, etc. it is quite impossible to keep a ledger and know at the end of the year what you have spent on clothing, school supplies, gifts, etc. You have seen your mother all your life keeping almost daily accounts of all our household expenditures so that she can tell year after year just what we are spending and if we do not watch carefully our expenditures we would certainly be in the poor house before this.

Accounting has saved us many dollars and it will do the same for you and that is the reason why I want to get you started doing it right. If you do it systematically you need not spend two hours at the end of the month trying to balance a fifty dollar account. It's part of your training to learn to keep accounts accurately. So come along and see what you can do next month.

In February of 1926, Helen wrote Mrs. Taylor:

Our guests all left us the fifth of January and then for a few days I just rejoiced in having the children in school and no one in the guest room. Then we began our annual January illnesses. This year it was the flu and Stewart, Martha, Margy and I all suffered. I think I never felt worse in my life than I did those few days. I really would have died without a struggle and with a very deep feeling of relief. Martha took it of course rather hard as she does everything and is not herself yet. I had kept her in bed eight days of the Christmas vacation just to fatten her and rest her a bit and she was just beginning to improve. Now with the flu she is pale and thin again. We are only letting her go to school in the morning and have a nap after luncheon. Elsie is so robust and healthy looking. They have just been promoted to second grade. That ends their babyhood. When a child passes into second grade, she seems so much more grown-up.

Again writing Mrs. Taylor:

In this mail we are sending Margy's application to enter Lake Erie this next Fall. She has been registered for four years at Wellesley and hates to give up going there. But there are several reasons for the change. She had no better preparation than Helen and Helen did not pass College Boards; and the date of the examinations this year is one week later and we had already engaged passage on the 22nd of June and we would have to give up going around by Europe...Margy is anxious to take this trip. Then Wellesley is this year, with the other Eastern colleges raising the rate to $1000. That seems an enormous price to pay and then add to it all the extras....Helen seems to be happy and getting something out of her course, besides just study....Of course I hate like everything to give up both Eastern colleges: perhaps it would have made me too proud to have my daughters at such institutions and for that reason this change is being forced on me....

Mary writes very little to us nowadays but all reports tell of improvement. It is a comfort to know she is better and we are looking forward to seeing her in September.

Mrs. Taylor upset Helen greatly in her continuing criticism of the liberalism of the college, and that Helen, Jr. was not working to earn money, but was selling Chinese things on commission. Her mother's defense was strong:

When we sent her home [to the U. S.] we told her we did not wish to have her do anything to earn money in college this year. We made this decision upon the advice of Dr. Woolsley and several other women who have known a good bit about college girls. She feels that the first year in college, especially for girls coming from another country, it is not wise to burden them with extra work. She thinks they need a year to get adjusted to being responsible for themselves, a year to get grounded in their studies and then they can start the next year and earn part of their expenses. So it would not be fair to Helen to blame her for doing nothing this year. She put her name down almost the first week for summer work of some kind and has expected to take care of herself. She has already applied for office work to the college and has our permission to do so. She asked us about doing four hours of work a day and we think that is too much and have advised her to ask for two hours. And only on the condition that the Dean things it fair for her to take it since she is accepting a scholarship. For sometimes there are not enough jobs to go around.

I did four hours a day at Teachers College and it leaves one very little time for study more than that enough to get the daily lesson, and little time for exercises. I'd rather she got more out of her course, and had more time for required reading and study. My exercise, of course, came with my college course. She has been to a co-educational school all her life so far. She found that many boys were stupid and that some cheated and lied and some were splendid boys. She knows that there is still a halo around her father, for me, even after nearly twenty years. The kind of men that we have in our home and that we enjoy are men who could not have been plain every day boys. I don't want her to get an idea that all men are stupid, nor that all men are common and ordinary. Nor do I wish her to think that they are gods. She is young and has not had much experience and she will make mistakes. I hope that you will not be too hard on her.

As for selling things that is the way that many of the school children from here have paid for their way and it is natural that if the girls wanted things she had, she should let them have them and order whatever they wish. It seems to me a perfectly legitimate way to make money; just as legitimate as to sell *Peters Chocolate* as did a man I knew at Princeton; or to take orders for suits of a certain brand of clothes as some of the Shanghai boys do at Oberlin....

Eighteen weeks from now and we sail for home. I wish of course that we were going a shorter way but it will be a fine thing for the children to have this experience. Joe too needs a vacation for we have not been away for a summer since we last came home from furlough....I am looking forward to having

Mary with us for a few weeks, for I realize that she is getting tired of the isolation of the Watson Home. It will do her good to get acquainted with her family and some normal children. But when I think of the sewing and packing and other work that lies before me, it seems that eighteen weeks will not be long enough to get everything done[1].

Around Easter Helen again wrote Mrs. Taylor, this time about a trip inside China:

Last week I actually went away for four days. It is seldom that I do that it is quite an event. I went to Nanking and stayed at Ginling College. The new buildings are lovely, the prettiest that I have seen in China. I loved the whole place, buildings, girls, atmosphere and all. You know perhaps that the Y.W.C.A. Physical Education Training School moved up there last year and has joined Ginling much as Boston Normal School of Gymnastics became a Department of Physical Education at Wellesley. I have been on the YW Board for so long and interested in the School that I wanted to see whether I approved of the present combination. I am most enthusiastic over the working out of our plan and I am especially enthusiastic over a Chinese College for girls here in China.

On June 20th Helen again wrote Mrs. Taylor:

This is our last Sunday in China. We sail Tuesday afternoon and next Sunday will be on the way from Hongkong to Manila. All the five smaller children are in bed and Big Joe and Margaret are at the lap supper at the Y.M.C.A. compound for the families who are going away. Martha was sick again and I stayed with her. We are very much troubled about her. She has these repeated attacks of asthmatic-bronchitis and does not seem to get over them....We have rented our house for the entire time and now it is cleaned and ready for the new occupants. Everything is packed and ready to go. The rest of the children are in splendid health and all promoted. Margy has graduated and is ready for college. She has had a very happy two weeks with lots of things going on and a lot of gifts. She was in the Senior play and had a lot of fun out of that....Joe and I have been to six Chinese dinners in nine days....Last night his senior class gave us a dinner at a new hotel. Last year's class had us for dinner Thursday night. I have never had so much Chinese food in so short a space of time.

Helen, Jr. Leaves the Nest

In late June 1926 the family sailed for their furlough from Shanghai. The ship stopped along the way at Manila and then went on across the Indian Ocean, up the Gulf of Aden, through the Red Sea and docked at Suez. To add a little excitement to this long voyage, it was decided that Helen should take the three older children (Margaret, Joe Jr., and Ruth) to visit the Pyramids in Giza. Instead of letting them join a regular tour group, Joe dickered with a local camel driver to take them on camels and then to meet the boat at Port Said. So off they raced on camels, the local driver determined to beat the more orderly tour group. However, he had no desire to race to Port Said. Much to Joe's distress and final relief, the group arrived just forty-five minutes before the ship was to sail on to Marseilles.

Meanwhile, as Joe and the others went through the Suez Canal aboard their ship, it was so hot in their cabins that Joe put the top of his trousers around the porthole and directed one leg to the upper and another leg to the lower berth in an effort to get inside what breeze there was.

The other excitement of the trip for the children, in addition to feeding pigeons at St. Mark's Square in Venice and visiting the London Zoo on a double-decker bus, was the chance to meet Gertrude Ederle, who had just completed swimming the English Channel. She boarded the *Berengeria* to award prizes to the young swimmers aboard. (Later that year the twins had another opportunity to meet her when she gave swimming lessons at the Y.W.C.A. in Atlantic City.)

Awaiting the family's arrival in the U.S., Helen, Jr. had applied to the Hiram House Settlement in Cleveland for a six week course in social work; the field work in the course was to be centered on recreational activities for the neighborhood children and adults. She was also able to talk the playground director there into letting her work additional time as her assistant. This was Helen Jr.'s first experience in social work.

In September she went to Pittsburgh and then took Mary with her on the train to join the family, altogether for the first time in many years.

Family picture from 1926.
From left: Elsie, Helen, Joe Jr., Martha, Margaret, Ruth, Joe, and Stewart.
Helen Jr. and Mary were in the United States at the time of the photograph.

CHAPTER ELEVEN

A YEAR OF DECISION
1926-1927

The 1926-27 furlough year in Ventnor passed quickly. Helen, Jr. and Margaret were both at Lake Erie College and Mary was finishing high school at Watson Home. Joe was placed at Peddie School for the eighth grade. Ruth was in 6th grade, the twins in 2nd grade and Stewart in kindergarten in Ventnor.

In a letter on September 12, 1926 to Mrs. Taylor, Helen wrote:

> This is our twentieth (wedding) anniversary and it was fine to have all our family together....It is wonderful to have Mary back again. She gets around on this floor which has a bedroom and bath. We found a wheelchair in the basement and though the steps off the front porch are steep, we manage to get her down. She enjoys getting out for she was so closely confined at the Home. Little Joe can take her to the movies. It is not possible for her to go to school here.

In October Helen voiced one of her infrequent complaints:

> Joe is in Philadelphia and will not be back until tomorrow night. It certainly seems strange to me to be keeping house with just four little children and without Joe so much of the time. I do not know how I will get through the winter. The older children are so companionable and bring such wide interests into one's life.
>
> Last Saturday we drove up to Hightstown to see little Joe. He is in a fine school but it was hard to leave him. I miss him dreadfully. This year is just what he needs however. His work is to gather up the silver after each meal and the glasses and put them on the side board. It takes about fifteen minutes. All the serving there is done by the boys. It reduced his expenses three hundred and fifty dollars during the year. He lives in a cottage with nine other boys, an older boy who is their "master" and then a man and his wife and his children live there and are in charge....
>
> I do not know how I am ever going back to China with three girls in this country.

There were other factors, too, causing them to seriously consider their return to China. The May 30, 1925 incident became an historic event in the struggle of Chiang Kai-shek and the Nationalist Party,

which then contained many Communist members and which was trying to extend its control over more of China. Sun Yat-sen had just
died. The Communists were fanning the anti-imperialistic, anti-
foreign, and anti-missionary feelings of the people. Helen, Jr.'s diary
refers to the demonstrations of students and factory workers and the
fighting between Chinese and foreign troops, noting that her father
"is working hard to arrange meetings as well as plan for the extra
medical services needed." About the time the family left for America,
Chiang Kai-shek had withdrawn from his activities as a leader and a
kind of stalemate prevailed in both fighting and politics.

A small pamphlet titled "Are Missionaries Wanted in China" included a number of letters from groups urging Joe not to resign and
to return to China. Dr. F. L. Hawks Pott, President of St. John's University, wrote referring to long-range plans:

> As I understand the situation, the only men who are not
> wanted in China by the Chinese are those who are decidedly
> anti-nationalistic. Now everyone knows that you sympathize
> heartily with the aspirations of the Chinese people and that
> you are a sincere friend of China....Both Bishop Graves and
> myself feel that the future development of the proposed
> Medical School depends a great deal upon your help and ad-
> vice. I trust that all doubts may be removed from your mind
> and that we may count on your return in the near future. We
> are very anxious that there should be no interruption in the
> work of the Medical School until the new organization has
> been effected.

The letters from the Chinese Members of the Medical Faculty,
from the medical classes of 1928 and 1929, the Acting Dean of the
Medical School, and the University of Pennsylvania Alumni Club of
Shanghai all request his return. The message from the Chinese members of the Medical School's Faculty included the following:

> During these days you must be reading sensational things
> about China in the American newspapers and wondering what
> we are trying to do over here. Anti-Christian, Anti-Foreign,
> Anti-British, Anti-American, Anti-Japanese and what not!
> Even we, who are right in the midst of it all, sometimes find it
> difficult to comprehend. You may perhaps be glad to get a
> brief word from us to clarify the situation and to show how
> much we need your leadership in China at this time.
> In China today we are really going through a most gigan-
> tic revolution with which the Revolution of 1911 cannot begin
> to compare. The present Revolution affects not only the po-
> litical but also the economic life of our people. Our interna-

tional relations are also involved--hence the nation-wide movement for the abrogation of unequal treaties--and the activities of the anti-foreign control movement. The success or failure of this Revolution is going to exert a tremendous influence for good or evil on the entire Far Eastern situation, which in turn will affect the entire world.

The Philadelphia Alumni Association of St. John's University wrote the following:

Are Missionaries needed in China today? This burning question--the by-product of the reaction arising from the recent political upheaval in China--which essentially constitutes a part of the necessary revolutionary process that must accompany the growth and development of a country, is fast becoming a significant problem of international importance to the peoples of the United States and China. It is a challenge to the Christian world--a test of fire which Christianity must undergo to prove its strength and purity of structure. It is the signal indicating the advent of a new force, which in general is antagonistic to Christianity. But the machinery upon which this force operates is doomed, by its process of sifting out the undesired individuals among the Christian elements, to serve at its final destination a very valuable purpose to the future foundation of Christianity in China.

This flaming issue to which we have alluded has recalled to our minds a missionary friend whom we love and admire. It is our firm belief that China certainly needs more missionaries of Dr. McCracken's personality and type. The problems of a missionary in China at the present day are much more complicating and perplexing than they were fifteen or twenty years ago. For this reason, it is evident that no one other than Dr. McCracken, who has lived among the Chinese for more than twenty years, is better equipped by virtue of his extensive past experience and knowledge of Chinese customs and life to shoulder the great task and responsibility entrusted to him in China. We appreciate very highly the tremendous sacrifices which he has already made toward the fulfillment of these duties, which were performed without the least hope for wealth, fame and glory.

In Dr. MacCracken we have found a sincere teacher, an enthusiastic worker, and a true friend. The ideas of righteous living embodied in his noble personality, as exemplified by his personal revelation of a life in unselfish service, has been, and will continue to be, a source of powerful inspiration to the youths of future China--a guiding star to those who hope to reach the summit of that aspiring type of leadership which has for its basic foundation the background of character formation. Every student of Dr. McCracken who has been together with him for any length of time cannot help loving a kind, sincere and open-minded friend, teacher and adviser. As a doctor, social and religious worker, educationalist, and promoter of international fellowship, his sphere of influence knows no barrier and penetrates far and wide into every circle directly or indirectly associated with social and religious life. His popularity among the Chinese, particularly the students and physicians, and the people of the American community in Shanghai, is a genuine example of the ideal type of leadership which China wants today. We all realize that China cannot afford to lose so valuable a missionary as "Daddy" McCracken. We do hope that, after the termination of his furlough, he will again return to China to offer his much-needed service to St. John's. As the Dean of the Pennsylvania Medical School, being the Medical Department of St. John's University, we wish him greater success than he has ever enjoyed before. May God bless him and his future work in China, is the sincere wish of his obedient students and loving friends.

On June 14th the University of Pennsylvania conferred on Joe an honorary Doctor of Science degree at the Commencement Ceremonies. He left the family in Pittsburgh visiting with friends in order to attend. The accompanying citation read:

JOSIAH CALVIN MCCRACKEN--Son of this University. During your student days in the College and in the Medical School you won for yourself by your character and influence the respect and affection of all who knew you. Your excellent scholarship, your prominence in the work of the University Christian Association, your achievements as a member of several athletic teams, made you notable as an all-round man, humanly interested in all that concerned student life. Since your graduation your career and your personal qualities have given you a place in the hearts of men on two continents on which you have lived and devoted yourself to your lifework--that of helping others and relieving their sufferings both spiritual and physical.

With the prospect before you of a useful and successful career as a physician and surgeon in your own country, you deliberately waved aside such advantages as were yours here and went to China, where you felt that your skill and knowledge were needed more. You were as a physician the representative of the University and its Christian Association in

Canton and Shanghai. Your work in China as Professor of
Surgery and Dean of the Medical School of St. John's University, Shanghai, is of the finest. There has been used of you
a phrase of Dr. Weir Mitchell that you have given a fine example of the conduct of the higher professional life.

In a speech delivered toward the end of his furlough, Joe reviewed
his experiences first in Canton and then in Shanghai at St. John's
University:

> Nearly one hundred years ago, it was an American who
> was first sent to China as a teacher. And from that day to this it
> has been the American missionaries who have felt the call to
> teach the boys and girls, the young men and women of that
> country. A pupil of that first educator came to Yale University
> and it was his vision and his enterprise that resulted in the
> coming later of a group of boys of nine or ten years of age, to
> grow up in this country and absorb its ideals. That first com-
> mission was recalled by the old Empress Dowager for fear that
> they might absorb too much and too revolutionary ideas but
> nevertheless the men who composed it have had their influ-
> ence on progress in China. This was the beginning of a stream
> of students that has poured into this country to the various
> colleges east and west. And in other directions have gone
> scores of American teachers, who have built up schools in
> China, reproducing as far as possible the schools of their own
> land. Starting with primary schools where children were even
> paid to come, and gradually enlarging until they had secon-
> dary schools, colleges, and even universities, this idea of uni-
> versal education has taken root.
> China twenty years ago abandoned the system in use for
> many centuries and started, on paper only at first, a govern-
> ment plan for the education of her people. There are today
> government schools which have under instruction about 4
> million, or about one per cent of the estimated population.
> These are not free public schools as we understand the term.
> There are practically no free schools in all of China. Often the
> teaching is quite inadequate. Government schools are always
> interrupted by political disturbances.
> Education is the most important opinion forming and citi-
> zen training agency, and "modern returned students" have
> been influential in emphasizing education.
> There is now a "National Educational Association"--a
> "Mass Education Movement" which is an attempt to put edu-
> cation in the terms of the vernacular; "Daily Vacation Bible
> Schools" taught by volunteers who are themselves students;

and a "National Association for the Advancement of Education." These educational beginnings make less noise than the militarists, but are the foundations which in the years to come will be more effective in bringing about a new China than the present clamor.

In 1906 our own University Alumni sent me to China to investigate conditions and ascertain what kind of foreign work the Christian Association might undertake. I spent seven months in and about Canton and soon made up my mind that there was no place where a man might so acceptably give his life, his knowledge of medicine and his belief in Christianity. In Canton the first American physician had also made his mark. But among the millions in South China there were only a handful who had ever heard of, or were willing to trust to any modern treatment of disease.

One of the items in a list of American beliefs about the Chinese, compiled by a student in America for the recent China Number of the *Literary Digest* is that "in China, doctors are paid as long as their patients are well and that the payment ceases the moment the patient falls ill."

That statement is about as unreliable as would be the diagnosis of the untrained native doctor in any case of illness. I have seen women, hundreds of them, kneeling in a temple before a hideous god, shaking a container full of bamboo sticks. When one stick rose above the rest she took this stick to the temple priest who gave her the prescription called for by the number. She then could go [to] the native drugstore and buy this prescription which she thought was prescribed especially for her complaint by the idol. But the "snaps and snails, and puppy dogs tails" of the childish rhyme are as nothing compared to the ingredients of some of these prescriptions. I hesitate to tell you for fear you will not believe me; some of the remedies I have known to have been tried on some of my patients before they came to the hospital.

There never was a "clean up" week in old China. There is today, outside of foreign controlled cities, no sanitary disposal of waste; there are no health boards, with regulations to protect the citizens. Bubonic plague, smallpox, leprosy, all contagious diseases are never isolated. It is a new idea to most Chinese that "large man can give small baby sickness."

There are hundreds of thousands of cases of preventable blindness and the latest statistics given in a recent paper from China, estimate that the number of Chinese lepers is one million. Until within the last few years there has been no knowledge of science and its applications to modern health movements. We have no idea, living in this country here today what this means to the conditions of a country with millions of people.

But it takes more than a few foreigners to make any impressions on the ignorance and superstition and our plan twenty years ago was to train Chinese leaders, men who given the knowledge and with it the ideals and standards of Christian citizens, would go out and help their own people to help themselves.

We spent seven years in Canton, studying the language, healing the sick who came from the nearby villages; buying land which in itself means many contacts with the country people for to buy twelve acres it took about five hundred transactions; and teaching classes preparatory to the boys' study of medicine. But no students were at that time ready to begin real medical work and in 1914 we joined St. John's University in Shanghai.

This is the oldest and the best known of any of the colleges in China. It was already doing medical teaching and had been since 1881, but with a very limited faculty. The number of students was small but they were well prepared to do their work in English. Three of the faculty were Pennsylvania men, Dr. H. H. Morris, Dr. W. H. Jeffreys, now of Philadelphia, and Dr. E. H. Tyau, a Chinese who had taken post-graduate work at Pennsylvania.

Twenty-five years ago, practically all the teaching of medicine was done by the busy foreign doctor who was not only the teacher, but was also the superintendent of the hospital, business manager, internist, surgeon and often head nurse. Students wishing to become doctors would walk the wards with this busy man and endeavor to absorb some of the medical knowledge. It was this kind of medical training which the late Dr. Sun Yat-Sen received and with only this very limited opportunity some of these students went out and rendered real service to their people.

Progress has been made along the line of medical education. Instead of these "one man schools" we have seven schools which are rated as A Grade. They all require at least two years of college preparatory work which must include special science courses. They all give four full years of prescribed study and most of them require one year of internship before they grant the degree of "doctor of medicine." These seven schools are located in different parts of the country.

The St. John's-Pennsylvania School is at Shanghai and is the oldest. It is of American origin. The teaching is done in English.

The Mukden Medical School is in Manchuria and is the effort of all the missions from Scotland and Ireland in that district. The teaching is done in Chinese.

The Peking Union Medical School is the outgrowth of the united mission work of that city but is now under the Rockefeller Foundation and is most thoroughly staffed and equipped. All teaching is done in English.

The Shantung Christian University Medical School is a union of British and American mission boards. The teaching is done in Chinese but English is taught as part of the required curriculum.

The Yale School which has just closed, also used the English language for all teaching work. It was located in Chansha, Hunan Province in central China.

In Szechuen Province, the most western of all, at Chengtu, is the Union Medical School, the united work of the American and Canadian missions and it endeavors to meet the needs of some 67,000,000 people.

There is also a Women's Medical School at present in Shanghai, a new school, teaching in English.

All of the six schools previously mentioned, except St. John's, accept women students with men. We are already cooperating in Shanghai with this new school and hope some day that the two may unite.

But these seven schools are inadequate to meet the needs of China for trained physicians. There are graduated altogether, not more than one hundred doctors a year when 10,000 are needed. Since doctors are not made synthetically the only way I know to meet the need is to continue as rapidly as possible to train young men and women in the art and science of medicine.

I would like to tell you of some of the men who have been graduated from our medical school and something of their work toward the betterment of their country.

Dr. F. C. Yen graduated in one of the earlier classes and has since taken post-graduate work in America and Europe. He has been for many years the moving spirit in the Hunan Province Red Cross and Public Health work. He was for many years the dean of the Yale Medical School and is now President of that School.

Dr. E. S. Tyau graduated with Dr. Yen and is now Professor of Tropical Medicine in the St. John's Medical School and now its Acting Dean. He has done post-graduate work in our own University and is considered one of the most skillful diagnosticians in China.

88

A Year of Decision (1926-1927)

Dr. W. L. New, after graduation, spent in England several years of study and work in surgery and is now the largest surgical practice in Shanghai. His brother, Dr. W. S. New, did post-graduate work in Harvard and is now doing orthopedic surgery in Shanghai. Both are members of our faculty.

Time will not permit relating the splendid work of others in other parts of China nor of the excellent research work done by one of our graduates in Harvard University. It is by work such as this that our graduates help to bring modern medicine to their people, and to encourage us to think that our efforts are worthwhile and worth continuing.

And today China is not the China that has been written about for centuries. China is changing; merchants, missionaries and diplomats hesitate to make any prophecies about the country....Politically the term Republic of China is an empty phrase. The economic life of China is almost at a standstill. Advancing and retreating armies squeeze the very life blood out of the long-suffering people. China has on hand today not only a revolution in government but also in industry, in religion and education. During the last twenty years when few took interest in the government the change has brought to this so-called republic hundreds of political agitators as well as a number who are really interested in government reform.

In his descriptions of the situation in China, some of Joe's insights even seem to foreshadow what would happen so many years later in Tiannamen Square:

We see the beginning and rise of a great force known as the Student Movement, a movement full of possibilities both for good and evil For good, because it means that the country is awakening; for evil because the student is young, inexperienced and impressionable. Country wide student organization and participation in national affairs originated during the Peace Conference in Versailles in 1919. The Powers there assembled were trying to decide the disposition of that part of China previously held by Germany. The students of China sent a cable to the Chinese representatives urging them not to sign the treaty if Tsingtau were to be given to Japan and not handed back to China where it belonged. The Treaty was not signed by the Chinese delegation.

A year or so later three unusually corrupt officials in Peking were selling to foreigners the very birthright of China. The students again rose up in their might all over the country, a mass movement was started. A big parade was staged in Peking and several students lost their lives but these three officials had to make rapid exit to Japan. Ever since that time the student class has been a power and influence in the politics of the country. They are radical, aggressive, apt to follow rash methods, and eager for a change of any kind.

The recent radical changes in education result in radical thinking along political lines. These younger men are steering the ship of state out on an unchartered sea, the load is heavy, the sea is broad and deep, the wind of the agitators is treacherous.

Sun Yat-Sen, one of the first to be imbued with the spirit of change for China has become their George Washington. He was most active in bringing about the overthrow of the Manchu dynasty and was the first president of the Republic. Now his principles have become the creed of the people.

The object of his Three Principles is not destructive but constructive. According to his own statement the object of the "Principle of the People's Nationalism" is to hasten the attainment of international equality by the Chinese nation. The object of the "Principle of People's Sovereignty" is to hasten attainment of equality in government. The object of the "Principle of People's Livelihood" is to hasten the attainment of economic equality. Revolution is only one method and is the means and not the end.

He advocated the revival of the former virtues of China and also emphasized China's former intelligence and strength. But he recognized that "if we do not learn the best the foreign countries have to teach we shall still fall behind....The outstanding feature of the foreign countries is their knowledge of science....It is because of this progress in science that human strength is able to make such marvelous use of natural forces."

He devised the following program for the gradual establishment of a national government, according to Mr. T. Z. Koo, an educated Chinese writing recently in *The New York Times*:

This national urge toward self-determination and self expression has three objectives. First, it is a struggle towards the political unification of China under the authority of a national government based upon the will of the people. Second, it is a struggle towards an economic life of the masses which will be further removed from the starvation point than it is now. And lastly, it is to regain its self-respect and a status of equality in the family of the nations. This national

90

government is to be organized around two kinds of powers, namely the four political powers of the people and the five governmental powers of the administration.

The political powers of the people include the power of election, the power of recall, the power of initiative and the power of referendum. Through these four political powers the people could check and control the government. The governmental powers are the executive, the judiciary and legislative which form the traditional divisions....To these Dr. Sun proposed to add two others; first, the examinative power, that is to lead examinations for all candidates for public office; second is the power of impeachment....The establishment of such a national government will go through three successive stages. First, the military stage, which is the period when twenty-one provinces of China are to be brought under the authority of one government, by military force if necessary.

The second stage, which will follow the military stage, is what Dr. Sun called the training stage, when the people of China will be made acquainted with the process of popular government. Dr. Sun's plan was to send groups of instructors to all the centers of China to explain to the people the principles of democratic organization and the duties of citizenship in order to prepare for intelligent participation in the government of the country. The third stage will be the real democratic stage when a government of the people, by the people and for the people will be established.

This program as laid down by Dr. Sun has been enthusiastically accepted by a large portion of those living south of the Yangtze River and by the student class in all parts of the country, as well as by the Chinese students in America. In the opinion of many friends of China it is a program which will take many decades to carry out.

The first stage, the military, has been on since 1911. After the breaking up of the monarchial form of government, the military generals divided the country into several camps and usurped the powers of the government. These war-lords have organized large armies which have produced nothing but have lived off the country by fair means or foul. There has been constant warring of one section against another. The turnover has been frequent and when the new victor comes in he makes new demands for the support of his armies.

It would appear to anyone who has not made a study of conditions that under such leadership progress would be impossible. But the reverse is true. During the past ten years China has made great strides; in education both private and governmental; in interest in mass education; communication facilities have been increased; daily papers have sprung up in every part of the nation. It would be within moderation to say that in the past ten years more progress has been made than in any previous century.

A study of the Custom's report shows that the imports and exports during this period have increased one hundred percent. This shows that in spite of the lack of government assistance, in spite of war-lords and in spite of those so-called unilateral treaties, China's own vitality is pushing her forward. Progress under such conditions gives great hope for the future when peace and the safety of property is assured.

As one who has lived for twenty years among the Chinese people and has learned to respect them and appreciate them for their sterling characteristics. I would like to urge upon my audience and upon our government:

(1) Toleration. These are revolutionary times in China and with the best of intentions on the part of the would-be government to protect foreign life and property, someone may be injured and some property destroyed.

(2) Patience. Young leaders, unaccustomed to dealing with great national problems are stepping forward at great personal risk to help in the affairs of the country. Many of these young men are the pick of the country. Many have received their inspiration from our own land of freedom or from our own representatives. It may have been our own representatives who have taught them to honor the flag and desire to serve their country. Mistakes will surely be made. Have patience.

(3) Time. I plead for time. China has territory forty percent larger than our own United States and almost four times our population. Remember she has a civilization centuries old which must of necessity break up slowly. Remember that communication is difficult. China has only one mile of railroad for every forty miles in this country and that mile is being used now for military purposes.

(4) Sympathetic cooperation. I plead for sympathetic cooperation. During the past forty years America

has had many opportunities to prove her friendship for China. The thinking Chinese leaders recognize and appreciate America's friendship.

Mr. T. Z. Koo recently wrote in *The New York Times*:

> Our hope is that you will maintain your traditional attitude of friendship and understanding. Your statesmen like John Hay and President [Theodore] Roosevelt, your business men, educators, and missionaries have built up for you a fund of goodwill in China which is worth infinitely more to you in trade than all the territory and special privileges extorted from us by the Powers during the past eighty years. Our hope is that you will allow us to work out our own destiny.
>
> The struggle going on in China is comparable only to the emergence of modern Europe from the Dark Ages. Our own genius, temperament and capacity must work out its problems. External influence or pressure may deter or deflect this struggle for a time but its onward sweep nothing can check...Our hope is that you will deal independently of other nations. We have to remember that different Western nations have different objectives and motives in China. For example several countries have sent warships and troops to China, all with the same statement, "For the protection of life and property only." Deep down in our hearts the Chinese believe this of America but not of some other countries.

Americans today, as in the past, can render friendly assistance to China. She is still need and by the thinking Chinese, is wanted. Her warships are there now, as declared by our President, only to protect life and property and they should be withdrawn just as soon as peace and safety are established. Our government is committed to the revision of all unsatisfactory treaties.

The Honorable Charles Hughes, former Secretary of State and President of the American Society of International Law, said in closing the annual meeting of the Society:

> It is not necessary to resort to litigation when changing conditions justify new negotiations; this is

recognized in the common conduct beyond the question of what is the absolute right of a nation with respect to a particular undertaking. Rather should be taken into consideration the mutual relations implied in the existence of the society of States. The very fact that we realize the sanctity of the obligations entered into obligates the States to alter unequitable treaties. The nations interested in this problem should consider it as individuals consider similar situations in the higher business organizations. When changing conditions justify new negotiations they are undertaken in the interest of good business.

If when these new treaties are made, it becomes impossible for Americans to do business in China under Chinese laws, as in the past they have done business under Americans laws, then business must withdraw. If they make it impossible to conduct mission work in China without special privileges, then missionaries will be compelled to leave the country as they have had to do in Russia where all treaties are abrogated.

While there have been during the past few months communistic acts toward foreigners and foreign property committed by those said to be in the Nationalist party, which do give us some concern, it is our belief and hope that this radical element will sooner or later be entirely eliminated. So that when new treaties are made on the basis of equality and mutual understanding they will be satisfactory not only to business but to all engaged in mission and educational efforts.

Whenever peace in China is established and friendly relations with other nations have again been created, I predict a period of great business prosperity, a time when foreign assistance in all legitimate forms will be sought and a time when all those who wish to come in the spirit of the Master, to preach, to teach, to heal the sick will be welcomed with open arms.

At the present time it is quite impossible for anyone to predict what is going to happen in China from day to day or what will be the outcome. It is going to be a long struggle. Business and missionary work is greatly disturbed over a large area. Trans-Pacific boats are full of passengers coming away or going either to Japan, Korea or home to their own countries.

"Why then," you may ask, "do you propose to return with your family?" I am returning, first of all, because I believe that the Chinese are sincere when they write letters asking us to come back. Second, I feel that there is work there for me to do. We have not only our own medical school which is

94

continuing at the present time, but we have also twenty-some students from the Yale School in the interior who have had to leave their school and join ours. As long as our hospital is open and full of patients needing surgical care I feel that I should be there to help. Our work is concentrated within Shanghai and is not dependent upon out-lying districts in the disturbed area.

When a ship is in trouble is not a good time to desert, as long as it is possible to render assistance.

If ever China needs friendly sympathetic assistance she will need it in the next five years. Religiously they are breaking away from the old; by remaining with them we hope to help make the new shine out more brightly.

In closing, we therefore plead again with you for China, for toleration, patience, time, and hearty sympathetic cooperation.

Having thus made the intellectual decision to return, Helen and Joe set off once more for Shanghai. Helen confided to Mrs. Taylor, "I cannot tell you how I feel about leaving America, or rather leaving the girls in America. It is truly a time to test one's faith."

Joe detailed their trip across country:

From the time we left Atlantic City until we ran the car on this boat we drove over fifty-nine hundred miles and averaged sixteen miles per gallon and paid from 16 to 40 cents per gallon of gasoline. The car gave us no serious trouble at any time. We had only two punctures, one as we drove into the yard of cousins Frank and George and the other just as we drove into another town so we never had to change our own tires. I let the battery go dry once and had some trouble starting and twice had to get help. We went over every mountain we cared to go over and did not find a hill the car, with all our load, would not take us up.

We found many ways of loading a car but found none we thought as good as our way and one that had more load around the car. We did not need to add anything to our equipment and we found all we had useful but I think again I would not take stools. The tent with a floor was a great comfort. My weight on the cots was too much for them so we did not use them all the time but slept on the ground. On cold nights, and we had a good many of them, that was the only way we could keep warm. Some nights we all (7) slept inside the tent 9.5 by 9.5 feet, which was some crowded but warmer. Only a few times did we take a wash inside except when we were with our good friends. After sleeping on the hard ground for a few nights a good soft bed did feel mighty good and prevented me from getting bed sores. Our friends and relatives were so good to us. We started out with Frank in Philadelphia who many times during this year took us all in over night and this time over Sunday. Elizabeth and Frank have a fine home and are so hospitable.

The next stop was Gettysburg with [a former medical classmate] whom I had hardly seen since graduation and he took us right into his big house even though his wife was not there....The next day we landed in Pittsburgh and the family stayed there while I went back to Philadelphia to get my honorary degree conferred upon me by the University.

And then came our ten days all together in Helen's brother's home in Cleveland where we kept house but had a maid. It was a wonderful ten days and then we bade Helen and Margy goodbye[1] and the next day brought Mary back to Watson Home, bade her goodbye and then went to Wheeling, West Virginia that night and set up camp for the first time. It was a cold night and we almost froze to death. The next afternoon we pulled into Urbana [Ohio] and were welcomed with such great quantities of good things to eat and softbeds. Two more nights of camping before we reached Kansas City where we stayed overnight with my friend Dr. Oatland. The next evening we were off to Sterling after 296 miles of travel over not the best of roads. That was the day too that we had to stop and care for a young man who had been thrown under his car and nearly killed. You all know what a good time we had in Sterling. It was too short but we were glad to have that much time to get acquainted again. And then came the nice, restful day with Gib and Flora in their home.

"About a thousand miles from Seattle" Joe wrote a letter back from shipboard in August:

The sea was terribly rough the first morning after we left Seattle and was getting rougher. Helen took the younger children to breakfast at seven and they all except Stewart went out on the deck and vomited it up. Helen and I went to breakfast and ate some fruit and porridge--afterwards I went to my cabin and went to sleep over a book. Helen woke me at eleven and said she was all in and that the children were vomiting all over the deck. She went to bed for the rest of the day, vomiting at intervals. I went up on deck to look after the children. No one wanted to go down to lunch. I stayed with them until one and then I went to the cabin to sleep a couple of hours. When I woke up I did not feel very sure of myself but I thought I must go up and see the children. Elsie was the sickest so I brought her down and put her to bed. Joe [Jr.], Ruth and Martha wanted to remain on chairs on the deck--Stewart was lively as a cricket and never sick at all. On my way back to the cabin I knew my time had come, and by the time I had reached our cabin I was ready to heave up Jonah. I got all the children to bed that night without either dinner or supper. Elsie was sick some during the night but all slept well and by morning the water was calm and everybody got ready for food and fun again....

We went to bed Sunday night and when we woke up it was Tuesday morning so this will be a short week. Every time we cross the 180 meridian going west we drop a day and when we come back going East we pick it up on the same line.

Life on the ship has begun. I have been elected chairman of the Sports Committee and we have to arrange for all the games this week and raise money and give suitable prizes....Altogether you can have a mighty good time on a steamer when it is not too rough weather. We have had a most satisfactory furlough and hope we will be able to jump right into hard work for another term of five years.

Joe received an honorary Doctor of Science degree at the University of Pennsylvania graduation ceremony on June 14, 1927. The group of those honored with various degrees included (from left): Dr. J. C. McCracken, Dr. Geo. D. Rosengarten, A. S. W. Rosenbach, Dr. C. W. Richardson, Dr. Penniman (provost), Miles Farrow, A. W. Thompson, the Rev. A. C. Baldwin, M. B. Medary, and H. S. Dennison.

CHAPTER TWELVE

BACK IN SHANGHAI
1927-1931

When the family returned to Shanghai in the late summer of 1927, Chiang Kai-shek was renewing his efforts to purge the Nationalist Party of Communists, extending his control of land into the Peking area, and seeking recognition of his government by foreigners as the National Government.

Shanghai was one of the world's largest seaports. Not only did it have a greater concentration of business and industry than any other part of East Asia, but it was the Far Eastern headquarters for this commerce and for both Protestant and Catholic missionary and educational organizations. Its population was some three million, including about 75,000 foreigners of almost every nationality and race. Shanghai was still an "oasis" for everyone. Some efforts had been made to get the United States to support intervention to protect Shanghai and make it a "free city," but the United States government continued its non-interventionist policy and took no positive steps to change the treaties and "gunboat" diplomacy, issues that were being used by the Communists to rile up more and more anti-foreign, anti-capitalist, and anti-religious feelings. Many missionary groups were having to bring their foreign workers out of the interior due to the turmoil.

At Thanksgiving (1927) Joe sent a letter to his supporters with a report on conditions:

> We have received here a hearty welcome from both Chinese and foreign acquaintances, who have made it clear to us that we are still wanted in China. The political situation is most confusing. The Southern National Movement certainly did allow itself to be led astray by Communism, which has almost wrecked the party. There has been considerable destruction of property belonging to both Chinese and foreigners and there is still much mission property occupied by soldiers; but the dangers of Communism, as such, have been recognized by the Chinese and everything possible is being done to rid the national movement of this destructive element. The country is still in the grip of half a dozen warlords whose armies feed off the people and do about as they please. Discipline is lax and it is from these uncontrolled soldiers that most is to be feared by those foreigners who are trying to live away from the treaty ports. We feel progress towards something better is being made, but so far it is mostly psychological and not material.

The common people are waking up; they are beginning to want something better and are becoming dissatisfied with everlasting wars and banditry. The privations of the poor, the sufferings of the innocent and the fears of the rich are beyond comprehension. In the midst of all this, and in spite of it, our hospitals and educational work go merrily along. Our classes are nearly double the normal enrollment, since we are now the only mission medical school teaching in English. The students are thankful that they can come to this protected area and continue their medical studies. They are a fine lot. In addition to teaching Surgery, I have a third year class in a Discussion Group (à la Pennsylvania). Here we study together frankly some of the problems, temptations and ideals of life. Last week our subject was "A Man's Temptations" and this week we have "The Duties of the Ideal Doctor". This class gives me a chance to know the students better and at the same time to give them something more than just surgery.

Another forward step--for thirteen years I have held the position of Dean of our Faculty. Upon returning to this country this time I refused to continue in that position and insisted that a Chinese should assume the responsibility of that office. Another Pennsylvania man, Dr. E. S. Tyau, who in addition to our degree holds a D.P.H. from Pennsylvania, has accepted this position. No better man could have been chosen. Another forward step is the calling of Dr. C. H. Tyau to join our Faculty. He is one of our alumni who is now in the Graduate School of Medicine, which he will receive next spring. Gradually the Chinese are assuming responsibility. Another interesting feature of our work is the cooperation with us this year of the Provincial University of this great province. This University, being unable to finance a medical school by itself, has become responsible for the first two classes of our school. We hope that this cooperation may lead to the organization of a Shanghai Union Medical School as a private institution with Provincial Government assistance. Hospital work has been unusually heavy, with some very interesting surgical cases. We are glad to be back and to be helping to make it possible for seventy boys to continue their medical education.

With "only" five children, Helen wrote Mrs. Taylor on November 20, "I have found it hard to find enough to occupy me." After describing some classes in the Emergency School of Chinese Studies-- Early Chinese History and Chinese Contacts with Other Countries since 1800, she continues:

Back in Shanghai (1927-1931)

I have been taking the Fourth Grade in the daily exercises. There is no teacher of physical education in the School, only students acting as instructors and a woman in charge of hockey and someone taking the high school boys. The class had ten minutes of a day with their own teacher and I am taking it off her hands for awhile. I may take two or three more if they wish me to. I do so hate for them to have no training along these lines.

She constantly speaks of looking forward to mail, of wanting to know just what her daughters are doing and how hard it is to have them so far away. In the fall of 1927 Mary enrolled at Lake Erie College. She shared a first-floor suite with her sister Helen, Jr. In her second and third years she roomed with her sister Margaret. Mary was also equipped with a pair of wheelchairs--a large one she could propel for use in the dormitory and on the grounds, and a small one fitted with two poles which slipped through the chair's arms. Margaret, Helen, Jr., and later her friends, could carry her around to the other buildings and up the steps. She and her braces and this lighter wheelchair were a heavy load. Old Bentley Hall had all the science classes and labs up two long flights of stairs. One of the teachers recalls Mary "flying in at about ten miles an hour," for her friends had to get to their own classes, too. It is remarkable that she was not dropped and injured.

At Lake Erie Mary was taught to swim, a recreation she enjoyed the rest of her life. Mary had been in pools and somehow swimming for some years, but she was being taught to breathe properly and this was difficult--in fact the teacher almost despaired, for Mary would get so choked, but she improved rapidly, as Helen, Jr. was able to report in a letter to her Mother:

> You do have the hardest time with us, don't you--but I wouldn't worry about us here at college....The faculty are so interested in Mary and tell me she is getting around so well and they enjoy her in their classes. Mary likes history now and I am so glad. Miss Tyler is thrilled at her progress in swimming--and she even has her diving off from the side of the pool.

For Helen, Jr.'s twentieth birthday, January 29, 1928, Helen reported:

> I am very faithful this year about going to church, no matter who preaches or what he says. It gives me time to think, quietly, to pray for you three thoughtfully, to try to get a right attitude toward my own life. I always come home renewed in

101

spirit, ready to tackle again the sins that so easily beset me....I wish many things for you this year but all the material things are unimportant or else summed up in the desire that you may grow in character, in honor and truth and purity of mind and heart, and be kept "unspotted from the world."

Back in Ohio, Margy was not altogether happy at Lake Erie, and wrote about the possibility of transferring. In a letter to Helen, Jr. about Margy's problems, Helen confided:

We all at times fret in the place we are in. I happen to find it hard sometimes, just now, to stay here in China. That is one thing that makes me enjoy so much this school teaching. That gives me good hard work and I get physically tired and ready to sleep. I would just pass away if I did not have something like that to do. I work like a dog that hour, trying to get the children to put themselves into their class. I had just gotten the girls to doing the kind of work I meant they should do and Mr. Anderson (Principal) asked me to take the boys, too. That means large classes, forty or more to a class. The boys, of course, thought they were going to have a high old time. Physical training means to them just waving their hands in the air. I have had the boys some days now and they are getting into the spirit of the thing. But it is the problem of it that "intrigues" me, getting it across to the kids, demonstrating to the others what I have always meant by physical training, showing what can be done in fifteen minutes a day. I really love it.

Now I must tell you about two of the children. I gave them all the first day, running high jump, which I have been doing with the girls for some time. I have a precious rope of my own which I take over and we hold it and they run and jump over it. Dick Pettit went home and told his mother that now they had Mrs. McCracken, they just "had girls' stuff." So I called him up on the phone and told him that the intercollegiate record for men was 6 feet and 7 inches and asked him what he thought about it. He is a changed boy as far as that stunt goes. Then yesterday I gave the third grade a folk dance. The girls had had it and so after giving the steps to the whole class, I made them take partners and because they are so silly that they will not walk with each other, I had each boy take a girl. I wish you could have seen the consternation that followed. While quiet was being restored, one little bit of a wizened up girl, just promoted last week from second to the third grade, stepped up and whispered to me, "My mother wouldn't let

102

me do that with a boy!" I nearly exploded. I told her as there was one too many she could stand and look on.

The summer of 1928 passed quickly with Helen, Jr. and Margy going back to Pocono Lake and Mary to the Watson Home. This time the girls had a better second-hand Ford to carry them about. Students were not permitted to use cars, so they jacked up their 1924 Ford behind the heating plant on the campus where it would be out of the way of college authorities, until they used it again in 1929.

In October of 1928, Joe wrote to "Our Dear Daughters":

Every now and then it comes over us how little we know about what you girls are doing or saying or thinking or who your friends are or what you are ambitious to be or do. If we cannot see you for another four years we will need an introduction you will have changed so much. Your parents will not have changed so much. We are proud of the way each one of you are getting along in and out of school and we are confident that each will live up to the best that there is in you but it all seems to be going on so far distant from us and we are so helpless and yet so interested in everything that you do or think or are....

Nothing very exciting is happening in Shanghai just now. On the surface things seem to be quiet but there are many who predict that it can not last long and I suppose there will ever be such as long as the world lasts. So long as the ship of state seems to be rising let us blow hard to keep it rising rather than throwing our weight on it, hoping to crush it to the ground. Reports from Nanking are to the effect that there is great corruption in official circles. We Americans might remember that in the early history of our own United States a Secretary of the Treasury was filling his pockets so rapidly someone complained to the President about it who replied that the man already had his pockets pretty well filled so would not likely take as much as a new appointee. And too we must remember that "squeeze is almost a legitimate business." The modern trained men are in the harness as never before so we hope that they will have greater moral stamina gained from their contact with honest people and the Teachings of Jesus. I know of no other source from which they can draw power to live honestly.

At Thanksgiving (1928) he sent his annual letter to his supporters with Christmas greetings.

If the political campaign in our country has allowed you time to think of China, have you realized that we over here have been making history?

This country is once again united under one government which already has been recognized by other countries. Most of the warlords have been suppressed or else they have come into this New Nationalist Government. Communism has been put down although its fires are still smoldering and may flare up at any moment. The younger generation is in office as never before, and men and women have equal opportunity of leadership. But changes cannot take place at once....One advance which interests us is the establishment of the government national health bureau....

Our medical work at St. Luke's has continued to be active. The hospital is always full to its capacity and as yet there is no place for the overflow. The Shanghai Municipal Council increased its annual grant to enable St. Luke's and plans are being made to put up a temporary building in which to care for convalescing patients. This will allow us to take in a greater number of acute cases.

During the past year I have been out of Shanghai twice. In June, as physician to a "Y" conference, I visited Putoo, an island about 70 miles away. Here the Buddhist religion is supposed to have taken root, when it was brought over from India in the ninth century. It is still one of the three great centers in China of this religion.

We lived for ten days in one of their large temples, sleeping on their board beds and eating their Chinese food. They eat no meat whatever, not even eggs, for the Buddhist kills no animal nor even an insect. Fleas when caught, are carefully thrown away in the grass or in winter, buried in the sand. It was a great experience but how glad we were to get back to beefsteak and coffee! We saw a nun take her orders: part of the ceremony is the burning of four places on the scalp with hot coals. As we lived there and saw the hundreds of priests, offering their prayers, ringing their gongs, beating their drums, I was impressed with the gloomy, forlorn expression on most of the faces. I thanked God for my Christian heritage.

Last month I visited Nantung, the "model village," which has been exploited even in American magazines. It does have some wide streets, many old Fords, and some public gardens and compared to most Chinese villages, is a model. We were the guests of a Chinese banker who came down from there last summer suffering from a large growth on the neck which some doctors told him was incurable. After three operations and several weeks in St. Luke's hospital, he took his last will and testament which he had brought with him and returned to his native village, a well man. He contributed three hundred dollars to our hospital and invited me to his home town.

In one of Helen, Jr.'s letters giving her father her accounts, she reports that the college will give Margaret and her each $150 for the school year for working two hours a day in the office, sorting mail, delivering phone messages to the dormitory rooms by pulling by hand the heavy cables in the old elevator, etc.; that the three girls would also have $150 scholarships--at a time when board and tuition was $600 a year.

Helen, Jr. had also written her parents that she hoped to go to New York City for a job or to the New York School of Social Work. She had refused to prepare herself to be a teacher and was determined to get away from the small town life to which many of her classmates were expecting to return. On her daughter's birthday January 29, 1929, Helen wrote:

Twenty-one! I can hardly believe it....The New York School of Philanthropy (as it was first called) was started when I was at Sea Breeze Coney Island....I do feel that I can trust you in New York. Daddy is sure we have not prepared you for "life in the Raw." But I feel sure you are sound at the core and will do nothing thoughtless, reckless, not too modern. It means so many years of heartaches all around. I would like to have you in Philadelphia, for Joe will be coming and will need your sisterly care and steadying influence. Then too Daddy has made friends there. It is more homelike--and Frank and Elizabeth too are nearby.

This afternoon Daddy and I went to a modern Chinese wedding in the ballroom at the Majestic. I wish I had the gift to describe it to you; A good many would not go because this man has divorced two wives. First he was married to a country woman who spoke no English. She still lives with his parents tho' he is said to have gotten a divorce. Then he chose a gay, modern girl--and now he says she is crazy. So this new wife is giving Number Two $30,000 to give him up. When I first met him fourteen years ago I asked him if his wife spoke English. He said, "No, and I do not want her to know a word of it, nor my children either. I do not approve of these new women."

Now he has left all these ideas far behind. He was dressed in military uniform tho' as far as anyone knows he has nothing to do with the army. We went at 3 o'clock and sat around watching the people. Finally the Chinese band in uniform came in playing Sousa's Marches, and all kinds of things, looking quite well, but playing noisily and off key.

105

Then the groom arrived. At four the bride appeared. Then the Majestic orchestra played Mendelssohn's wedding march. They came out of the Winter Gardens and crossed the ballroom and up to a table. First came the maid of honor in lavender, then two bridesmaids in green, and the bride on her father's arm. She wore a delicate pink, with a veil which flowed yards behind and was held by a flower girl--and she carried a huge bouquet. She is a rich girl and her headdress was of real pearls and real diamonds. They fairly crept up the aisle and every six feet even stopped creeping and stood still. Finally they went on up and they had a civil ceremony, exchanging rings, made bows and it was all over. There was nothing solemn or sacred about this affair but it was interesting. The wedding cake was four feet high!...Mrs. Fitch wouldn't go and I told her I laughed all night at her. She wanted to know why and I said because she went to Chiang Kai-shek's wedding and Mei Long Soong was his fifth! She said, "Oh, that was different." I thought the difference not to his credit. But he is quite ambitious socially.

This is quite a long letter for me to write by hand but I felt like seeing you and talking with you and you are so far away....You are our dear, dear child if you are twenty-one and grown up.

In a letter written to Mrs. Taylor on Mother's Day, 1929, we learn of an unexpected opportunity for Joe:

Perhaps before you receive this letter you will have seen the girls and know that Dr. McCracken is coming to America....We had both so much wanted that one of us might see the girls this summer: five years is so long to be separated from one's children at college age. But we could hardly afford to pay for the trip, and I did not think I ought to leave the children. They are too young to leave by themselves and too old to leave with amah. We did not think of such a thing as Joe's leaving his work to go. But this is quite another matter. It is an opportunity to do something for this family, as well as for the boy....The cable went to Mr. Wood and I hope he lets the girls know right away. I can imagine their excitement when they first know it.

At last our children are at home and though not quite all right yet are nearly so. Ruth, her third week at the hospital, developed acute nephritis, getting worse in spite of careful watching and special day and night nurses, until she had one long, severe convulsion. Dr. Dunn hardly thought she could come out of that. She did however and after a few more days of anxiety she began to improve. Two weeks after that she came home but had to stay in bed for two more weeks. Altogether she was in bed eight weeks. She is still careful about diet and tho' in school has dropped some subjects and is not going in for much physical activity. When she came home we did not let Stewart go near her room for he had been exposed to measles and we thought he might be coming down soon. Ruth had not had measles with the other children. The very day after she came home, he took to his bed with fever and the next day broke out. He had a light case followed by ear trouble, had to have his eardrum lanced and is still having some discharge. It is almost well now, however.

Joe's trip to the United States came upon the urgent request of a wealthy merchant, the head of a mining company organized by Herbert Hoover. Joe had told him that his son, if it were his own child, should be taken to the Mayo Clinic. Within ten days Joe, the patient, and three of his brothers were off to Rochester with plans made for the young men to be placed on a boat for England where they would stay for seven years to complete their education and training so they could become certified accountants. Later the father would send the other nine children to be educated in the United States!

In an interview with a Philadelphia newspaper Joe gave an explanation:

> Conditions in China at present, though outwardly peaceful, are not particularly healthful for many of the Chinese wealthier classes, and the merchant was most anxious to send his children away at this time. Organized kidnapping is most prevalent and an armed bodyguard must be maintained at all times. The merchant kept a staff of five armed men on continual duty, and when his boys attended school they were at all times accompanied by an armed guard to prevent kidnapping. The victims are often held for his ransoms, and the father felt that his children would not only become well educated in the United States and England but would at the same time be more secure.

It was a wonderful event for the three girls to have their father at some of the Commencement activities. They brought the Ford out from behind the college heating plant and loaded it up for their trip to the Poconos, including Mary who would stay with them most of the summer. Helen, Jr. wrote that the Dean was horrified to have the car parked at the entrance to the dormitory along with the cars of other parents. "Looking at an old snapshot, I can understand better now her feelings, for it looked worse than those of gypsies."

Always resourceful and determined, and without the trunks we have in cars nowadays, the girls had tied to the runningboards and top everything they needed, including Mary's wheelchair. Room inside had to be saved for four people instead of two. For the girls it was fun and a means of getting to their jobs.

Helen, Jr. wrote her mother:

> Our drive to Pocono was not so bad--but I guess Daddy wouldn't want to do it again. It seems odd to have him footing all our bills. And it's the first time we had had the assistance of a man....
>
> One day I left my job and met Daddy in New York City to make some plans for what I would do. Much as I wished to return to China I knew that I did not want to attend a school for missionary training and that there was plenty of service to others which I'd prefer.   But I was fortunate. At the National Headquarters of the Y.W.C.A. they spoke of two fellowships for graduate study at Schools of Social Work in Pittsburgh and New York--a beginning recognition that Y secretaries needed full professional training. It was not until late in August, and only by pushing the New York City Y to accept me, that I learned I would go there instead of Pittsburgh where I had been accepted. This was a two-year fellowship paid by the New York City Y.W.C.A. to attend the New York School of Social Work--$75 a month for the first ten months and then $100 a month for the second year, with my field work being the thirty hours I put in at the West Side Y.W.C.A. near the old Madison Square Gardens. Fortunately for me, this money was put aside and was not affected by the Stock Market crash of late 1929 which led to the Depression. I was also more or less expected to put in at least two years of Y.W.C.A. work full time as part re-payment for such an opportunity.

Just before leaving to return to China, Joe gave an interview to a columnist of the *Evening Public Ledger*:

> China is peaceful now, but, of course, we never know out there when warfare will break loose. The Nationalists are in power and control four of the eighteen provinces of China. They are supposed to have "one united party" but it is united in name only, for there are thousands of persons in the outlying provinces who are not in sympathy with the central Government but are not yet strong enough to furnish effective opposition. At present those in power are strong enough to check any movement of opposition that might come from Canton or another outlying province. If, however, some war-

lord gathers sufficient money and men about him and thinks there is a chance to overthrow the present rulers he will strike and China will once more be on the front pages of the American newspapers. No one can tell when this will happen.

I will not live and you will not live to see China a united republic, such as the United States. The reason is that its four hundred million persons are scattered over a vast area of territory and not connected by splendid highways, automobiles and radio as they are in America. So it may readily be seen that hundreds of years will pass before China will be the kind of nation we would want her to be.

What encourages us most is that she awakened psychologically to some extent during the last ten years. The people are beginning to think for themselves. In a nation such as China is today, the only hope of progress is mass education, which will teach the people to think for themselves. But this is just beginning and there are centuries of work ahead....

We are really just beginning in medical work also, but there, too, the start is encouraging. After a fifth of a century of hard work we have now 1000 recognized physicians in China. That isn't much for four hundred million people but it is a start.

While Joe and the girls were in Cleveland, Mrs. Taylor had them all for dinner and gave him a check for $1,000 for the Community Church. On August 13, 1929, he wrote her:

You will see that we are able to sell your check in gold for M$2,392.31. The Governing Board wishes me to express to you their very deep appreciation and may we ask you to remember the Community Church and us in your prayers that his church may become a mighty force for the Kingdom in this great Oriental City.

The family all met me at the Bund and it was a sight worth seeing. I do not know anyone who had so much to come home to nor so much to leave behind in America.

The next day I started to work in the Hospital and I am now in full swing. For a month I will have the heavy operating usually done by three of us. Yesterday I was operating six hours on seven cases. Helen and Joe [Jr.] have been studying Algebra all evening. Helen is trying to get Joe up on the subject so that he may pass it off this fall and not have so much to carry during the year.

In the fall of 1929 Joe wrote to Helen, Jr. in New York:

Mr. Chester and I have had a wonderful trip up the Gorges. I have been away sixteen days now and it seems an age. We only brought clothes for a four-day trip. When we left Shanghai we thought the Gorges were clean out of the question. Mr. Chester has given me a wonderful trip and I am grateful to him. He sends his love to you. He is very much pleased with the gorges and is very glad he went to the expense of the trip. Expenses to him these days does not bother him much. He came off the farm a poor boy but he says the only reason he has anything now is because from the time he began to earn money he put away one-third of it and has it yet. What a mighty fine practice. The only reason your mother and I have anything more than a bare missionary salary is because, from the time we married, we insisted upon saving something each year.

Again in February he wrote:

And so our summer plans have finally worked out and you are now in the International House. I am glad that you are even though you may find it a little more expensive to live there. You will meet a great many kinds of people--good, bad, indifferent. You will need to make your choices very carefully of those with whom you care to associate. Living there will open up to you a great many interesting things and people all of which you will enjoy. You will have a chance to study international human nature and to develop the international mind which few people have. Try to get acquainted with the Edmunds and take my kindest regards to them. Also tell the Dickensons how much we think of them. Those kinds of people are the backbone of our nation.

Yes, there are many educators and some leaders who leave God out of their thinking and so it has always been, but they are not the ones who have helped most to make America what she is today nor do I believe they will ever be a very important element in our society. It seems to me that more people today see God in and through science and nature than ever before. Why do you not ask for an appointment with Henry Sloan Coffin and ask him to suggest two or three books you might read to counteract so much of the social service reading you have to do these days which so largely leaves out God. I am sure he would be glad to see you, and if you do see him give him my best regards. Let us know what you are thinking about and the people you find helpful. I venture to think that Christian people as a class [demonstrate] more responsibility for unselfish service to others than any class of Godless people.

Helen's letter in the spring is typical of the times and situation:

> Daddy sent Margy fifty dollars extra in the last mail and we hope it will cheer her up a little. A little cash sometimes is such a help. I have had unusual luck selling linen lately and ought to have a check for fifty dollars coming my way. Daddy is trying to get me to put it in the bank, for if I do not teach next year I shall feel hard up.
>
> I just got word that I am expected to teach and they wish me to sign up now (for 1930-31). I have said I would not teach. But what would I do without something to do, and my sixty dollars every month. I do enjoy it and love having the money.
>
> Mary has that money in a trust fund and we have never touched it all these years hoping not to have to for many more years so that it would help her out and keep her independent of you girls after we both die. We do not want any of you to feel that she is to be a financial burden in the future. If we can let this money accumulate she will be able to support herself with what she is able to do and take care of herself. But she will need help in physical ways, help about plans and getting about.

Helen, Jr. represented the family for Margaret's graduation, magna cum laude, from Lake Erie College in June of 1930. Margaret decided to return to Lake Erie for 1930-31 to take its fifth year graduate program in Physical Education. Mary was a senior and also a brilliant student. Joe came over in late summer to start two years work at Peddie School. Though he had graduated from the Shanghai American School, he would need much better preparation than he had received in China in order to compete at the University of Pennsylvania. Helen, Jr. spent the summer of 1930 doing casework in the Harlem section as part of her training, and was earning additional money by acting as receptionist at International House. In the fall she added classes at New York University so, along with the Certificate from the New York School of Social Work, she would have a Master's degree in educational sociology.

In the fall of 1930 Joe had an unexpected opportunity to come to the United States with all expenses paid. Tragically a lonely woman, who called herself a missionary, and had gone alone to the interior of China, became so emotionally ill that she had to be sent to New York State, her last place of residence, for treatment. Joe and two nurses were employed to bring her, so he was able to visit his three daughters and son as well as accomplish some business.

In a letter written on shipboard in November, 1930, Joe expresses his concern for Helen, Jr.:

A way out here away from work and worry, a fellow has more time to think and wonder what another year will bring forth for us all. With so many units to observe and be responsible for there are a good many moves to be considered every twelve months....

What I have to offer will be in the way of suggestion. I know living at International House and meeting so many people of different standards of ideals and backgrounds that of itself is enough to greatly influence one's way of thinking. On top of that living in New York and studying such subjects and working with such people might be enough to quite upset a less steady girl. While you are right in the midst of things you may not fully realize the strength of these forces and the necessity of watching your p's and q's most carefully. You cannot be too careful in the choice of men with whom you travel. I am old enough to know there are many wolves in sheep's clothing. And be careful about places you will allow yourself to go. There is so much in New York no girl needs or wants to see or hear. I am sure I do not need to warn you even once against any of the alcoholic drinks that may be offered to you. If you do, you are playing with fire and no one knows what it may light up. If you could only know how much your mother suffered on account of a drinking father--how they lost their beautiful home, how it broke up the family and finally sent her father to the soldiers' home to live until he died. I am sure you will never knowingly let one drop of that stuff pass your lips and that you would be as ardent fighter against it all your life as has been your mother and dad.

For the summer of 1931 Joe, Jr. went to Camp Tecumseh, Mary returned to Watson Home prior to enrolling at the University of Pennsylvania in the fall for graduate work, and Margaret traveled to Europe with Mr. Chester and his niece before attending hockey camp. Helen, Jr. completed her work at the School of Social Work and was continuing as Director for the programs for industrial girls at the West Side Branch of the Y.W.C.A. The Depression was beginning to affect job opportunities, but in the fall Margaret went to a boarding school for Indian children at Ardmore, Oklahoma and Helen, Jr. left New York for a position as Business and Industrial Girls' secretary at the Lynchburg, Virginia, Y.W.C.A. In Shanghai, Ruth began her junior year in high school; the twins were in 8th grade and Stewart in 5th grade.

In that July Helen wrote a most interesting description of the memorial service for Silas A. Hardoon, a businessman who played a great role in the economic development of Shanghai and was connected with the Sassoons Family, who were the Rothschilds of the East:

> We have just come from Hardoon's Gardens where they are holding a memorial service for Mr. Hardoon who died five weeks ago today. It is pouring rain but we went just the same, parked the car outside and went in. Mrs. Young had one of her husband's cards; Mr. Young is an adviser to the Chinese government. When they saw that they let us in.
>
> They have spent $200,000 on the decorations and this service. 300 policemen and assistants are showing people around. There are lama priests from Peking to do chanting and there are both Buddhist and Taoist priests taking part. We walked under a covered way, mat shed lined with white and with a white fence at each side, to keep us in the straight and narrow path, all over the place.
>
> Finally we reached a place where his tablet was in a sort of shrine. They had places on either side for the bands to sit and they played foreign music while people went up and paid their respects. The Chinese all had servants walking ahead and carrying their red old fashioned cards high in the air and calling their names. As we stood there waiting a foreign-dressed Chinese youth came along and asked us what we wanted to see. He told us if we would like to go into the inner room, we could if we made three bows. So Ruth, Mrs. Young, Elizabeth Young, Elsie, Martha, and I all went in and he told us to bow three times. So we did. Just as we began to bow they turned on the lights and took a movie of us all bowing at the shrine. That was somewhat disconcerting so we probably were too surprised to look natural.
>
> Then we went on around and saw where he was buried, right in the garden. The grave was covered with flowers and the enclosure full of wreaths. At the head of the grave was a life-sized wax statue of the man, dressed in evening clothes and wearing his decorations from the government. It looked more natural than a corpse in an open casket....If one bowed he was presented with a fan with Mr. Hardoon's picture on it and also an ordinary washcloth with Chinese characters on it. At the gate each was given a button with his picture and a paper flower, yellow camellia, to wear.
>
> Hardoon was a Baghdad Jew, brought up in the orthodox way, who came to Shanghai in 1891. He died worth one hun-

dred million Taels. He married a Chinese girl from a small
village in Fukien; she is a Buddhist. They had no children and
so they adopted eleven of them. When they were married they
had both Jewish and Chinese ceremonies. He always ate foreign food and she Chinese food and neither knew much of the
other's language. He built and gave the synagogue here to the
Jews in Shanghai. He had done or translated the Koran and
other Buddhist and Taoist books. He had 200 mow of land
there on Bubbling Well Road and a staff of 900 servants, some
of them being from the old Imperial Palace. He made them all
bend on one knee when they served him in the old palace
style. And yet he was buried according to orthodox Jewish
rites, no coffin, just wrapped in a sheet. It happened that it
rained the night before, after his grave was dug, and he finally
was laid to rest in a little pool of water in his garden. It is quite
interesting to see all this, something never before seen on such
a large scale in Shanghai and probably will not be seen again.

There is an interesting comparison from one of Joe's letters
dated July 25, 1931 and used in a January 19, 1932 appeal for
funds by the Christian Association. "To run a leading medical
school in America requires over $400,000 a year; to run St.
John's University Medical Department, Dr. McCracken spends
less than $3,000 gold a year."
The appeal continued:

As acting dean I have this month been receiving applications for admission to our school. I am surprised and mightily
pleased over the number of well prepared boys who are applying. Already the Freshman class is nearly full. With the
staff we have, we really ought not to admit over twenty but we
may go to twenty-four. I believe that we will have over fifty in
our three medical classes next year. We so much need more
teachers, in the preclinical subjects especially.

I am now working on our budget for next year. To try to
run well a medical school on fifty thousand Mexican plus my
own services is no easy job. The last year or two we have not
spent much for equipment and now that we feel sure that we
are going on, we must spend aplenty.

Sometimes I wish I could give up surgery and just try to
raise money for this school, and then again that is the last
thing I want to do. We will just have to carry on the best we
can hoping that we can do what will be worthwhile.

Helen's letter of August 29, 1931, reports:

Daddy and Ruth have gone to the French Club where Ruth is to swim the fifty yards breast stroke. She hopes to get second. I am sure she could have gotten first in the back stroke if the strap to her suit had not slipped down over her right arm. But she was second and has a cup like Joe's for diving. Martha has high hopes for a cup next week in diving. She can do six good dives. I tell her that I shall give her a dollar if she wins and shall pay for all her lessons with Mr. Bright this week. She is such a cute diver. (Ruth has just come back to say she came in first but was disqualified for she did not use her feet properly.) Elsie shines best of the three in tennis. She swims well but does not dive well. Elsie had been pinning her hair back into a small knot behind. She looks so grown up I hardly know her. I feel like calling her Helen!...

I am having a tea on the tenth for the Dunlaps and have invited 150 people....I have never had such an affair before. We are not going to have it on our anniversary (25th wedding). I do not like to have people think they must give us something. So we are going to do something together as a family to celebrate that.

In Joe's letter to his supporters, written to be sent as Christmas greetings, he makes the first mention of a continuing problem faced by so many mission schools including St. John's--that of whether or not to register with the Government:

Yes, there are wars, floods, famine and great need in China today and I could write pages about these conditions, but I believe that you will be more interested in reading about how we are trying to meet some of the needs of China.

In the first place the medical alumni of St. John's University are residing in eight of the eighteen provinces. As far as I am able to find out, all of them are practicing their professions and are doing their part towards the betterment of the health of the country.

Our alumni have spent in either mission or public hospitals or health services, eighty percent of the aggregate number of years since their graduation.

We have this year fifty-four young men studying medicine, which is the largest number we have ever had enrolled at any one time.

Up to the present time St. John's has not registered with the Government because of certain religious restrictions imposed upon registered schools. Our graduates are not given a license to practice. Notwithstanding this fact they are all practicing and the government itself is employing every available one.

As acting dean this year I have the arduous duty of trying to keep our medical school expenditures within the budget, which is not an easy job when the cash budget is equal to not much more than the salary of one good teacher in America.

This summer one of our alumni offered himself and was sent by a local Chinese Christian church into the interior to open up medical missionary work. This is the first instance where a local Chinese Church has sent a doctor as a missionary to another province.

We are thankful for the opportunity we have to serve the people of this land and are grateful to you and our many friends who have stood back of the Pennsylvania end of this work all these years, especially so this year when I know that you must have many calls for help all around you.

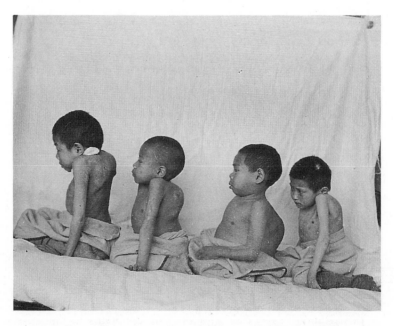

Typical young patients at St. John's Hospital (1930s)

CHAPTER THIRTEEN

THE UNDECLARED WAR BEGINS
1932-1935

The war which came to Shanghai in 1932 involved the family for the next ten years. The Japanese had been expanding their influence and control of Inner Mongolia and Manchuria. A manufactured "incident" at Mukden on September 18, 1931, gave Japan the excuse to make this area openly a Japanese dominated state. Pushing down into Northern China around and below the Great Wall and Peking, the Japanese sent troops into Shanghai and bombed the Chapei District January 28, 1932. The League of Nations took no steps which might involve member nations in a war. But after a few months a kind of cease-fire was arranged for Shanghai while the Japanese turned to concentrate on North China where, through puppet governments they were able to exploit that area's resources and markets and, by selling narcotics, weaken the social structure there. Later it was recognized that this "Mukden Incident" marked the real beginning of World War II, though it was five years before the "Marco Polo Bridge Incident" outside Peking, which started the official Sino-Japanese War.

The Japanese provided Chiang Kai-shek a visible foreign power with which to contend. But he had a worse problem with the Chinese Communists who established the Communist Soviet Republic in Kiangsi Province in 1932. Chiang Kai-shek undertook many campaigns in the next few years to try to rout the Communists and ultimately force them into the Long March in 1934. This campaign ended in their setting up a Communist Republic in the far, far west, at Yenan in Shensi Province. The Communist leader even then was Mao Tse-tung.

A January 31, 1932 letter from Helen described the situation:

> Sunday again and what a day! We are in the midst of war. I wonder what you are hearing and what you are thinking. And I do not know where to begin to tell you what is going on. The Japanese began going into the Chinese city Thursday evening at midnight. Since then they have bombed Chapei which you remember is the district outside Szechuen and Range roads....Ever since there has been shooting, bombing and burning in the Hongkew section of the city. All the foreigners have been brought out of such sections as Scott Road and Allen Court. Chinese refugees pour into the rest of the city....They have not been allowed to enter the Settlement and Frenchtown but of course they do stream in in some places.

Daddy was busy all day Friday and Saturday operating on the wounded civilians. The soldiers who are wounded are not allowed to be brought in, but there are civilians who have been knifed or shot or hit by shrapnel. Friday night some rough Japanese soldiers forced their way into St. Luke's, looked around and left. Mr. Powell told Daddy that in Manchuria they did that and, claiming that shooting was going on, went around and killed men patients in their beds. Today Daddy went down early and has not come back. There is fighting around the hospital and near the Japanese Club. He thought it safer to stay there than to try to come back for dinner and then go back. We cannot get the hospital by telephone but he can get us; of course I want to call up dozens of times to see if he is all right.

Saturday night [our Chinese friends] the Meis telephoned and wanted to refugee with us. We told them to come along, bag and baggage. They had already moved from their home to his office and then to the Y.W.C.A. I am really proud to have the Meis turn to us and am glad I can take someone in and feel I am doing even a little.

At this point Helen had six of her family, two Bakers, and now added five Meis.

After describing about $200 worth of groceries she had bought she continues:

I know that when Daddy comes home he will say why did you not take your checkbook and go out and buy more stuff? But it seems so unbelievable. We may all have to leave town. Some say the Americans will be sent out, and wouldn't I hate to leave a storeroom full that I had just paid for? Already prices are going up. I know, too, that nothing would induce Daddy to leave if he were needed and I want to be with him if he is here.

This is the first time I have ever forgotten one of you children's birthdays. I forgot utterly Helen's in all the excitement and Tuesday will be Mary's. You can now know my mind has been taken up with wars, rumors of war, food, responsibility for the family and so on.

On February 19th she wrote:

St. Luke's Hospital was evacuated Friday afternoon. Daddy arranged it and had a lovely time. He had motor trucks, ten ambulances, private cars, quite a parade. As fast as they were filled they moved over Garden Bridge and lined up and then all went out together. First four policemen on horse-back, then the Fire Brigade truck and then Daddy and then ambulances and cars. By eight at night every patient was lying on the floor in a dormitory at St. John's, his mattress under him and bedding over him and a nice white bedspread on top, and all had had their supper. I went with Daddy yesterday to see them. By that time they had gotten out beds and half were up and in beds. They moved 110 patients and 60 nurses, or-derlies, cooks, etc....

Stewart is thrilled because there is to be a Father and Son Banquet at the Church this coming Tuesday evening. Mr. Hunt has arranged for Theodore Roosevelt Jr. who will be in town that one evening to come to the dinner and make a speech. The Scout Cubs, of which Stewart is an enthusiastic member, are to be the guard of honor to receive him and Stewart expects to shake hands with him. I have had his uni-form washed and his tie washed and he thinks he is ready to do his part. He had his hair cut yesterday and has his new shoes. Such excitement.

Back in the States, both Helen, Jr. and Mary were experiencing bouts of homesickness and of feeling uncomfortable in their careers. Both girls missed the social position and status they would have en-joyed in China as their parents' daughters.

Helen wrote them:

I remember going out by bus with you two girls to Paines-ville, and saying to you then, that what I felt you girls would miss more and more, was home background. I said that you girls did not have the home to go back to at holiday time, and to give you stability. It has come over me more and more and was the reason I am so anxious to get home this year. I am afraid that it is something we cannot create in a year, but we can have each other for that time and give Mary a family feel that she does not have.

I think we are really coming home. Daddy talked with Bishop Graves today about our going and it may be that they will ask Dr. Tucker to return the first of July. We still have our passage engaged on the *Coolidge* for the 26th of June....Both Daddy and I want to go this summer. I shall come alone if we do not but we want so much to keep the family together.

Helen continued "talking" to her four children in the States, keeping the letter in her typewriter until she learned that a boat was leaving. Then she found someone sailing who would take mail; it was cheaper and more reliable. On February 21, 1932 she wrote:

Again it is Sunday, the weeks fly by for we are so inter-ested in all that is happening that we forget the time. Four months from now we shall be packed and ready to go....I hope you will like us all as much as you think you do. It is five years for some of you and you may have created an ideal that we shall not be able to attain. I am staying home again from church, actually I have not been but once so far this year and then got up and left because I was so concerned about Daddy down at St. Luke's that I could not sit still.

A week later, she added:

Since the patients at St. John's who went out from St. Luke's Hospital were getting well, and Bishop Graves did not wish them to take in more, Daddy found himself with time on his hands. So he began looking for something to do. The Chinese Refugee Committee opened the old Bickertown Hotel this week for a hospital for soldiers and Daddy and two of his assistants are to do the operating there. They took over the house one day and started to clean it up and the next after-noon admitted twenty-five soldiers and by the next morning they had 110. Then they took over the house next door. Hos-pitals are being opened all over the city by the well-to-do Chi-nese and by this refugee or relief committee which has re-ceived money from overseas Chinese. Daddy came Friday with a bolt of cloth and wanted abdominal bandages. Mrs. Dunbar and Mrs. Boynton cut them out and I sewed and later Mrs. Arnold did some and we all made thirty-six.

Most of my spare time I spend knitting baby sweaters. There were sixty new babies last week at St. Elizabeth's and no clothes to put on them. I made one little Chinese baby garment and amah certainly laughed at it. She said it was not Chinese fashion. But it was terribly cute. It seems as though one could not be idle in the face of all the need. It has taken our minds completely from flood relief.

On March 6, a further addition:

Fighting is supposed to be over but one cannot trust the Japs. They are still continuing down near Liuho (about thirty miles away). Having said they would stop if the Chinese re-treated they let them withdraw and then followed them right up. In the meantime St. Luke's is to move back to Hongkew tomorrow and the medical school is to open in two weeks.

The Undeclared War Begins (1932-1935)

Everything depends upon what happens next, but I think you can count on us getting back before September.

Gradually the situation in Shanghai became less acute and the 1932-33 furlough seemed possible. Joe remained in Shanghai to get the medical school going in the Fall. But Helen and the four youngest children sailed in late July. In Seattle she bought a new car and drove across the country to Cleveland, where Margaret had just taken a job with the Cleveland Y.W.C.A. Ruth and Helen arrived Saturday night about dark at Camp Ruthers, where Helen, Jr. was staying with a group of girls. It was always difficult for the family to be demonstrative so there was not a great deal of open excitement. But the next morning Helen, Jr. awakened early with a miserable rash completely covering her arms and legs. They finally located a doctor about noon, discussed Helen's case and included the fact she had just been reunited with her mother after five years. He suggested it was probably a reaction and to wait and see if it did not clear up by late afternoon before coming to see him. And it did clear up!

Joe joined the family in the late fall and immediately became engulfed in all his usual activities with the Christian Association and mission boards, speaking engagements and efforts to learn the latest in medical knowledge and the administration of a medical school. During this year, Helen, Jr. was in Lynchburg, Margaret in Cleveland, Mary and Joe, Jr. at the University of Pennsylvania, and the rest were in school in Atlantic City and Ventnor, where Joe and Helen were housed.

In the summer of 1933, a trip west for the family was possible because Margaret had a car in which Ruth and Helen, Jr. could return with her. Motels were not so fancy or prevalent in those days but it was fun. Helen became adept at cooking on a hot plate or a picnic grill. They managed a long day at the World's Fair in Chicago--quite an undertaking with Mary in a wheelchair--then a visit to Grand Canyon before saying their goodbyes in Phoenix, Arizona.

Mary was to return to China with her parents so that she could attend medical school. That fall she entered the Women's Christian Medical College in Shanghai, where she did so well in anatomy that the second year she was there, she taught it. Ruth was enrolled at Oberlin College for the fall, while Helen, Jr. was very anxious to return to China and pick up a job in Shanghai with the foreign Y.W.C.A. Despite her interest, Joe talked her out of this; he was sure that war with Japan was coming. So Helen, Jr. stayed in the U.S. and completed the last six hours for her M.A. degree at New York University's summer session. Joe, Jr. worked the summer at Camp Tecumseh.

Again it was difficult for Joe and Helen to return to China in the late summer of 1933, especially for Helen, who would have only four of her "twigs" to bend and could only share in the lives of the other

121

four through letters. A clipping from the *Philadelphia Inquirer* of September 18, 1933, delighted them when it came in the mail. It was entitled "McCracken, Jr., Came from China to Penn Team His Father Once Graced." The dateline was Camp Wyomissing, Minisink Hells, Pa., where the University of Pennsylvania football squad was encamped for a 10 day pre-season training period.

China, land of antiquity and ancient curios, has produced many strange things, has seen many strange happenings and developments in its thousands of years--but it is doubtful if, in all history, the oldest extant civilization, which has survived countless revolutions and has come through so much turmoil has ever fostered so strange a love of alma mater and of American football as in the heart of Josiah Calvin McCracken, Jr.

McCracken at 165 pounds is the lightest man on the University of Pennsylvania football squad....the son of that Josiah C. McCracken who is among those legendary Penn heroes of the nineties--the huskies who made "guards Back" famous. His father, indeed, was that redoubtable "Cal" McCracken who in '99 was guard on every duly recognized All American team. The son hopes to follow in his father's footsteps as quarterback and if you take the word of diverse and sundry persons who have seen him perform in the workouts on Camp Wyomissing's rain-soaked field, he is at least due to fit into his Daddy's boots as a Penn star....

Billy Morris, veteran team trainer and rubber-down, has not yet had time to spare from his liniments to watch the second McCracken generation perform. But Billy, admittedly, is stirred with memories whenever he tapes the lad. To Bill the presence of a new McCracken is like turning back the hands of the clock. You see Billy fulfilled the same duties to young Joe's father more than 30 years ago as those he is fulfilling for McCracken today.

A dreamy, far away look came into young McCracken's eyes. Dad used to tell me about those he had known when playing for Pennsylvania. But he never talked much about himself. I have since learned a lot more about him from talking to those who knew him or had watched him play than he himself ever told me....

Yes, I played football in China. The students of the American School there formed a team three or four years in a row....Our only opponent was a group of Chinese graduates of American schools whom we met three times a year.

Joe's letter to his supporters which was to take his Christmas 1933 greetings is more "newsy" than some:

> We are glad to be able again to broadcast from Shanghai. Upon our return we had a warm reception from many warm friends, for the thermometer was about one hundred in the shade.
>
> How quickly one drops into the regular routine of work to be done! The second day my colleague in surgery left for his holiday and hospital responsibility for me began. The hospital was full; so much so that all painting and repairing must be done on the wards with each bed containing a sick patient. "How terrible," you will say; but would you have us put into the street patients with broken backs, or fractured legs, or operated hernia, or operated peptic ulcer, or with some other equally serious condition? There is no other place to put them. You would do, if you were here, just what we did. You would be exceedingly careful to protect your patients from unnecessary annoyance and exposure, and with extra work on the part of those in charge, you would be able to have the entire hospital repainted without any deleterious effect upon the sick.
>
> The medical school opened two weeks after our return, with an enrollment of seventy-five, the largest in the history of the school. Seventy-five is as many as we can satisfactorily teach with the present equipment and faculty. We will do well to hold this large number for we have had to increase our tuition to one hundred and fifty dollars, which is more than any other medical school in China is charging. And too, our school is not yet registered with the National Government. Some students come to us because we are a mission school; others prefer a registered school for fear of trouble in securing a license to practice. The Government has licensed all of our graduates up to the present time but we have no assurance that future graduates from an unregistered school will have the same privilege. St. John's University will not register the institution until the Government will allow it to do so as a Christian school. A little over half of our boys are Christians, forty-one out of the seventy-five. The largest percentage is in the senior class.
>
> All but one of the fifth year students are taking their intern year in mission hospitals; that one is in the Rockefeller School in Peiping. (This is the new name for Peking.) In this way our school is making a definite contribution to mission hospital work. Eight men are in the four hospitals of the Episcopal Church; four are in Methodist Hospitals and two are in

123

Hangchow in the hospital run by the British Church Missionary Society. Many of our graduates are giving their entire time to hospital work in various parts of the country. The call is ever increasing, as the missionary boards are compelled, because of lack of support, to withdraw their medical missionaries from work in China.

This demand for Western medicine works itself out in some unusual ways. At present St. Luke's Hospital can hardly maintain its nursing staff; after a few months the men leave to make more money practicing medicine! Some have even joined the army to be army surgeons. Just last week it was found that the operating room coolie, the night-watchman on the medical side, and the two coolies in the receiving ward, had opened a hospital of their own. The operating room coolie was chief surgeon, the night-watchman was the medical chief, and the two coolies in the receiving ward were contact men and turned patients toward the new enterprise. Can you beat it?

The operating room coolie was fired and we surgeons are now protecting ourselves by not allowing the new coolie in the room when we are at work. The night watchman medical chief has been arrested for dealing in opium; at least he was kindhearted enough to wish to keep his patients free from pain. Drugs are sold over the counter here with as much freedom as candy or cloth. Recently our school ordered carbolic acid for the anatomical department and instead of receiving crude carbolic acid we were sent Lysol. Very little effort is made to find out the cause of death so we can only imagine the effect of selling powerful drugs so unconcernedly. If you lived here for a while, I think that you would join with me in saying "More power to the Government" in its effort to regulate the sale of poisonous drugs and impure food.

We receive very good news from our four children in America. Helen, our oldest daughter is the business and industrial girls' secretary of the Y.W.C.A. in Lynchburg; Margaret is in the Physical Education Department of the Y.W.C.A. in Cleveland. Joe Jr. is in his second year at the University and Ruth has entered the freshman class at Oberlin. We are thankful that each has a real job. We too are glad that we have a sizable job. Some of our friends have retired at sixty, but I would hate to think of being on the shelf in a few months. Nothing could be worse when we still have our health and strength to keep busy.

Margaret and Helen, Jr. were together for the Christmas of 1933 but Joe, Jr. and Ruth were in Atlantic City. Even before Joe, Jr. married Barbara Silvers, the Silvers family began to provide a home for the younger McCrackens for holidays just as their older cousins, Frank and Lawrence Ramsey had done for Mary, Margaret, and Helen, Jr.

In June, the four stateside McCrackens had a family reunion in Cleveland before Joe, Jr. went to Camp Tecumseh. Ruth decided to attend Western Reserve Summer School and then transfer to Lake Erie College. Margaret (also known as Peg) would be sailing to China in the later summer for she had accepted a teaching position at the Shanghai American School for 1934-35. Both Peg and Helen, Jr. had met the men they would eventually marry.

Helen, Jr. wrote her parents preparing them for the fact that they would have to adjust to an adult daughter in their home:

> Both Peg and I have been so independent and responsible to ourselves that it may be hard for Peg, though I know you wouldn't mean it to be. Sometimes I even think Tyler wants to know too much about where I go and why--it is just because he is interested, I know, but!...evidently you have said something to Peg about 'her resisting the evils of a big city' when she comes out there. I think she can do that all right; but she does enjoy going to dances and having a good time and you will have to expect that she will go a lot but you can trust her to be a credit to you in her behaviour.

In reply to a report on Mary's activities in medical school, Helen Jr. wrote, "I think Mary did wonderfully to earn so much her first year and to have a job for the fall plus a good time in Shanghai. Nothing like that could have happened in the United States." Mary had her own rickshaw and coolie which gave her independence not only to attend medical school but to develop her own circle of friends. Helen wrote in September, 1934:

> This week I am going to be fifty-seven; I cannot believe it. I weigh 110 1/2. This week [an American woman] came to visit Shanghai for a month. She is almost as wide as she is tall. When Daddy saw her he said he was willing to pay for me to go to the Y for gym for the rest of my life if I just kept my weight down!
>
> I am making wheat again; Mr. Rossitor got four hundred pounds of nice clean American wheat. I expect it will go fast. I ought to clear about $75 Mex for it for my own charity gifts. I gave $50 last year to the Auxiliary and the rest of what I made to other collections, YW, AAUW scholarship, etc. It is nice to have some of my own. I wish cross stitch would pick up a lit-

tle. I am hoping to get some new stuff before the first of November and then have a sale.

In January of 1935 she complimented her older son:

> Joe, I am so glad you have your gold football. That is a great thing to have looked forward to for twenty-three years and finally won. I too thought of it long ago when you were just born, that some day I would be proud to have you winning games on Franklin Field. I can hardly believe that your football days have come and gone; how can I ever be anything but proud of the fact that we had a son who followed in his father's footsteps, not only in football but in the Christian Association.

However, she also sadly looked ahead to the departure of the twins to school in the U.S.:

> So soon we shall lose the twins, and I cannot tell you how empty it makes it seem even to talk about it. They add so much to the life of the house.

Joe's letter of Christmas greetings to his supporters was wistful:

> Many of you have been, for more than twenty-five years, my friends and loyal supporters of the Pennsylvania work in China. Others have been, for shorter periods, just as much interested and are as much appreciated. It is for you all that I am especially grateful this Thanksgiving Day.
>
> When Dr. William Posey and Mr. Frank Gucker, treasurer of the Christian Association for so many years passed away, this work lost two loyal supporters, for they had been interested in Pennsylvania in China since its beginning. And, too, three football friends have gone during the year: George Woodruff, our coach, Dr. John Carnett and Billy Morice. When one sees his friends dropping off, it makes him realize that life is short and uncertain. It gives me somewhat the same feeling that Captain Robert Dollar expressed when at seventy-five years of age, he was seen rushing around the streets of Shanghai. He was asked, "What's the hurry?" and he answered, "I must hurry. I have only a few more years left."
>
> If it were possible in a letter like this, I should like to tell you the encouraging things which the National Government is doing. Only the failures are broadcast to the world. Twenty-five years ago, even ten years ago, this government took no interest whatever in the welfare of the individual and did

nothing to alleviate the miserable living conditions of the large majority of the population. The present government is beginning to see need and to feel responsibility for doing something in a concrete way. Mass education, first pushed by foreign and private funds, is now being encouraged and supported by the government. Millions are being offered for the first time, the opportunity of receiving a limited reading knowledge of a few of the commonly used words of their language.

It is just ninety-nine years since Dr. Peter Parker, a graduate of Yale, began to practice medicine in Canton. It is said of him that "he opened China at the point of a lancet." All through the century it has been the missionary who has practiced, preached and taught "western medicine" and it is through his long patient efforts that faith in and knowledge of scientific medicine is developing in the Chinese. This present Chinese government recognizes its value and is beginning to see the need of putting on a public health program. Some progress has been made but advance is necessarily slow with few doctors and four hundred millions of people. One busy doctor among seventy-five thousand of the population does not go far when it comes to health campaigns. Yet the need is now felt and an effort is being made, which is encouraging.

The "New Life Movement" is an effort to teach the common people how they can improve their own living conditions. General Chiang Kai-shek and his wife, a graduate of Wellesley College, both Christians, are vitally interested in this movement. In fact, they started it and are appealing to all Chinese, to help stop opium smoking, gambling, footbinding and immorality. They are asking the missionaries who know the language and the people to help direct this effort. With the needs of the common people realized by the government I feel that we may expect much greater progress in the next decade than there has been during the last century. Every advance made in any direction increases the call for more and better trained doctors.

Our own work continues about as usual except that we are more cramped for funds. Last June [1934] we graduated seventeen, the largest class we ever had. That day was one of the high spots of my missionary work. It gives me great pleasure just to think of seventeen fine young men prepared and ready to go out to help meet the great needs of their people.

We admitted twenty to the freshman class this fall and twenty is the limit of our accommodations. In this class there is one American boy, and there are Chinese from Hawaii, the Philippines, Java, Canton and Peiping. The American is the son of a missionary and wishes to prepare himself to do medical missionary work in China.

After a brief furlough in 1933, the family drove back across the U. S. to catch a ship to China. This picture was taken in Yosemite National Park and shows Joe and Helen standing; Martha, Stewart, and Elsie seated on the front bumper; and Mary seated inside their Ford.

The McCracken's cook, Da Si Foo, and his family.

The McCracken's housekeeper, Chang Sz Foo

Three of Joe and Helen's daughters played on the Shanghai team in the Interport field hockey league: Margaret (middle of second row), Elsie (second from left in front row), and Martha (second from right in the front row). Picture taken in 1936 before a game.

Martha and Elsie's legs following the field hockey game.

CHAPTER FOURTEEN

MARY SPREADS HER WINGS
1935-1937

In the spring of 1935, Joe and Helen came to America; he was having difficulty with a duodenal ulcer and needed to have consultations. They left the children in Margaret's care, until school was out and then in Mary's, for Margaret came to the States for the summer. While they were away, the American Oriental Bank failed because the director had gambled on exchange rates and used the stocks deposited in it for collateral. Helen had put most of the money she made selling Chinese cross stitch, playing at weddings, etc. in the bank and the stocks they owned in China were there too--all of it was lost. Fortunately for Margaret the money she had been saving was in a Chinese bank which had a branch at the school, so she was able to keep the family going until they returned.

Joe's Thanksgiving letter of 1935 tells more:

This has been an unusual year for me. For the first time in thirty years of service in China, I have had to take "time out" for sick leave. After four and a half months of "hard labor," resting and dieting, I am glad to be back in Shanghai; work is far more pleasant than such enforced idleness. Many thanks to the doctors and other friends who made my "come back" possible.

In June in Atlantic City I attended some of the meetings of our American Medical Association where there were about eight thousand delegates. Just this last month we have had in Canton, the biennial conference of our Chinese Medical Association and there were present about three hundred and fifty members, the largest medical conference ever held in China. Besides the usual group meetings we were celebrating the arrival, one hundred years ago, of Dr. Peter Parker, the first medical missionary appointed to China. Think of the courage needed to be the first to tackle the medical needs of this country. In reading about him before I went to Canton, I found that he did graduate work at the Pennsylvania Medical School in 1840 when he was at home interesting people in his work. Even as long ago as that the citizens of Philadelphia were being urged to take an interest in the health of the Chinese.

Canton is a changed city. Much of its fascination has been swept away by attempts to modernize the city. The old city wall is gone and in its place is one of the broad roads with traffic controlled by very modern looking policemen. It is still possible to find some of the narrow alluring streets with open shops on either side, but the general impression is of a modern city. In our day there were no wheeled vehicles in the city; sedan chairs or "shank's mares" took us from place to place. Now rickshaws, bicycles, motor cars, and motor buses are there in ever increasing numbers. The roads are well paved and are being pushed out into the country. A new modern bridge across the Pearl River is to them what Camden Bridge is to Philadelphia and the Jersey side.

Just as Canton was the first city to admit modern medical science so she was the first to initiate health administration. They have had a Bureau of Public Health since 1912 but its work is much limited by lack of personnel and by need for funds. On the way to Canton our boat stopped at Amoy, a coast city of three million, where we have ten graduates of our own medical school at work in the city's hospitals. You would have enjoyed seeing our boys, hearing their work praised by other American doctors, and realizing the pride they take in their profession. The boys took us to a famous old Buddhist Temple for luncheon, a grand feast without a bite of meat, and on the way we saw new modern roads leading out into the country; the roads are so new that the black pigs still "jay-walk" while the cars slow up to let them take their time to cross safely. The life of a dog or pig is worth considering.

These new roads represent ruthless cutting through houses, rice fields and grave yards. We must compare it to a necessary surgical operation which means life to the patient. Good roads mean better markets, better transportation, improved health conditions.

During the past nine months four American banking institutions in Shanghai have gone into liquidation. St. Luke's hospital building funds were placed in these banks while the new plans were being studied in New York; now the greater part of the money is lost and what is "left" is "frozen" for some time to come. Old buildings, crowded conditions, poor facilities for teaching must now be endured for years unless new gifts make available what is so sorely needed. New and better national medical schools are being founded but they teach only in Chinese and are for men with lower standard of preparation. Our teaching is done in English and requires a higher type of student, who can go further after he is equipped for the practice of medicine. We have had no lack of students ready to take our work, with seventy-nine enrolled this year, the highest number so far; but we are having more and more difficulty securing adequate faculty and supplies due to ever decreasing income from America. A teacher of pathology is sadly needed just now. Is there anyone in American able to teach this subject who would like to take a year off and spend it helping us out? We might give him his board and lodging.

Five of our graduates are this year in the post-graduate School of Medicine in Philadelphia. I recommend each or all of them if you are interested in seeing for yourself what type of doctor we are sending out. A few months ago a little orphan boy of ten or twelve came as a stowaway from the famine district to Shanghai. He was penniless and begged on the streets. In a few days he became ill with amoebic dysentery, a painful disease. He slept in an alley. One morning a passing rickshaw man heard him moaning. He stopped and told the boy he ought to go to St. Luke's Hospital. The boy said he had no money and did not know where the hospital was; whereupon the rickshaw man picked him up, put him in his rickshaw and brought him to St. Luke's. He was a desperately sick boy. After weeks of treatment he recovered and he proved to be bright and attractive. He is now happy in a school for homeless boys. I wish I knew more about that rickshaw puller--a real modern Good Samaritan. Life after all consists not in what we have but what we are. Let us, out of our abundance, in comparison with the rickshaw coolie, do our bit toward extending the blessings of medical science where the need is so great.

This letter speaks of the bank failures which would affect the plans for the medical school and new hospital. But events elsewhere in the world were also affecting the family's life and Joe's work. President Roosevelt was struggling with the problems created by the Depression, the drastic severity of which would affect contributions to foreign mission work. Hitler in 1935 re-created the German Army and in 1936 re-militarized the Rhineland, moving toward World War II. From 1936-39 Civil War raged in Spain. Italy began her aggressive moves in 1935-36, conquering Ethiopia. England and France were involved in an appeasement policy towards the Axis Powers (Germany, Italy and Japan) which led to the Munich Pact, worked out in September of 1939, intended to preserve a form of peace, after Germany had taken over Czechoslovakia in March.

Helen, Jr. had written her parents announcing her decision to marry Tyler Fulcher, enclosing a recent picture of him. In her reply (December, 1935) Helen commented that he did not stand up straight, and he was a Democrat but, "if he would make you happy, I'll be satisfied!"

December 22, 1935 Helen wrote:

This is the last Sunday before Christmas. I know you three are not together but hope that Ruthie is with Joe. Today Margy and the twins went to the Marine church; the rest of us went to our church. This afternoon Margy and the twins have gone to the Race Course where Margy plays a hockey game....Mary and Stewart are making some caramels and Daddy is about to go to sleep if the noise of my typing does not disturb him....

Daddy has had a relapse this past week; he has gone back to his diet, and I hope will rest enough and keep enough in his stomach to keep from getting any worse. It frightens me when I think of his getting ill again. Next year with four in college and one still in high school, the thought of his being ill is certainly disturbing. It isn't just because of that either; not just the problems of the family, and the adjustments that would have to be made. It is like having part of me disabled. We have been so much together for thirty-three years that we think alike and plan alike, often find ourselves thinking of the same things at the same time. To think of doing without him just appalls me. But I know he ought not to go on working if he has these spells. I think the doctors were too forehanded in letting him go back suddenly to eating everything, and to full time work. He has taken advantage of it. Now he will not like to give up anything. I would like right now to have him take a week off and stay in bed and rest. But of course you know he will be down in the operating room tomorrow at nine.

On December 25, 1935, she added:

Yesterday afternoon we all went down to the celebration at St. Luke's. Each received a towel, a cake of soap, three bananas, four oranges, some hard candy and a package of cigarettes, donated by the British-American Tobacco Company. We had a great time setting up Daddy's aquarium. On the boat coming out Daddy got interested in having an aquarium of tropical fish, so we planned to start it. Stewie bought the glass tank, twenty inches long and twelve wide and twelve tall. And the twins and Margy bought the fish.

In 1936 it was a busy household; the twins were in their senior years, Stewart was a sophomore, Margaret and Mary were living at home with their own circle of friends and activities. Helen wrote about attending the trial for the American bankers who wasted the money of so many individuals and organizations, adding "Daddy thinks such

134

attendance is ghoulish." Helen began to fill her guest rooms with "paying guests" in an effort to help with family expenses.

Her letter of January 19, 1936 started:

> Today's papers again were full of the three McCracken sisters and their hockey prowess. I shall be glad when these interport games are over so that we can calm down about hockey, yet it is fun to have them so interesting. Yesterday the Interport team played "the rest of Shanghai" and won 7-1. Martha made five goals and was well written up. Every one I meet asks me how I like having three of the eleven on the team [be] my daughters.

She added more on January 26:

> The greatest excitement of the week was the interport hockey; it would have been wonderful if they had won, but still the score under the circumstances was partly due to accident. The game was played in about four inches of mud. When anyone hit the ball the mud flew up in chunks and one could hardly distinguish the ball and the lump of mud....When they came home we put old steamer rugs on the car seats; the girls were mud from head to foot. Their faces and hair were splashed with mud and their legs looked as tho they had stockings of mud. I was helping Elsie get her clothes off and went to the bathroom with clean things; she stood in a tub of water rinsing the mud down and the water looked like the water of the Whangpoo River. Tommy and Henry came for lunch and then eight of them went off to the movies. These kids do have fun.

Meanwhile, in Philadelphia, the University of Pennsylvania held its first Founder's Day Exercises in honor of Benjamin Franklin on January 18, 1936. Josiah Calvin McCracken was one of the eight alumni honored with an Alumni Award of Merit:

> Because of his student record in many fields of Intercollegiate competition, which is one of the proudest pages in Pennsylvania athletic history, but much more because of his courageous and significant life devoted to the relief of human suffering and the spread of medical knowledge among a foreign people, a life which, in the highest degree, exemplifies self-sacrifice and noble purpose.

A more complete description appeared in a newspaper report in Shanghai:

J. C. McCracken Receives Honor

When a great American University selects eight of its 50,000 alumni for signal honors on the occasion of its first Founders Day, and when it comes as far afield as Shanghai to pick one of the eight, the event may be regarded as definitely unusual.

Dr. Josiah Calvin McCracken, Dean of the Medical School of St. John's University and surgeon at St. Luke's Hospital, has been so honored by his Alma Mater, the University of Pennsylvania.

The New York Times and the *Philadelphia Public Ledger* of January 19 tell the story of the awards which were made the previous day in Philadelphia as the institution celebrated the birthday of Benjamin Franklin. Others to receive scrolls of merit each of which bore an individual citation included Senator George Wharton Pepper, Associate Justice Owen Josephus Roberts of the United States Supreme Court, Mr. Effingham Buckley Morris, Chairman of the Board of the Girard Trust Com. And a number of professors each outstanding in a special field of endeavor.

Dr. McCracken graduated from Pennsylvania's Medical School in 1901. This June his son, Josiah Calvin McCracken, Jr., finishes a four year career at the same college that has been extraordinarily like that of his father. Both won their gold footballs as leaders of the University gridiron and both were presidents of the campus Christian Association. To those who remembered the father, it seemed singularly fitting that young Joe would be the one to take his place among the celebrated personages at the Founders Day ceremony to receive the award as proxy for Dr. McCracken.

The family in Shanghai first had news of the event through an amateur radio message which reached there by devious routes after the oldest daughter, Helen, in Virginia inadvertently happened upon the article in *The New York Times*. A letter from the son followed, and today Mrs. McCracken, the four daughters and son in Shanghai are rejoicing as they had occasion to rejoice twice before, one in 1921 when the U. of P. gave Dr. McCracken an honorary Phi Beta Kappa key and again when he was made Doctor of Science in 1927.

On February 23, 1936 Helen wrote the family about the Award which Joe received just before his sixty-second birthday:

This last week I sat by George Fitch and told him at dinner about Daddy's award. He told Marian who jumped at it for a news item. These young writers who are paid by the line like to get something to write about. She put it in the evening paper. Daddy nearly had a fit about it and went around demanding to know who had the nerve to put this in. We none of us claimed the honor and he does not know yet. The next day Randolph Raven put it in the *North China,* and someone else copied it in the *Times and Press* and they dug out old pictures of him and put them in. Well, it was fun for the family and I really think very nice for Daddy....With some of our best people being taken to jail, why not a little publicity for one who has always kept his name honorable. Some people here get a lot of publicity but Daddy does not often get a pat on the back here in Shanghai. I think on the whole it has done him good.

Soon after Helen had an attack foretelling the high blood pressure and arteriosclerosis she would develop. Joe reported to the family, " I do not expect any more trouble if mother will only be content to slow down and not fret about dirt, servants, etc."
Helen wrote on March 15, 1936:

This is the first morning I have been up for breakfast since the 26th of February; it did seem much nicer than breakfast in bed. Yesterday was the Father and Son day and Daddy and Stewart spent from five to eight at the Foreign Y in company with other fathers and sons. So I took the twins and Margy to see Eddie Cantor and then we went to Sun Ya restaurant for supper, Chinese food. Mary went to a movie with Peggy and to her house for supper. So it was quite a day....Since I can do so little I have decided to knit in the mornings and play bridge in the afternoons and so am going to my first bridge tomorrow; Mrs. Young took a table at a benefit and wants me to go. It simply shocked Daddy and perhaps he will loosen up on his requirements if I threaten to be a bridge fiend.

Just to sit and knit seems such a sappy way of spending a morning. I always knitted when I could do nothing else, at committee meetings and prayer meetings; but to sit down and knit from nine to twelve just bores me... I have been doing just one thing a day. If you saw all the medicine Daddy has laid out for me to take you would think I could go about to two or three things; one injection a day, three capsules of some kind of stuff and two tablespoons of something else, in the middle of the afternoon. I tell him that he has for thirty years brought me up on the uselessness of medicine and now it chokes me. Nevertheless--I am taking the stuff.

Before he went off to church this morning we were talking about the summer; he is supposed to have a good vacation. I found that he does not want to go far from Shanghai. He has operated on several people lately whose ulcers perforated the intestinal wall. He says he does not wish to go too far from a good hospital. I had not realized that such a thing was at all imminent but he says they do sometimes act that way. We would not wish to go away until the first of August when the twins have gone and so I expect we shall just stay at home. If he does not work for a month that would be something, but that is hard on him too. I expect Daddy and I both feel happier being busy even tho it does shorten our lives. I am still tutoring the second little boy but will finish this week. I should have $100 from my two jobs. Let us hope there are a few more to be helped.

Early in May, Helen and Mrs. Young were able to take a seven day trip to Hangchow [now Hangzhou], Nanchang, Kiukiang [now Jiujiang], Kuling and Nanking. She wrote a five page letter telling of her unusual trip and the pleasures of meeting so many interesting people:

We visited Dr. Ida Kahn's hospital; she was the first Chinese woman to go to America and study medicine; she went to Ann Arbor. Her hospital is large and spacious and spotlessly clean. It is still run by Chinese doctors. The grounds are wonderful, with lovely trees now many years old; it is one of the beauty spots of Nanchang. All these old missionary compounds are lovely; land was cheap and they bought a lot of it. They all loved to plant trees and shrubs and now their successors reap the benefits....Think of the courage and vision it took to start such far-reaching work as they did! I would ask how many boys in this school--two hundred and fifty. How many girls are there--three hundred. And how many here--a hundred in the primary. And now all of the schools are under Chinese principals and Chinese control, handed over, and the foreigners helping and taking a back seat. The longer I live in China, the more I see of mission work, the more I read of missionaries in the early days, the more I honor those who thought of coming out here and starting it all. They had an ever-increasing purpose, the bringing of Christ to this enormous population. It was a tremendous task. They made a good beginning. Now the Chinese can begin to take over and carry on.

Mary Spreads Her Wings (1935-1937)

This trip gave Helen an unexpected opportunity to see the progress being made by the Nationalist Government in problems dealing with the Japanese expanding control of northern China and the fighting to keep them and the Communists from securing more land. She was able to see the new roads and trains; rehabilitation and construction which Chiang Kai-shek was pushing in Chekiang and Kiangsi Provinces; the rural reconstruction, agricultural education and experimentation, and the increasing cooperation of the missions with the governmental education programs. But all too soon the Japanese "peaceful occupation" of northern China would end and the real Sino-Japanese war begin.

In June Margaret was packing and preparing to return to the States by way of the Trans-Siberian railroad, because the American School budget could no longer support a physical education teacher. The twins had graduated from high school and Helen was getting them ready to take the boat through the Panama Canal to attend Colby Junior College in New London, New Hampshire. Helen reported:

> Yesterday the Chamber of Commerce and both university clubs had a luncheon at the American Club for the Chinese and American school people who are to go to college this summer. It was given at the Club which is usually sacred to men. They had a good crowd and Daddy and I decided to go since we would not have many chances to go with two children. This is the first time that twins have graduated....Last night was the athletic banquet; we had to go there for Stewart is getting a letter in tennis.

On June 19, 1936 Helen, Jr. married Tyler Fulcher. Joe wrote his eldest daughter:

> I really do not know how to write to a married daughter. I have never attempted to do so before. Since it is probable I'll have the privilege to write to more even than one, I'll begin to practice upon you. We were so glad to receive your cable telling us of the exact date; we were at least thinking about you and wish we all could be there. I am sure you and Tyler will have great fun and happiness building up a home for yourselves and others. Really I think it is better to begin in a small way and add as time goes along. Our married life, all of it, has been a very happy one but I believe no part of it has been any happier than the seven years we lived in that little bungalow in Canton where you and Margy and Mary were born. It only took me four months to build it and it had no running water, electricity or central heating. While it is nice to

139

have material comforts they are not the most important things which make for a happy married life. Here is hoping that you and Tyler may be just as happy in your married life as your mother and I have been for these nearly thirty years. May God bless you both.

Helen's letter of June 21, 1936, is typical of her:

This is the first Sunday that we have had nine children. [She was now counting Tyler as part of the family.] It seems like quite a family. But we are quite thrilled to have Helen's cable....We were awfully glad to have Ruth's letter about all her athletic successes, and also about her [honors] in chemistry. It can be done, can't it, Ruth, and you must have some brains, after all. I always knew you had.

We went over to the Boyntons the other evening to tell them we had another son, and told them too of all the rest of the honors in the family and especially did I emphasize Joe's being third honor man in his class. He told us that Ruth had the highest I.Q. of the family when he was principal of the school. I told him, "Yes, you told me that; you also told me that Joe was practically a moron and look what he did." He could hardly believe that he had ever said such a thing but he really did tell me that Joe had a very low intelligence test score and made me furious. I told him years ago that no boy who read as little as Joe did, could pass the usual intelligence tests but that did not mean he was a moron.

Mary tied for first or was first in every examination she took in her medical work. Daddy is quite proud of her, and of course I am too!...Yesterday St. John's had their Commencement; I went just to see Daddy march in the academic procession, but could not hear a word of the program, and if I could have heard, most of it was in Chinese. You know how the Chinese are; the whole family comes. Amahs carry the babies up and down the aisles, proud papas take the little boys out to the bathroom. If there is anything going on in English the Chinese all talk and if it is in Chinese the foreigners cannot understand.

Joe and Helen went to Weihaiwei for three weeks after the twins and Margaret and their belongings were gotten off. With so many empty bedrooms in their large home, Helen made a greater effort to take in boarders, both children and adults. One of her most interesting experiences was with "the little Britons," ten and twelve-year old boys who stayed for the fall. They were the sons of British consular service parents stationed in the interior. She wrote:

Yesterday, [a friend] took Stewart and me with them and we went to the British Country Club and, within its sacred doors, we went into the "swimming bath." As she introduced me about and said that the children were spending the winter with me and going to the American School, I felt exactly like a British nursery governess. But I am glad we have the chance to take them and the extra money will help a lot, besides the fun of having a larger household. They think Stewart is wonderful and follow him around all the time he is at home.

Yesterday I took the two boys and their mother to the zoo to spend the afternoon. I had not told you that they arrived with a fox and a porcupine in two large boxes for Jessfield Zoo. I never smelled such smells as from our front porch while those two boxes waited to be transported. They have a pet tiger at home which is being sent to the zoo in Regent's Park, London.

Joe's 1936 Thanksgiving letter to his supporters is the last before the declared war with Japan began:

Submerged by the campaign and election news, foreign affairs have doubtless been given a small corner in American newspapers. However big things have been happening during the last few months in China. The country is now unified under the Nanking government, a goal sought for years by all who have the country's welfare at heart. Just as we read that political parties in America are planning to work together in loyal support of the newly elected President, officials out here, of the various provinces are pledging loyalty to Nanking. This move adds to the government, airplanes, money and men, enabling them to face Japan with more backing and more security than they have had in the past few years.

To be sure Japan holds "Manchukuo," is trying to force "Autonomy" in the North, and already has a foothold in Fukien. Students, faculties and other large groups are sending petitions pleading for "no acceptance of Japan's demands." But three years have made a great change in China's "preparedness." The changes in these last two months have softened the "demands" and we hope that delay, discussion, and an ever increasing array of military equipment may prevent actual warfare.

Each year I write to you that we never had a finer group of students. Yet again it is true, and we feel that the eighty-three enrolled this time are an unusual lot. Three Americans are in the classes: ne is the grandson of the doctor who founded St. Luke's Hospital, and one is our daughter Mary. We have had applications from other "foreigners," but as the Chinese are given the first chance and many apply, we have had to refuse them. A Chinese student wrote to me, three years ago, saying that he wanted to study medicine and had saved about one hundred dollars in U.S. currency towards his medical education. I wrote to him to come along for I liked the tone of his letter. He is now the honor student in his class. It is always a special satisfaction to pick a winner.

Hardly a week passes by that I do not receive requests from country hospitals wanting me to help them to find a good doctor. Already eight hospitals want our fifteen interns next year. We shall have only three to spare. This last week we entertained in our home, a club made up of first and second year men of our school and the corresponding classes in the women's medical school. About fifty young people came; they had arranged for the program and helped us to serve the refreshments. Thirty years ago young men and women did not meet socially in this way, nor was there co-education in colleges. This is one of the great changes we have seen.

One of our students, a Chinese Honolulu boy, is the captain of the St. John's football team and last Saturday his team won a victory from the Shanghai America School team. You can see that these are modern young people, preparing to live in a modern world. Boys graduating from non-government and non-registered schools are now allowed to take the government examinations and receive a license to practice in any part of China. That makes it easier for our young doctors.

In April, it will be thirty years since we began medical work in China. Looking back over these years we realize the strides the country has made in every line; government, education, transportation, the position of women, patriotism, medical work, universal education, child labor and factory conditions. The millennium has not yet arrived. But turning out well-trained doctors has been and will be a part of this progress. Some of you have been loyal supporters of this work for thirty years.

We run our school on the proverbial "shoe string" but if the "shoe string" holds out we shall continue to prepare men for service to their country. We need equipment, more faculty, and more money; but we have the students. Where is the young doctor who would like to give a year of his life to the job of teaching out here in our school, and at the same time meet some of the finest people in the world? Or where is the pre-medical teacher who would like to spend his off year helping to meet the needs of our school? Next year we could use a teacher of physiology, a teacher of pharmacology and a teacher of bio-chemistry. May the New Year bring us the help we need.

Easter Sunday Joe wrote about his resignation as Dean of the Medical School:

> I think the University will be registering by the end of this year and while it is not absolutely required that the Dean be Chinese, it is desired because of the many Chinese reports which have to be made and, too, all the government regulations are in Chinese. We have a fine younger Chinese doctor, a graduate of Johns Hopkins whom I think will undertake the responsibility and will do it well. When it is registered, I hope that we will be able to get more local support, more personnel and equipment than we have had in the past.

Helen's letter from that time describes dinners or movies every night the past week, a track meet at school, a luncheon at the church and then says:

> But you know that I have almost nothing to do and every day after eight my family leaves the house. I have no sewing, I cannot knit all day and have not much knitting to do, and I cannot go down town all the time, and some days I just feel as if I had nothing to do but walk the streets. I should have a project; I do have the work committee at the church but that takes two meetings a month...So I will accept all invitations to play bridge though it is rather tiresome; and now Nellie Mae and I are going to art lectures and visits to see special collections. So you young people take warning and choose something to stick by you in your old age, some hobby or some interest in reading; I am going to try everything.

But not much later she had decided she "has a most interesting life for a woman her age."
In April Helen wrote:

> Mary is away for the weekend at Hangchow which is across from Chinkiang. She was so happy to be going somewhere. She took her coolie. We thought she might not be able to go, for Thursday afternoon Soong put down the shafts of the rickshaw and took off his license on his arm and said he would not take her any more; that was in the middle of the street. He finally brought her home, and packed up to go. Mary was just sick about it. We did not know what was wrong.

As we had guests he stayed to bring her down to dinner. I saw him in the kitchen preparing spinach for supper. I seized the opportunity to tell him what I thought of him for leaving abruptly a person handicapped like Mary who had lessons the next day and was going away Saturday. By the time we finished dinner the storm was over. He told her the thing he did not like was walking with her in the rickshaw. She has a way of walking home with Peggy; he said it was not Chinese custom to walk when anyone was in a rickshaw and he would not do it any more. He never said a word about it before and I think it is just that he took that as an excuse to save his face and return. But anyway it saved the day and he is staying on. He really is a good man for her and lots of fun.

I wish she would send you her new passport picture. It shows the complete change in Mary. Compared to her other pictures it brings out her maturity and independent-ness. Of course being able to go where she likes, do as she chooses and be an individual has made changes and I think this picture shows it....I wonder if Mary will ever be content in America where she is so dependent or whether she will just want to go for a trip taking a coolie with her to carry her. Some day she will be making enough to afford to go where she pleases.

Helen's letter of June 3, 1937 indicated:

Mary has sold 300 c.c.s. of blood and received fifty dollars for it. She certainly was pleased. She and Miss Lamberton and Stewart start the 25th for Peking. Soong-sz-foo is going, too. Mary has been asked to teach anatomy next year at Margaret Williamson and offered a thousand for the year. Dr. Tucker thinks she can do it and finish her year's work too....To have them ask her for her time and offer a hundred a month with all the Chinese New Year vacation, and to be able to do her studying too, that pleased her a lot. I am sure that some day Mary will be famous.

In spite of the difficult conditions in China, Joe and Helen's letters continue to show concern for Elsie and Martha in their second year at Colby Junior College, and for Stewart as he settled down at Peddie School for his last year of high school.

Helen's letter of June 7, 1937 was sent to Elsie:

I got your special letter sent to me at the hospital last week. I am always especially glad to receive these extra special letters and to know what you are thinking about and discussing with each other and what's on your mind. We human beings are so constituted we are all the time changing, physically, mentally and spiritually. It's the latter I want to write about in this letter because you wrote that you felt "muddled" and did not know just what to believe. Well do I remember that same feeling very soon after I went to the University although it is over forty years ago. I thought the professor said we were all descendants of monkeys--that disturbed me a lot. Everybody who thinks has these moments or times when they hardly know what they do believe, what they should believe or want to believe. It is important especially during those times to keep on doing what you know to be right and what you know to be the highest ideal and keep yourself in touch with the best Christian people and these problems of belief will settle themselves. We do need to take time to read our Bible and meditate more than most of us do.

Helen's letter of June 24 is one of her funniest, with due respect to the DAR (Daughters of the American Revolution). The letter described the formation of the "Order of the McCrackens of Shanghai."

My dear children: The mail came about an hour ago and Mary, Stewart and I enjoyed ourselves for a half hour or so....Mary is thro with her exams and she and Stewart are doing stamps this morning; they leave Saturday night on their travels to Peking....

Yesterday I had one of the funniest mornings. Mrs. Wilbur called me the afternoon before to say that two ladies, "very high in DAR circles were in town and she was having the DAR in to meet them." The DAR affords me much amusement anyway because she makes so much of it. I promised to go out and meet the ladies and drink coffee with them. And did. After awhile she asked this one woman to tell us about their chapter and what it was doing. She talked over an hour! As you can imagine they had a very active chapter. Then she showed us all her badges. When she came she had gone into the guest room and emerged with a blue sash over one shoulder and many decorations hung on her bosom. I told the family I now know why so many of the DAR officials are so fat; they have to develop room for their badges. After her talk she began to tell us what the badges stood for. I may not remember all of them but will do my best. DAR pin, State Regent's pin, Vice Regent pin for whole DAR, Badge for being present at laying of the cornerstone of Constitution Hall in Washington, Badge for being present at Dedication of this Hall, Past regent's badge for her State, Nine bars because of nine ancestors in the Revolution. Then she had a lot of other things which were not on at the moment but she generously showed us: Colonial Dames of America, Nine bars to go with it, Badge which showed that some of her ancestors came to Virginia between 1607 and 1620 (no earlier and no later), Order of the Barons of Runnymede (descendants of those who forced King John to grant the Magna Carta), Order of the Crown (only worn by descendants of William the Conqueror. That of course, goes back to 1066)...everyone was so serious about it.

I hope it will be a solemn lesson to me not to take too much stock in ancestry. I thought of the man on the steps of the Vendome in Paris (the 1926 trip through Europe en route to the States) who would not go in; he stood outside and smoked and talked to Daddy and played with the twins. He said, "I am tired of seeing things five hundred years old. I would like to take these people back to California and show them something we have done in 1926." I feel that way about ancestors--not what they were but what we are. We decided at tiffin that we would start an order to hand on to our descendants. How would it do to have a badge only to be worn by descendants of the eight McCrackens born in Shanghai or Canton, or who lived in Shanghai, for we must have Joe [Jr.] in this. We thought it would be easier to start one and add badges as we go along than to go back to 1066 or even 1215. Go back and we find cattle thieves among the McCrackens in Scotland, goodness know what on my father's side. I believe my grandmother did not speak English when she was married. But go on in the future and we are responsible for what they do. So now we might plan for it, the *Order of the McCrackens* who lived in Shanghai.

Of course the family had no way of knowing that the undeclared war with Japan would break out again in Peking while Mary and Stewart were there. Helen wrote more about Mary's coolie, Soong:

Soong went with Mary and he *was* excited; two days before they left, he told Mary [that] his wife was going to have a baby in about a month and also he had a toothache. I came up that night and Mary said, "Tomorrow I have to see about his teeth and get his wife to the pre-natal clinic at St. Elizabeth's. What a day! But his teeth were fixed and the wife has a card for the clinic and if the family want anything they are to report to ME. Soong bought new white silk clothes and new black "slick" clothes and new sneakers and a hat very much like Daddy's new summer one. Mary bought him a Chinese

146

suitcase and he put everything in it but his shoes. There was no other place for them so I wrapped them in many layers of paper and put them at the bottom of the luncheon basket. Everything else was in tins so I thought that would be all right. Tonight they get off at Taishan and go up the mountain for the sunrise.

In the midst of their good times came the famous "Marco Polo Bridge" incident on July 7, just outside Peking; the Chinese and Japanese began fighting. Mary had expected to remain longer for a course in Physical Therapy but a telegram from her father and local warnings changed their plans. It took her, Soong, and Miss Lamberton several days more of sightseeing, shopping and packing before they started. It is amazing that without reservations, with the fleeing refugees, the changing of trains and all the confusion, this helpless young woman got back just before the trains stopped running at all.

Mary Elizabeth McCracken, about 1935.

147

War descended on Shanghai in 1937. From the top: smoke rising as a result of Japanese bombing of the city; a convoy was used to move the hospital to a safer location; and refugees crowding to flee to the countryside to escape the Japanese bombing of civilian areas halted the convoy near the station.

CHAPTER FIFTEEN

THE SINO-JAPANESE WAR IN PROGRESS
1937

It is difficult to describe the spread of the Japanese armies over the countryside, the bombing and fighting from Peking down into the Yangtze valley, the evacuation of Japanese and other foreigners, the destruction, the hysteria of the masses in those regions and the building up of the Japanese forces in the Shanghai area, especially in the Hongkew district which had been their headquarters in the fighting in 1932. Mr. Powell, in his book *My Twenty-Five Years in China,* speaks of a million and a half people crowding into the International Settlement and the French Concession. The climax came on "Black Saturday"--August 14, 1937. Bombs fell in the inner city, killing about 2000 and wounding about 2500. Gradually the armies moved further away but the Japanese took control of the territory surrounding Shanghai, including the family's section of the International Settlement. The Japanese began to reorganize business and industry for their own purposes and to exert pressure on the leadership of the International Settlement and French Concession for greater power in their governments. In December there was bombing of British and American gunboats and shipping. Then came a period of uneasy tension which would last until the take-over at the time of the bombing of Pearl Harbor December 7, 1941.

Helen kept her children informed in letters and newspaper clippings. She had strong views about the start of the war: "I cannot understand how any nation acquainted with World War I and its sufferings can start a war." At the same time she was furious that the other powers were not taking more positive steps to threaten Japan and force her to get out. Europe and Russia and the United States were more concerned with the activities of Hitler in Europe.

Joe's annual letter to his supporters, sent in November 1937, provided an overview of the year's events:

Not being a war correspondent, I must let you depend upon your daily papers and magazines for information about the political affairs in China since the outbreak of this so-called "incident." My part is to tell you more or less about the things which you have been interested in and have helped in making possible. The first eight months were quite prosaic. We graduated sixteen doctors in June. With the co-operation of another mission we had made plans to increase the size of the entering class from twenty to twenty-four. By August there were more than enough qualified applicants.

Great changes occurred during the next three months. As you may know from hearing of our experiences in 1932, St. Luke's Hospital is located in that part of the International Settlement where most of the Japanese have lived and that is the part always taken over first by the Japanese army. The Japanese Club where the army makes its headquarters, the Japanese consulate, the Japanese flag ship and St. Luke's Hospital are within a quarter of a mile of each other.

When the Japanese war ships steamed up the river in August, we were looking for a place to which we could move St. Luke's Hospital. We could transfer to St. John's University as we did in 1932, but that location is also much exposed and, we felt would not be safe. During the second week of August, tens of thousands of Chinese were rushing out of our section of the city carrying with them such possessions as they could snatch in a hurry and put on their backs, or if they were a little more prosperous, could put on someone else's back or on a truck or wheelbarrow or rickshaw. On the 13th, the bombing of the railroad station began and continued during the night. By morning I was convinced that we could no longer take the responsibility of keeping two hundred people in the hospital.

I got up at half past five and went to consult my colleagues and we agreed that we must immediately move to St. John's campus. I promised to have ambulances, trucks, our school bus and private cars ready to start loading at nine o'clock. We sent an S.O.S. to the Settlement Fire Brigade who have city ambulances in charge, to the American Marine headquarters, to the Shanghai Emergency Committee who had previously been notified of the possibility of our needs. By nine o'clock an ambulance, our school bus and a truck were loading from three separate exits. To load and to make the round trip of twelve miles through crowded streets, required an hour and a half. The streets were packed with people getting out of this Hongkew district. Bombing planes were in the air and anti-aircraft guns from both the gun boats and land batteries were often busy during the day.

About noon there was a sudden unusual commotion with a lot of rifle firing. All workers retired into the building as the Japanese marines threw a barricade across the street a block from the hospital. Fleeing civilians were cleared out of the streets nearby and we continued loading ambulances and trucks. In the afternoon we had a telephone message telling us to be out of that district by four o'clock. Patients and nurses, more than two hundred were out by half past three.

The senior resident Chinese physician, the acting superintendent Miss Lamberton and I remained to close and lock the

150

windows and doors. We left the hospital at five minutes before four to follow the patients to St. John's. We passed through streets where a half hour later bombs burst and killed and injured over seventeen hundred civilians. The next day it was impossible to get trucks to go into the hospital district, but by using our own private cars, the school bus and our ambulance we were able to remove much needed supplies and small equipment. Several times while we were at work the shelling and bombing were so near and so severe that we all had to remain indoors until the spasm was over. I did not know before that a building could shake so much and not tumble down.

The following day we were loaned trucks and brought out beds and sterilizers. We had what we thought necessary for a short stay in our new quarters on the University campus. Just two weeks later American officials and military advisors urged us to move away to a location nearer the center of the city. We scouted around for some suitable place and finally the trustees of the Cathedral School for girls offered us their beautiful building, equipped only as a day school. In two days we built an outside kitchen which could provide Chinese food for two hundred and at the same time we had to erect a mat shed large enough to house the fifty cooks and coolies. We moved in on Sunday August 29th. The chemistry laboratory became the operating room, the assembly room a large ward, the other classrooms small wards. The next Sunday morning we had to make room for twenty-seven injured civilians from the bombing by Japanese of a small village just beyond St. John's Campus. Two operating tables were in use all day and one until midnight. What mutilated human beings! Legs, arms blown off. Big holes made by shrapnel in the abdomen, chest or head. Two died before anything could be done for them.

If General Sherman could see war as it is played now with these horrible air raids, even he would not be able to find a word adequate to meet the demands of the occasion. We took the girls' school with the promise that we would evacuate on two weeks notice. That notice came the first day of November and we were given until the twenty-first to get out. In two weeks we visited twenty-two possible locations before we found one available and usable. Every nook within the foreign concession is full to running over with refugees. We have now decided to rent the Cathedral Boys' School down in the heart of the business district, for the next nine months.

We are moving for the third time this week. We expect to be able to put up one hundred and thirty beds and our patients should be more comfortable than they ever have been in old St. Luke's for this school has a central heating system.

However to run it we must earn or beg enough money to buy coal and pay the rent. With war all around us it was impossible to think of opening the University on the eighth of September; but before the end of the month the faculty and alumni felt that the University with its medical department must continue to offer opportunity to study to the hundreds of men and women still in Shanghai. An alumnus, Mr. T. L. Soong, brother of Madame Chiang Kai-Shek, Madame H. H. Kung and T. V. Soong were able to arrange with the St. John's Alumni Club for the use of its rooms with other space in the same building.

The Middle School for boys, St. Mary's Hall for girls and the University including the medical school, opened classes on the 18th of October, with a total enrollment of over one thousand students. St. John's campus was not considered safe and the alumni did not wish to have students living on the campus because of the danger from bombing planes blowing up nearby railroad and creek bridges. But a medical school cannot be run for long without laboratories so we were given special permission to send the first and second year classes to the campus for laboratory study. This worked well until the Chinese army made a "strategic withdrawal" and the campus became a hot spot, with Japanese soldiers possessing the athletic fields which are across the Soochow Creek. We have had to make temporary arrangements to teach Anatomy, Pathology, and Bacteriology at the downtown center.

When we will be able to move back nobody knows. The present war is not yet over. I do not expect to see China stop fighting for some months to come. She is fighting for her very existence. Her men, poorly equipped and without long training, have and are putting up a magnificent struggle against tremendous odds. Their bravery and tenacity as we have watched them around this area, have won them the admiration of the world. As Mike Murphy used to tell us, "A team who won't be licked can't be licked." I do not believe a people who have the qualities possessed by the Chinese will be "licked" for long. China during these terrible days, needs the sympathy and support of foreign friends as never before. We are grateful to you who have made it possible for us to continue our work in China.

Helen contributed her own account of events. On August 1st she wrote that they had decided not to take a vacation. Joe was on the special defense committee and they were too worried about getting back to Mary and Stewart. Then she confessed:

I thought about Margy and her wedding all last evening. I could not get to sleep thinking about how nice it would have been to see the wedding myself. [Margaret and William Yates were married July 31, 1937.]

I meant to tell you all that Mrs. Beebe says I have knocked off ten to twenty years from my age, with my new clothes, a little color in my face and lipstick; so you girls better look out at home or we shall be taken for sisters by the time I get back on furlough.

The letter of August 7th described the growing tension and refugee problem, adding:

Daddy, as you know is Chairman of the American Community Committee and as such is a member of the American Emergency Committee; they have arranged for twelve concentration points in the whole of Shanghai where at a signal the Americans can move and then be taken to other places. Our nearest point is the American School. We would find ourselves taken off to Manila.

Within two days, Joe and Helen had made up their minds to send Stewart home to America so he could continue his education. He would go to Peddie for his senior year of work in high school. Margaret saved a newspaper clipping from *The [Cleveland] Plain Dealer* of September 9, with headlines "Boy Arrives from Shell-Torn China:

Stewart McCracken, 15, who sailed from Shanghai August 16 on the *President Taft*, the last refugee ship leaving for the United States, arrived in Cleveland last night at the home of his sister, Mrs. William Yates. His father, Dr. Josiah McCracken, surgeon at St. Luke's Hospital, a missionary hospital for Chinese in Shanghai, and his mother packed him up on half a day's notice, when the bombs began falling and it became evident that the schools in the international quarter would be closed indefinitely.

Helen wrote of the bombing of the hospital:

The old building in Hongkew has been hit by a shell and the operating room blown open. No one can go to see what further damage has been done for no one is allowed to cross the Garden Bridge as yet. The finances of the hospital are terribly hit; everything is going out and no money coming in. The refugee patients they have now are not able to pay anything. The service built up after many years of caring for employees of firms, which gave them an income to run the hospital, that service is impossible now. Practically all local income has ceased but expenses continue. When (St. John's) wishes to re-open, the patients must be moved again and every move costs money. Probably any equipment will have been destroyed by this time. St. Luke's must struggle for existence this winter.

In the large vacant lot next to our group of six houses here in Frenchtown, is a Salvation Army camp, conducted by them for the International Relief organization. They are ready to take care of 5000, and to date have 3800 under their care. They have built huge matsheds, each caring for about 200, or the double ones for 400 people. The ground is their bed, with just a piece of matting or an old quilt under them. As fast as they can send people to the country to their homes, that is being done. The other day I saw two crowded trucks taking people away, but at the same time a third truck was unloading another lot of arrivals.

Helen's letters for the fall reflect her concern for Joe's health. October 1, 1937:

Daddy is having a return of his old trouble and today is to stop work at the hospital for ten days and take to his couch and his diet. The strain of the past six weeks is telling on him. All the younger men had their six weeks vacations so Daddy bore the brunt of the responsibility.

On October 7 she added:

We went to Hongkew. I went to see the place and to keep Daddy from working; I thought I could do the coolie work....We drove in behind the surgical building and saw the open side of the operating room where the shell hit. We went in to the buildings used by the medical school to get out books; we moved out cases and then filled them with books. It was sprinkling then and before long it was raining hard. There were three Russians helping out with the truck and they worked awfully hard. The rest of the people scattered into the various buildings bringing out more stuff. I could not get over the fact that that hospital has belonged for seventy years to Americans; it is their own land and these are their own buildings, and this is international territory, and yet here we were working to get things out by the gracious permission of the invaders. We had to abide by their rules, go in and out together, after submitting lists of what was wanted, and obtaining

154

passes from the Japanese army officials. Imagine having to move a library in the rain, in a hurry, in order to keep it all. They say after this week no one can go in to remove anything. They had not men nor trucks enough to bring out the chairs and tables for classroom work, which are going to be needed for the school. When the books were out we went over to the hospital library building but had to leave most of these books behind. Never had I had a chance to see the operating room so we went upstairs. The inner wall that was untouched bore in the middle a bronze tablet:

To the Glory of God
And in the Loving Memory of a
Little Girl Child
Elizabeth Miller Hobart
August 10, 1896

Opposite this wall is the outer wall, wide open to the skies and all around is wreckage of this room which was dedicated to the saving of life. Compare seventy years of service in Hongkew, nights and days, weekdays and Sundays, most of the work done for poor people, and the destruction done in a few minutes. I could have sat down in the midst of it and cried for I know how much Daddy has done of that kind of service "to the glory of God" ever since he came in 1914.

When these old buildings are dismantled they show under what handicaps this hospital has worked. Now one sees them in all the glory of their inadequacy and shabbiness. But the medical school buildings are even worse; two shabby old houses, inconvenient, crowded they have supplied all the rooms they could; servants quarters, backhalls, former bathrooms, verandas and closets have housed this work which has turned out doctors who can enter any graduate school in America. A Shanghai doctor said in my hearing the other day: "Without a doubt a degree from St. John's Medical School carries with it a prestige that no other can give."

The Medical School opens the 18th of this month; some of the classes in the Continental Bank Building where the University is to function. Mary is to teach the first year anatomy; she was to have taught in the Women's Medical but they have not been able to open except for their 3rd and 4th year classes. St. John's is taking in a new class and is taking in girls. One of the doctors thinks if they once get into St. John's they will never transfer to here; but Daddy thinks if the girls wish to come and they are well-equipped he will be unable to refuse them....It may force cooperation later between these two schools. So Mary is teaching the first year class at St. John's, so far nineteen students, two of these girls. They had filled all their places with twenty-four men but some were coming from Honolulu and now are not getting here.

The missionaries returned to their inland stations, and Helen wrote on October 15th:

I think that takes guts. For men to go back to all these cities along the Yangtze River and open their hospitals to soldiers when the Japs are bombing everything from here to Chengtua, that takes a good bit of courage. Coming to China as a missionary is like getting married; it is for better or worse. We have had thirty years of the good and now we must "take it." In no other place in the world could one sit on the veranda and watch bombing two or three miles away.

I was stitching yesterday on small Chinese garments and could see the Japanese planes sailing by and then hear the peculiar sound of the dive and then the explosion of the bomb....Nine weeks of war and the Japanese have not even yet gotten the North Station; they try every day and now are dropping very heavy bombs which shake our house....A Japanese letter in the evening paper said, "If the people do not want to be hurt, when they see our planes coming they can get out of the way." He ended his letter by saying that "if our criticizers do not like what we do they had better be careful or they will find the flag of the Rising Sun flying over the Sun Yat Sen Memorial in Nanking, the Times Building in New York and the Arc de Triomphe in Paris." Aren't they ambitious?

Enough about war; I am tired of it. Daddy is giving me for my birthday organ lessons. I began last week. I have wanted to play the organ all my life so now it seems a good opportunity to begin. I am not expecting to become a soloist but I do expect to get a lot of fun out of playing. I need something to do. My days are so long here alone. I cannot sew or knit even on war things all day long. There are no social things and none of us go downtown, women, I mean, unless it is necessary. So it leaves me with empty hours to fill. I am learning to play scales with my feet.

On October 25th Helen wrote:

I went up to an adult Bible class yesterday and heard Mr. Hudspeth; he is a Briton whom I like very much. We had been talking the day before about how angry all this makes us and how stirred up we get when the planes go back and forth and drop bombs and the windows rattle and we get so sick of it all. Ruth said she had just lost her religion sitting up there on the roof of the Y apartment seeing the Japs do as they please. Mr. Hudspeth read as his introduction the 37th Psalm. "Fret not thyself, because of evil doers." It reminded me of the hymn I like, "Although the wrong seems oft so strong, God is the ruler yet." It may be hard to believe it sometimes but I am convinced it is true.

Helen became active on the project sponsored by the International Relief Committee to set up committees to visit and investigate refugee camps in an attempt to put them on a uniform basis and provide better feeding and sanitary measures. Horrible as the conditions were in many places, she also found some camps which were better. Helen was grateful for a challenging opportunity to be contributing.

Helen's letter of November 11 described the ironic situation:

This has been a queer Armistice Day, with guns booming from the crack of dawn until about three o'clock....I went to market very early in the morning hoping that around eight o'clock when the ceremony at the War Memorial was going on, the Japs would stop firing. They did not.

I had terrible shocks at the prices....This morning Daddy left to do an operation at eight o'clock at the hospital. About twelve a man telephoned me and asked if I knew where he was. I said I supposed he was at the hospital. The man said, "Do you know whether he is the American doctor who has gone down with some nurses behind the Jap's smoke screen to evacuate a hospital." I told him I did not know and he said the man answers his description and the Hospital is called "Base Hospital Number Two." Imagine how I felt!

About half past twelve he telephoned to me and said he would be late to luncheon which seemed a small matter after hearing his voice. He had been trying to get wounded soldier-patients moved and had trouble getting the ambulances into that district past the police. He and two nurses have been helping to organize an evacuation, having had some experience.

On November 12, she added:

Everything is over around Shanghai. 2500 soldiers came across the Siccawie Road at Avenue Dubail and laid down their arms for the French. Fighting now moves from this immediate neighborhood....There are many forecasts as to what will happen. The Japanese have issued two warnings to the Municipal Council; one advised them to control all publications so that no anti-Japanese feeling is expressed in anything printed in Shanghai. The other is that they are to harbor no political refugees or people liable to have anti-Jap feelings!

As fall turned toward winter, Helen continued to reflect on the situation:

I think people have the idea that we are doing something noble and unusual out here. We are just going on about our ordinary business. That there happens to be a little gunfire around the borders of the Settlement does not change ordinary hospital work into anything glorified. You all know that living at home in Shanghai isn't anything. It is not nearly as hard as living at home without any money and jobs, as Americans have had to do during the Depression....

In the last *Pennsylvania Gazette* there were pictures of the new grounds given to Penn out near Valley Forge. It just seemed wonderful to see rolling country with lovely trees and good roads....I could not help but think of these awful camps I have just visited, nineteen to date. The people have nothing to go back to. The Chinese are the ones to be sorry for. They have lost so much, the whole business is sickening. It is that sickness of spirit which is hard to bear. I hope that we can live long enough to see them come back, in spirit, morale and courage, and regain their lost ground. They need backing and encouragement and friendship more than ever right now....

Daddy has been busy all day long trying to get a new hospital started for sick refugees; it is very much needed and some of the American Red Cross money is available for the purpose. They expect to take over a building and set up a branch of St. Luke's Hospital. Tomorrow at eleven they sign on the dotted line, a lease for the building. This building is now under Chinese control but they are expecting to lease it and then fly the American flag and use it for Red Cross purposes....

Perhaps you can realize how impossible it seems to us right now to leave Shanghai. He is just as much needed as he ever was. They have opened this new hospital in the *Academica Sinica*, a scientific institution started with about 500,000 of Boxer money and conducted by the government. They have rented it to St. John's Medical School and St. Luke's Hospital (for a dollar a year though that is not for publication as what they wanted was to get it into American hands) and opened a hospital for men and women refugees.

To pick up and leave Shanghai just now would be a poor finish to thirty-two years of work. It will be thirty-two years the
first of January since Daddy first left for China (1906). It was
thirty-two years the first of November since he first signed up
with the Christian Association....

It is not just the hospital either; he is still Chairman of the
American Community Committee, is on several other emergency committees, and for this International Red Cross is on
the medical committee. Last week he was given a check for
$10,000 Mex to start this new hospital and will need much
more if he keeps it going for the winter months. He is a person to whom the business men trust money and responsibility.
How can he pick up and leave just to get away from this war?
It is not safety he is looking for. So do not expect us to come
home until the war is over. After saying "Hello" to all of you,
what would we do with ourselves?

On November 20, 1937, Joe received a singular honor when Sterling College, in Kansas, named its new athletic field McCracken Field
in honor of his early life. Joe's sister Daisy and her niece, Grace
Browby, represented him at the ceremony, despite a car wreck in snow
along the way. The dedication speech was given by Dr. H. R. Ross,
then acting Secretary and Director of the Division of Public Health
Education of the State of Kansas. In his closing remarks, Dr. Ross
quoted the poem [by Josiah Gilbert Howard (1819-1881), published
in *Wanted*, 1872] which had been used at the reception held at the
United Presbyterian church in Sterling in 1906 when Joe was on his
way to China to start his life work so many years earlier:

> *God give us men a time like this demands,*
> *Men whom the lust of office does not kill,*
> *Men whom the spoils of office cannot buy,*
> *Men who possess opinions and a will,*
> *Men who have honor, men who will not lie.*
> *Men who can stand before a demagogue,*
> *And brace his treacherous flattery without winking,*
> *Tall men sun-crowned, who live above the fog,*
> *In public duty and private thinking.*
> *For while the rabble with their thumb worn creeds,*
> *Their large professions and their little deeds*
> *Mingle in selfish strife, lo, freedom weeps.*
> *Wrong rules the land, and waiting justice sleeps.*

Dr. Ross continued:

Today Sterling College honors herself in dedicating this field to clean athletics, the only type worthy of a Christian institution. Such ideals have been upheld through the years, in the example and in the life of sacrificial services of our distinguished friend, former student and citizen, world athlete, physician and surgeon, teacher, scholar, missionary and withal the Christian gentleman, Josiah Calvin McCracken. May this name inspire higher, nobler and purer ideals, in all who in the future use this field, and may Sterling College ever encourage and uphold such ideals.

Helen fell and suffered a slight concussion in December. Joe wrote Christmas night (1937):

We had a Christmas celebration in the Hospital on Friday afternoon with a service, singing on the wards and a large bundle of presents for each refugee. They have forty nurses, most of them women nurses and quite a number of Mary's class living there and helping on the wards. It is reported that the Japs are going to begin policing Zack a Doo and the territory around our hospital January 1. We are waiting until that time to see what effect it may have on our continuing. If there is no trouble we expect to increase our bed capacity to 175 during January and maybe 200.

This 1933 Buick carried Joe around Shanghai until he had to give it up in 1938 during the Japanese occupation.

160

CHAPTER SIXTEEN

LIFE UNDER JAPANESE RULE
1938

In 1938 Joe sent an "extra edition" to his friends and supporters, written and then mailed February 1:

> This extra edition of our annual letter is written in order to give you "news while it is news," as our radio reporter here says; we feel that if you are interested at all in China, you will be glad to hear what is being done in Shanghai, during this major catastrophe. One of you sent me a card for Christmas with this verse on it:

> *If folks crowd round your apple cart*
> *And upset it*
> *Just prop the old thing up again*
> *And forget it.*

> Our apple cart was upset in August; we are propping it up but it is impossible to forget it. The Medical School opened the fifteenth of October [1937] and it is the only medical school giving a full curriculum between here and Chengtu, about 1500 miles away in West China. St. John's University, still unable to use its campus, is continuing all classes in a downtown office building. St. Luke's Hospital, driven out of Hongkew, moved from the University campus to a girls' school, and asked to evacuate so that the school could re-open, was fortunate in being able to rent a former boys' school building and is more comfortably housed than for years, with steam heat and modern plumbing. But moves and modern housing are all expensive luxuries. The hospital has had help from American Red Cross funds which will enable it to continue for a few months. Unless conditions change, it cannot return to the old buildings, as that part of the city is still under the complete domination of the Japanese. No Chinese can go in and out of the district, without a pass; it would not be safe for the Chinese staff to live in that section and the sick would rather die than go there for hospitalization.

> The last week of November we were offered the use of the *Academica Sinica*, a group of buildings for scientific research built with government and indemnity funds. In response to the need for beds for sick refugees, and with the help of American Red Cross funds, we opened a second hospital, St. Luke's

Number 2, for refugees only. With buildings which had to be emptied of machinery and other apparatus [using] no equipment at all, we began to gather things together and opened the first of December. Now we have two hundred beds full, including a maternity ward and a children's ward. The staff is made up of volunteer workers: Chinese doctors, interns and 4th year medical students of St. John's Medical School, and refugee missionaries. Several groups of women are helping to make hospital clothing, bedding and dressings. We have opened an out-patient department, financed locally and also with some Red Cross funds, which is seeing seventy-five patients a day. Not only are we running a hospital in this building, but also we have taken in two groups of Chinese nurses, from Mission hospitals in Ningpo and Shaoshing. This gives them a safe place to stay and the Ningpo training school can continue its courses. Graduates from both schools can work in nearby hospitals and refugee camps. Our building is large enough for four hundred beds and if funds are forthcoming we may expand. The need is urgent. The refugee situation is terrible; it is difficult even to describe to people in America the conditions under which these people exist. The newspapers give daily reports of the number of camps in the International Settlement. Today's reads:

Number of camps.............   179
Number of refugees..........93,412

Add to that the number in the so-called "safety zone" in Nantao, the old Chinese city, about 250,000 destitute. Add to that the number in the French Concession, a total that I do not know but the camp in the vacant lot next to us had 4500, and one mile away, there are 17,500 living in the buildings of a Chinese government university. They have been herded into these camps, some for weeks and some for months. They left their homes in warm weather with what they wore and could carry. There have been epidemics of measles, dysentery, many cases of malnutrition, some diphtheria and some scarlet fever. The camps provide some food but the diet lacks vitamins. The Salvation Army camps, the best of all the large ones, feed the people on three dollars per person per month; that is Chinese money and means less than one dollar in American currency, and is spent for food and fuel to prepare it. Some people in town are sponsoring a "Save a life" movement whereby each member pledges himself to support one person a month. Our Community Church, as one of its Christmas projects, provided for one large camp, not Christmas greens, but greens (fresh vegetables) for Christmas.

Life Under Japanese Rule (1938)

In the camp of 17,500 out of forty people who died in one day, two only had been seen by a doctor; but that is better organized now. When the refugees come to our hospital they are in such a condition from exposure and malnutrition that nearly half of them die in the first forty-eight hours. As they arrive they are a sorry looking lot; they have to have baths, haircuts, and their clothes deloused. They are given clothing, food and a clean bed. The Chinese believe that burial is of the greatest importance, yet in the streets of Shanghai during four months, the Shanghai Public Benevolent Association (Chinese) picked up and buried 41,045 bodies, most of them refugees and about seven-tenths of them children. Their relatives were too destitute to provide burial. From here all the way up the Yangtze River the six hundred miles to Hankow, the same situation prevails in cities and towns. Either everything has been bombed to ruins or the Japanese are in control which means no promise of security or safety.

What can a penniless refugee do if he returns to his former home? There is no little hut, no farm ready to plant, no seed, no water buffalo to pull the plow. By this time of year usually the ground is worked over, prepared for the seed, winter vegetables are growing, the winter wheat is well along. Or suppose a man returns to Hongkew: he may have had a small shop or factory. We drove through that district when it was open to foreigners. For about ten square miles there is not a whole building to be seen. In that part of Shanghai, where usually a million people live, asking nothing more than a chance to do their work, we saw just two Chinese. Do you wonder that after hospital care it is difficult to discharge patients even if they are well enough to go?

There is also risk in leaving the Concessions; the Japanese take able-bodied men to work for them. If they do not understand when spoken to or do as they are told, there is, to the Japanese soldier, only one answer. When you read about or see pictures of the Chinese welcoming the Japanese you may be sure that out of sight there is a gun or a threat. Recently the Japanese staged a "victory parade" in Peiping, to celebrate the fall of Nanking, the Chinese capital city. There are the regulations sent out to the schools of the city..."teachers, administrative officers and all pupils assemble at the school...each to carry a small celebration flag and proceed to the route of the parade." In the event of "any failing on some pretext to join enthusiastically in the celebration when the times comes...the same will mean that the persons concerned are guilty of deliberately evading compliance and they will be punished with the utmost severity as for complicity with Communism, nor will any mercy be shown."

Everything modern and progressive in these provinces has been destroyed; postal services disrupted; airmail discontinued; school buildings and hospitals, and beautiful government buildings in ruins. The Japanese say they have no interest in the continuance of missionary work in schools and hospitals; they, themselves will do all that is necessary. We know how they will do it. Hundreds of wounded were taken out of hospitals and killed. The districts where there are Japanese soldiers are unsafe for women. The houses of foreigners and Chinese have been looted of everything of value, after the taking over by the Japanese. People here in Shanghai have seen their own household belongings being moved out of their homes, in trucks driven by Japanese soldiers. There is a shortage of rice; there is a shortage of vegetables; there is shortage of fuel; there is a scarcity of houses. Little children sat on the curbs of Avenue Petain waiting for the leaves to fall from the trees. Hardly a leaf touched the ground before some child dashed out regardless of traffic, to grab it and put it in his basket. They go about picking up small twigs and sometimes breaking them from our shrubbery. Along the railroad track near one of our parks there was a nursery of young trees. Not one is left on that acre of ground. Now small children hack away at the roots. There are beggars at every corner and at all the bus and streetcar stops.

Missionaries and business people, Protestants, Catholics and Buddhists, have all poured out money in aid of the refugees. Shanghai's people have been generous with time and money in their relief work. But the end is not in sight. Nothing equal to this has come to China since the Taiping Rebellion eighty years ago. Famines have come and gone and taken their toll in lives; but the destruction of property and life today is unequalled. Rehabilitation and reconstruction will take years to accomplish. All this suffering, all this waste, all this long drawn out terror has been brought to these peace loving hardworking people by a heartless, aggressive "neighbor" who is better armed, better equipped, better trained in warfare. It is an "undeclared war" on an unprepared people who were building up a new united China.

Helen's letter of January 29th describes some of Mary's activities, for she and several others are helping to run the Out-patient Department:

Out of my wheat money I bought a thirty yard piece of pink and white flannelet and we are making baby garments, for the hospital is opening a children's ward. The work being done would interest anyone, and the stories we hear are wonderful, sometimes wonderfully horrible and sometimes touching and sometimes funny.

Daddy is really having the time of his life being a superintendent of a hospital, running it his way, and having with him the people in St. Luke's that would make a different type of place. Miss Lamberton and Miss Hurst are so nice and they adore working for him and being bosses in their departments, too. I think it will be a good thing for the mission to see what can be done. But that is just for you children to know.

In a later letter accumulating Helen's thoughts, she wrote on January 30, 1938:

This evening I have been trying to realize that I have seven children in America; in church this morning we had an elderly rather old-fashioned preacher and as I was not interested in the sermon, it gave me a good chance to catch up on my thinking. I seem to have been so busy lately doing things and not thinking very much about anything. I just began with the oldest of you, who was thirty yesterday, and each one had a turn, and I took in Tyler and Bill, Allan [Ruth's boyfriend] and Babs [Joe Jr.'s girlfriend] as I went along. How nice you all are and how I wished we could see you. When letters are so delayed you seem farther away....Tonight I felt lonely for you all and played on the piano for awhile and finally sang a few hymns as we used to do Sunday evenings. I do not suppose any of you is old-fashioned enough to do that. But do you remember how we did, and later each of you took turns playing the one she chose? It is nice to remember things we did together.

Today our servants gave us a big feast. We never had servants to do that before for us. Chang, Soong, the Dumbbell and amah all joined and we had awfully good food. They had had an old hen running about the basement for several days, and a whole head of a pig. We had twelve varieties of food and I had no idea they could cook such things. Then the servants ate what was left over, I guess, for it sounded very hilarious downstairs. We have never had such good feeling below stairs; they are like a big family there. It is much nicer than ever before. I feel that they feel differently toward us now that we have opened our doors to two new babies plus the little girl and make so much over them.

On February 24, Helen wrote:

This was great week in the history of the McCracken Family; the American Community gave a big dinner for Admiral and Mrs. Yarnell on Washington's Birthday, 360 people, Americans only, present. Daddy and I stood in the line with the Admiral and his wife and shook hands for perfect ages with all the people. Then at a small round head table we two sat with Judge and Mrs. Helmick and the Admiral and his wife. It was almost too much glory for me. The Admiral is very nice; he made a very nice speech about Daddy when he talked. First Daddy welcomed the community; then he read Ambassador Johnson's telegram; then Judge Helmick made a speech introducing the Admiral and then the Admiral made his. He was at Annapolis when Daddy was a football star....For Daddy to be chairman of the American Community at a time like this, is quite an honor. This was the largest dinner of Americans, and one of the nicest functions ever held in Shanghai.

On February 28, Joe added to the letter:

The medical school has begun its second term with over ninety percent normal enrollment. Some of the Fourth year men have had an exciting experience doing war work. All of them seem to have conducted themselves under very trying conditions in a creditable way. All of the third and fourth year students are now living in the Refugee Hospital and help on the wards. We have now an average of over 235 patients, forty-five of whom are children under 12. We have never had such splendid material for teaching purposes. Many of those patients who die we are able to do a post on. I think we shall have enough money to keep us going until July at least if the Japs leave us alone.

On April 28, Helen's next letter spoke of the difficulties and feelings of being so distant from all of her children (except Mary, at this point):

I love to hear of you children getting about to see each other; it means "family" to me and I do want to think of you as caring a good deal about seeing each other often. At this distance, of course, it is easy to make suggestions that it might be hard to carry out over there. I do not want ever to make plans for any of you or seem unreasonable about what you do

166

or do not do. We are too far away and it takes too long for our letters to get to you, for us to try to plan anything. I have felt lately as though next February would never come when we could start off to see you all.

As for the twins, we want them to study next year and not stop to work. The Association has given each of you older ones five years of college allowances; four for college and one toward special training. With that to count on you have a chance to get very good training in some line of work or other. We shall continue to try to help you if anything unusual comes up. We shall help Joe [Jr.] through his medical course and training and hope to see each of you established in doing what you want. So count on that much. If anything happens to me, Daddy will still be able to help you and if anything happens to him, the Association is pledged to do that much for you, even Stewart, until he is pretty well along.

On May 8, 1938, she wrote of being so distant on such a special day:

On Mother's Day any woman with twelve children [that is, eight of her own, and four married--or nearly so], thinks a good bit about them; I have thought about all of you all day long. In spite of having eleven of you on the other side of the world, we are pretty lucky first to have you at all, and then to have you as your are, doing well in your lives and your work, nice to live with, pleasant to know and very dear to your parents. Stewart, tomorrow is your birthday. I hope all your gifts reached you safely.... We are going to see if these letters will go before next Sunday. It would be nice if there were a mail; we shall see. Much love to you. You are, remember, the McCrackens of Shanghai. You are to carry on the traditions. After all there is something in handing down the best, generation after generation. That is why I like the Episcopal church service; it has meant the highest ideals for so many people for so many years.

Joe added to the letter:

This being Mother's Day it would seem quite in order that Daddy write to his children. I still think that you children have the finest mother in the world and that she has the finest children in the world and that I am a most fortunate man and have every reason to be one of the happiest men in the world.

Joe and Helen had decided to rent the big house and take an apartment for the months before they hope to take their furlough, especially as Mary would be moving to the hospital for her internship. Helen was kept busy going through the accumulations of fifteen years at 5 Avenue Petain. With Stewart's leaving in August of 1937 there were no McCrackens at the American School for the first time since 1914 and no children at home at all.

On June 9, 1938, Helen wrote:

Tomorrow the Y.W.C.A. has a tea and a Pageant, showing the development of the work there, thirty years. I am one of the women taking part in the first board meeting. There were five foreign and five Chinese ladies and all are to wear old fashioned clothes. We who do not pay much attention to the differences in Chinese clothes from time to time have to laugh at their clothes thirty years ago as much as at our own. Then all women wore this short upper garment and now they all wear the long gowns. I am wearing white mull dress I made by hand at that time. It was up in a tin-lined box and yellow with age. I have washed it and can wear it nicely except that the waist belt does not meet by about an inch. I am wearing a sash with a bow in the back to cover up this deficiency. The collar is high with whalebones to hold it up and I have a pair of white silk stockings and an enormous white hat to which I am adding a wreath of flowers. Most of the women are wearing their husband's shirts and skirts for the old fashioned shirt waist outfit but I look like a real lady. It is lots of fun and we laugh at each other, Chinese and foreigner.

Helen's letter of June 28 reported on Mary's move:

Mary moved last week and will have very little time off; every other Sunday and one afternoon a week, I suppose. I shall miss her a lot. She passed with good grades in her medical work and now has about twenty-five beds for which she is responsible to a resident doctor. Graduation this year was a historic occasion. Seven missionary institutions had their Commencement together in the Grand Theater. Five hundred graduates marched in two by two, and had all the front portion of the theater. Then followed the faculties of all the institutions and then presidents, deans, guests of honor, etc. They did not hand out the five hundred diplomas but present[ed] each class [as] a bunch. Daddy, however, had to call up his seven doctors and all M. A. students and specials came up to the platform and received their honors.

On July 5, Helen's letter reflected the loneliness of being so far away during important family events:

> This morning's paper tells of Ruth's graduating June 14 from Lake Erie College, receiving her degree of B. S. and a certificate in Physical Education and a state certificate as a teacher. Today it was brought home to me just how alone I am in the apartment; Daddy went off for the day at half past eight and probably will not get back before six-thirty. There was not much for amah to do--she comes twice a week for the mornings. Daddy found a room for Sung and his family and two children at the hospital where Mary has moved. The boy is downstairs fixing his rice. Daddy is rejoicing because he just received a promise of $15,000 Chinese currency for his medical school from the Boxer Indemnity Fund....He is the only man I am sure in Shanghai who could wangle a thing like that. They turned him down at their April meeting because St. John's is not a registered school but he applied again at the June Executive meeting and is to have the money. He wants a big year for the school next year. How shall we be able to go home with a hospital and a flourishing medical school to leave?

On July 13, Helen wrote:

> Having given you twins the extra $25 you had coming back from the college, we sent nothing more for your graduation gift but I wish we had been represented in the lists of gifts you had. I am so glad people are so good to you. Elsie, of course, you must have a typewriter. Daddy meant to tell you in his last letter but I think he did tell you that we would help you more this year and that is one of the necessities. You did well to earn money and to get such good marks and a scholarship prize as well. I am terribly proud of each one, and of Stewart's doing so well in only one year as to be asked to the Cum Laude Society. I wish I had been around. But I might have cried and you would not have liked that; cried because I would have been so proud to see it all.
>
> Mary did not graduate yet; you see the internship is required here first before they graduate. She will get her degree next June. You will all be interested to know that what is left of the Blind School is moving to Daddy's place. There is one large school building empty out there and Daddy is turning it over to them. Since their buildings were destroyed and Mrs. Fryer died and Mr. Fryer went home, the school has been out at the China Inland Mission and now they cannot continue

there. Isn't it just like Daddy to open up and give them room? Daddy is so busy. I hope the heat will not be too much. All other doctors in the mission are taking August, of course, as their holiday.

The July 28, 1938, *Shanghai Evening Post and Mercury* included pictures of the American Refugee Hospital and a long report of its work since its doors opened December, 1937, with Joe as Superintendent. Staff is made up of doctors and nurses and technicians from St. Luke's Hospital, from St. John's Medical School and from persons refugeeing in Shanghai because they cannot return to the interior. Support is coming from the American Red Cross, the Shanghai International Red Cross, the Child Welfare, Inc. of New York and gifts from friends in the city and abroad. There are five departments--surgical, medical, maternity, children's wards plus a large out-patient unit with the appropriate specialties clinics in the morning and general clinic in the afternoon. Efforts were made to collect one cent from those registering at the clinics to get the patients to have a feeling of participating in paying towards the cost of treatment.

August 14, 1938, marked one year since the bombing of Shanghai. Helen wrote a summary of the changes:

It is a year today since the bombing of Shanghai and it will be a year Tuesday since we sent Stewart off in the midst of the shrapnel fire on the tender manned by W. S. crew, the first time our Navy has taken over a boat on the Yangtze River. Such a year. Yesterday was the anniversary of the beginning of the war around Shanghai. It seems to be the custom to call this affair by other names, such as incidents, hostilities and so on, but we call it war.

Shanghai began a week or so ago to prepare for this anniversary and yesterday was like an armed camp and yet a deserted city. Pictures in today's paper show that almost no people were about on the downtown streets. The Bund was empty. Stores were closed. Amusement places of all kinds were closed. People were supposed to stay at home so as not to cause "incidents" and so as not to be hurt in case of trouble. The funny thing is that the people who were arrested for causing disturbances were Japanese Some were in Chinese clothing. Some were in Japanese civilian dress. The men arrested by the Marines all had guns....That bears out the feeling that most of us had all along, that these terrorist acts are inspired by the Japanese just to make trouble and give them excuses for taking over more and more policing of the Settlement.

Life Under Japanese Rule (1938)

Mr. J. B. Powell gave a good summary in a talk to the doctors and their wives at the French Club and compared what we could do a year ago and what we can do now....

Daddy's hospital now has about four hundred a day in their clinic and there are 300 beds in the hospital. We took a woman out there last week and after she had seen this surgical clinic and all the abscesses and sores and then taken a look in the children's ward, she felt faint and Daddy put her down on the hospital floor with her head on his arm until she was able to get up and go to one of the offices and lie down. The other lady had tears rolling down her cheeks at the sight of so many sick people.

I feel more or less like that myself and often think it would have been better for Daddy to have married a nurse who could go out there and work. Mary seems to be able to stand it and must be my representative in the hospital. I have to take out my feelings in work at home, making the bandages that wrap up the arms and legs and heads, and dressings and clothing. I have now finished fourteen suits and hope each one made some child happy when he had to leave the hospital and go back to refugee camp.

Much as I love you all and wish to see you I am glad to think of you living in a free country where you can take your car and go for a ride, and move about freely where you wish to go. And when you turn on the radio you can turn it on to listen to music or fun but not to hear news reports of war and atrocities or bloodshed, or what the Japanese spokesman says....You all have voted and must do your share to keep America free from a dictator and from such oppression as goes on in Germany and Japan.....Just be thankful you are Americans.

Joe and Helen began to hope that they might make a short trip back to America and see their children for a few months--after the medical school had gotten started and he had examined the children at the American School and arranged matters at the hospital for his absence. On September 28, Helen wrote of regret at their missing Joe Jr.'s and Barbara's wedding on September 17, 1938, and then adding comments on the situation in China:

I do not know whether you realize how much a European war means to Shanghai. There are nationals from all these countries living right here in Shanghai: Germans, French, British, Russians, every country in Europe and then Americans. It means not only a war in people's home countries but the consequences here in Shanghai are unpredictable. Japan has announced that she must stand by her allies, Germany and Italy, so it is expected that she would try to take over the International Settlement where the majority of control is in British hands, and Frenchtown which belongs to France as much as a city in France. What would happen to the rest of us and to the nationals of smaller countries, is another question. So rumors have been flying around, people listen anxiously for the broadcasts which are frequent, and no one knows quite what to expect.

The other great question is Hankow. How long can the Chinese hold Hankow. The Japanese have set various dates when they expect to take Hankow and have made plans for a big celebration here, in Peiping and Nanking.

Hitler's rise to power had led to recreating the Army in Germany in 1935 and the militarization of the Rhineland in 1936. During this same period Mussolini was taking control of Ethiopia. The Civil War in Spain was being waged during 1936-39 with Franco being assisted to power by Germany and Italy. It was in September of 1938 that Great Britain and France let their "appeasement policy" culminate in the sacrifice of Czechoslovakia by the signing of the Munich Pact on September 30th. Germany was moving into Bohemia and Moravia, and then came the invasion of Poland September 1, 1939. War was declared September 3 by England and France. The United States was trying to maintain its neutrality, but was being drawn closer to the Allies. Yet many historians go back to the Mukden [now Shen Yang] Incident in 1932 or the Marco Polo Bridge incident as the beginning of World War II, at least in the Far East.

Helen's letter of October 9, 1938 reported on goings-on amid the continuing difficulties:

It is a quarter past nine on Sunday morning. The sun is pouring through the windows as well as a very fine breeze. It is the kind of day one really should spend out of doors. Daddy has gone to the hospital and I have played the piano for nearly three quarters of an hour. I do not play as much here; sometimes radios are going and sometimes I am afraid I might disturb people, and I am tired of all my old music.

Monday night we had the usual Y supper and meeting afterwards, the first for this fall....Tuesday the Women's Club had its first tea of the year and I poured, supposedly as an honor but I always find it rather boring. I always like to be walking about seeing people but had to sit at the coffee table. I supposed I was asked as one of the oldest members. Certainly there are few here now that joined as early as 1914. I have joined a "current events" course for eight weeks and hope to learn more about the world. I am starting out on two more pieces of cotton flannel, sixty yards, to be cut out and made into children's warm garments for the hospital, and if we do the cutting we hope to get the auxiliary women to do some of the sewing but it comes hard. They do not mind rolling bandages nor folding dressings but the need is for winter clothing...

We have been again planning to sail on the *Empress of Canada* November 13th, though it is difficult for Daddy to make any plans. I think part of Daddy's extreme fatigue shows in his not being able to make up his mind. I tell you all frankly that [his doctor] says Daddy has some heart irregularities due to nervous fatigue and that he is having recurrence of his ulcer troubles for the same reason. This noon he came home, having seen the American consul, and feels we might as well be off. So he has gone to play golf and I am here dizzy with changing emotions. He is afraid that Mary might need us. I tell him all the mission is devoted to Mary and she would probably have more people running around to evacuate her than any other person in Shanghai.

[Joe's doctor] says Daddy wants to finish his life working on the field and he told him he had better go home and get to feeling better and then come out and do his swan song.

On October 27, Joe wrote:

The Shanghai Medical Society is meeting tonight and I thought I should go, but before night came I decided that I would stay home and have a simple supper and write some letters. I was out last night at the Park Hotel where a group of Chinese gave a dinner announcing the plans for the opening of an eye hospital. I had been asked to be an honorary Director. We had been invited to the C.F. Wong's for dinner and Helen went there. Tomorrow night we are to go to the Sawyers. When you have been on the go all day long I sometimes wish we might stay at home and early to bed.

Helen has been working awfully hard this week getting the freight packed and ready for shipment tomorrow. She has done all the packing and it is well done I am sure and ready on time....The annual letter, has to be written, printed and mailed this week. Helen has written most of it and addressed the envelopes, etc. Just to get on the boat and know that there will be no telephones and nothing in particular to do for sixteen days will be a great relief. With Canton gone without a struggle and Hankow in the hands of the invaders, it is almost the zero hour for China. I do not believe she will give up yet and yet she is going to be terribly handicapped from now on if she does continue to fight.

We had 292 patients in the hospital tonight and I saw some awfully sick ones leaving because no bed could be found for them. I hate to see them dragging themselves away for I know they have no comforts to go to and no medical treatment. With the hospital for T. B. patients moved in we have all the space available occupied so I think we have reached our limit and will have to stop expanding. I am trading the old car in for an economy Ford to be taken over in Dearborn. I hate to give up the Buick but then the next two or three years are going to be expensive ones. Nobody I know of ever heard of one family having five children in Universities at one time. We are glad you are all there for we feel that each one of you is trying to profit by the opportunity offered you to prepare for your life's work.

There is one more letter from Helen during this period, although it is undated:

Today Shanghai is waiting for the decision about war; as an international city this decision is most important to many people here. We feel that it is also important to us personally, because no one knows what will happen to this town and no one knows how it will affect Daddy's work. Would not you think Europeans would remember vividly enough the World War, so that they would not think of having another? The men in power now must have lived through war and know what it means. It seems terrible to contemplate; but at least it decides for us the question of going home in November. We can hardly leave if war is declared. Or as someone said, we may all be leaving at once. Such uncertainty these days....

People who grow old without anyone but themselves to think of do get very queer. I am thinking of a couple here in Shanghai this last week. They have never had a child and they are wrapped up in themselves, their aches and their pains and their own affairs. I feel as if my horizon was so much greater than theirs, my interests, my life so much fuller. I never intended to have eight children. Don't ever think that. But methods were not perfected in those days. Precautionary measures could not be depended on and now it would be hard for me to choose out of my family the ones I thought I wanted and the ones I would not have planned for. We always wanted a few and have enjoyed our crowd. I think I get a lot of fun out of having an unusual number, just because it shocks people to think anyone would have eight.

Life Under Japanese Rule (1938)

Helen wrote Helen, Jr.:

I am glad though you have a home to call your own, to develop, to give you security and roots in a community. That is one thing I have liked about our life, we have belonged to Shanghai for so many years, we are part of the community, but unfortunately it is not a place where we can pass on that past to our children. Not unless some one of you chooses to spend his life out here. And just now it is not the place for a person to plan to live!

Amidst all of the uncertainty, Joe and Helen sailed for the U.S. on November 13th, 1938. They then took a train to Dearborn, Michigan to pick up a new car, and then on to visit children and friends on their way East and to settle in a cottage at Ventnor. The Christmas holidays were memorable days for everyone, except that Mary was absent. As often as possible the seven children, their spouses and boyfriends visited or were visited.

They were among family for only about a month. All too soon on January 23rd they began to drive back to get their boat in Vancouver, stopping to see Helen's sister in Washington D.C., Helen and Tyler in Amherst, and Joe's sister, Daisy, in Tulsa, Oklahoma. Taking the southern route, they visited in Los Angeles and saw about forty China friends at a tea, and they then had two days in Berkeley.

The boat trip gave them time to rest and recover from a car accident they had en route in which Joe received two broken ribs and Helen suffered a head gash, broken teeth and extensive contusions. The fate of the car was worse.

Helen's letter of March 9, 1939 tells of the welcome given to them by their Shanghai friends:

Having left a letter for each of you in Kobe to go back by this same boat, I hesitate to write another so soon. But you will wish to know that we arrived safely. Mrs. Munson met us at the China Merchants Wharf in Hongkew and we turned all our baggage over to Cook's and got off the boat there, saving at least two hours of waiting at the Custom's jetty. She brought us right out to the apartment where we found the Wolcotts were not out but just getting out. We went up to the Olivers and Mary came and we had tea.

Then we went to the hospital where we were welcomed with a firecracker celebration such as I have not seen in years. One long string hung from a tree to the ground just outside the big entrance gate. When we came in sight they touched it off and from the gate in, every ten feet, was a coolie holding a giant cracker about ten inches long. He would touch his off and then the next and so on down the line. When we reached the entrance there were three long strings of big crackers going off at once. The noise was deafening and all the coolies, nurses and staff were out waiting for us, and coming to shake hands and greet us. It was a lot of fun. I believe it was the coolies who started this idea and they certainly did their job well. For a year and a half fireworks have been forbidden and I do not know how they got around that unless because it is off the Council Road.

The Japanese have not been there yet since we left but there are rumors that they intended to take the place over soon. Now that Joe is back, if he puts as much determination into keeping that place as he did to travelling in spite of broken ribs, we shall be there indefinitely. Daddy rented a car from the Ford Hire for two weeks and got it today. The Council gave away our famous license number although they had promised to hold it and so we shall never drive with 1346 again.

Mary looks fine; she spent the first two nights here, getting up and going back before breakfast. The first night after we got back I opened every piece of luggage to get out all her things.

Helen's letter of March 17 reported further on their return:

Teas and dinners continue but if they did not I should not know what to do with myself. The apartment practically runs itself. With Chang and amah I have little to do. Amah has to work or starve and I cannot let her and her little boy starve. I pay her ten dollars a month and five for doing odds jobs for Mary. But she has to pay five a month for rent and six to have someone take care of the baby while she goes out to work. Daddy is arranging for her to have a place to live at the hospital for which she will work one day a week. Our servants had rested in the thought that when we came back we would return to our house and they could bring all their families and friends and all come "home" again.

I am making wheat cereal again. I spend two dollars to get it and sell that amount for six dollars; I don't see why people do not make their own cooks do it but as long as they do not, I have that much for things I like to do in the Auxiliary, AAUW scholarship and so on. The alumni and students are planning a big celebration for Daddy's sixty-fifth birthday [March 30]. We received invitations yesterday. It is to be a big dinner at some Chinese place and what else I do not know.

As time went on, it became "more and more difficult to find people leaving who can carry letters out so as to avoid censorship by the Japs." Helen warned the children to be careful of what they wrote and what they did with the letters they received. On April 21, she wrote:

> I doubt if people at home realize the extent of the work necessary to distribute this American Red Cross money. Dr. Hylbert is chairman of this Advisory Committee and he does a tremendous amount of work. Each appeal is copied and sent to each member of the committee and at weekly meetings they talk over whether or not to respond and how to respond. These reports are quite interesting. In reading Daddy's [report] to this committee lately, I find that he has been responsible in six months for spending over one hundred thousand dollars on his work for the hospital alone. This committee has just promised him $24,000 gold for another year. It takes money to run a three hundred bed hospital when everything is free....
>
> Mary has shifted her work in the hospital and now is in charge of all pediatric cases. She is most interested in the children. I am, too, and have begun to make little garments again.

Helen wrote May 17 about Mother's Day:

> Mother's Day Daddy and I went to church; Mary sent me a lovely basket of snapdragons and came for luncheon. But the rest of the day I must say that I missed you all very much. You seemed so far away, as if we had brought you into the world, had you for a little time and then sent you off and let you go, with no further touch and so little knowledge of what you are thinking. It was a long afternoon. I ought to have gone to the Navy Y and done my share down there. Then I would not have been so sorry for myself.

Helen's June letter spoke of continuing activities:

> This is the day of the Dragon Boat Festival. So I had a holiday from my new job. It certainly is interesting to be doing something. I began Monday to sit in the office in the Mission Building, mornings, and interview European refugees. Dr. Hodgkins has been doing it and asked for volunteers. I know nothing yet about what can be done for these people, where to send them for money, summer clothing, places to live, etc., but I hope to be able to do some things after a few days. Poor

177

people. Some of them had good positions and comfortable homes. They are deported with nothing. Some are not Jews now, but on one side or another had a Jewish grandmother or grandfather.

There is this job in the mornings and in the afternoons I am practicing the organ again. Mr. Dent called me up and asked if I would be ready by August to take the church meeting. He is to give me a lesson a week and I am to practice at least an hour a day. Fun for me....I simply love to play. He has much more savvy teaching than the woman I used to have. He has started me off using both hands on different manuals and feet on the pedals. I feel as if I were trying to rub my head and stomach in different directions, or something like a three-ringed circus.

Daddy was down at noon for me and before coming home he ordered some clothes so I could have some of his old ones for my refugees. He has outgrown some of his anyway and ought not to be seen with them almost popping off him. He ordered a white serge (sergy as the tailor calls it) double breasted, a linen suit with two pairs of trousers and a white dinner coat and trousers of a black light weight material. He is always going out to dinners and I insisted he must have a new dress outfit. His tuxedo was new in 1926 and he can just get into it....

Mary is to get her degree Saturday morning. I promised her her calling cards with Dr. Mary Elizabeth McCracken on them. [Mary would graduate at the head of her class.] She still seems bent on going to America the end of October. I feel just the same about it. But she is twenty-seven or eight years old and has the right to do as she pleases but if she goes, it is against our wishes. I do not see how she can think of it without someone to help her. I can lie awake at night and think of all kinds of possibilities for trouble. She is so used to Soong-sz-foo that she does not realize how helpless she is. And she forgets how much you girls did for her...

I may surprise you some day and write my "Memoirs" but not now while I am having mornings with refugees and afternoons with the organ. I am too too busy this summer. I might write up the refugee situation. A second man burst into tears this week; that gets me. I cannot stand seeing men cry because they want their wives to come to China. I think of how I would feel, picked up and sent off miles and miles and unable to have Daddy come or I get back.

Helen's letter of August 12 told of the increasing stresses on them and those in Shanghai:

I really should sit down and weep. For Daddy and I have just left our house, having sold all the things left to a second hand dealer. He did not consider they were worth very much but if he had added the memories of all of you children they would have been worth a great deal more. Now the place is empty and rented to Germans. One era in all our lives is over.

I wonder what will come to Shanghai next; today exchange is over fifteen to one. People are glad of a Sabbath respite. Stores are not sure whether to sell or not; Shanghai money is worth so little. Rice is soaring. It went up five dollars a picuel in just two days. Daddy has contracted for two months supply, for he had five hundred people to feed. He has been told it will go higher. He has contracted for or rather bought one hundred tons of coal. He has a lot of responsibility on his shoulders. Now that he has his rice and coal for a few months, the house rented on a gold basis for two years, and all this stuff of ours cleared out, he can rest a little easier in his mind.

Daddy also bought four microscopes this morning. He has ten extra students in his first year class and is trying to get microscopes enough to go around. He really works as hard as if he were a young man, just out. Dr. Tsang told me the other day that Daddy, at sixty-five, worked harder than young men half his age, that he thought they ought to be ashamed of themselves.

We have just been invited to celebrate the anniversary of the bombing of Shanghai, at Dr. Gilmore's on Monday evening for an informal dinner. They are getting together some of the people here that August of 1937.

On September 1, Helen wrote:

We had welcome mail last night, and Elsie's [message via ham] radio with its swell news came on Wednesday. We are terribly pleased about her scholarship and I know she is happy over it. That will make up for some of the hard work you put in last year. Your checks all went some time ago. Daddy always has to be sure that they will and not get there before Mr. Wood puts the money into the Girard Trust. But I think you are all set for a few months.

The letter of September 24, 1939 indicated the increasing imposition on those in Shanghai:

Daddy had a call from a Japanese woman last week, sent by the military, saying that she had come to talk things over. She told Daddy he was not a Christian, that he allowed himself to be prejudiced against the Japanese people. He told her he was not prejudiced against the Japanese people, but against their army. He told her they would have to deal with the American consul. Mr. Gauss, the American consul, gave him a proclamation to put up at the gate and at the entrance to the hospital saying it was American leased property. The Japanese have written him they wish to take it over. It remains to be seen what can be done and where they could possibly move to, 522 sick people, a medical school, nurses, students, etc. It is very discouraging. Daddy has known that they were getting more active about taking it over but has hoped to hold them off.

Red Cross wheat bags provided stylish clothing for the "Fly Swatter Squad" during the early war years.

CHAPTER SEVENTEEN

THE END OF AN ERA
1939-1942

Joe's letters to his children plus his Thanksgiving letter to his friends and supporters describe their lives during the last part of 1939. On October 8 he wrote:

> We had communion this morning and the church was full. There were a lot of young people and an unusual lot of Chinese; thirty-one joined the church. Everyone likes Dr. Caughey and we are glad that he has consented to stay even a little longer than a year. He goes around for the most part in a rickshaw and I think we ought to give him enough money to enable him to have a car. I think we ought to treat our minister as well as we treat ourselves and I'd hate to have to give up my car. I may have to do so if gas goes any higher. It is now $2.80 a gallon. Our car gives us 18 miles per gallon.
>
> The hospital is full to running over every day. Hardly a day goes by we do not have to refuse patients and when we refuse them it means for most of them a trip back home to die, for few other hospitals will take them in. This morning while I was at the hospital we admitted an old man who had fallen and broken his back five days before. He was paralyzed and had had no treatment for five days. His back was already covered with bed sores and I do not think his bladder had been emptied since the accident. Probably we can not do much in the way of a cure but neither could we turn him away.
>
> Mary gets in her department awful scrawny little folks. She is getting excellent experience and is trying a lot of things which will be worth reporting some day. Already a paper which she really prepared from her own observations on her patients and which has been accepted by the American Medical Association, will appear under the name of Dr. Tsoa, who is the head of the Urology Department at the hospital.
>
> With all the rapid changes in the political situation the world over, ours remains here as befuddled as ever. Just now the acute point is the western district of Shanghai. Yesterday I went out to the hospital to operate at eight-thirty on a large hernia. There were lots of adhesions, so that it took some time to get him fixed up. Then I had a ward class with students, followed by considerable office work. After lunch I went out for two rounds of golf but my golf was not too hot so I came home and proposed to Mother we go to a movie. We saw *Man*

181

About Town and laughed a plenty....As we were eating supper Mrs. Arnold called up to see if we would not come over and play bridge for a little while. We did and came back about eleven quite rested. It was the first game of bridge we have had for months.

My appeal for fifteen microscopes is bringing in very satisfactory results. Our minister sent a copy of my letter to a wealthy friend of his and got back a check for $140.00 U.S. A Mrs. Yarnell who has supported us for thirty years sent in a check for $100 and Dr. Logan at Mayo Clinic sent a check for $100 and said he was forwarding a second hand microscope. The Executive Committee of the International College of Surgeons is sending a check for $150. By the way, I am supposed to be a Fellow of the International College of Surgeons and its representative in the Far East.

Joe's 1939 letter to his friends with Christmas greetings reported on the past year:

Notwithstanding war in the East and war in the West, we have much for which to be thankful. For our own country is not engaged in war and can lend her mighty influence to bring peace and justice to all people. We are thankful, too, for the many joys the year has brought us. Our short health trip to America gave us a new lease on life. We appreciated seeing our children in their homes and in their colleges, and having them all with us for the Christmas holidays in Ventnor.

We would like to be home in June, 1940 to see Joe [Jr.] receive his M. D. from Pennsylvania, Martha her B. A. from Vassar and Elsie hers, from the University of Chicago. That seems out of the question. Time did not allow us to see many of our friends last year, but enough of them to reassure us that friendship bridges over time and distance.

Because of the generosity of the American Red Cross, the China Child Welfare of New York, and friends in America and China we have kept the American Hospital for Refugees open for its second year as a free hospital. Those who have never worked in such an institution have little conception of the conditions of the patients when they arrive. On my wards now are three cases of appendicitis; one came in for the operation the tenth day of the disease, another the eighth day, and the third sixty hours from the beginning of trouble. Other patients come with infected wounds neglected for days and weeks, and from surroundings too filthy to describe.

A woman on my service came in recently from a district outside Municipal control, with the history that, a week before, bandits came to their home. The husband fled but she was caught and when she did not tell where their little savings were hidden, these men took firebrands and burned her in several places. On her hip an infected wound six inches in diameter. They got her belongings, but she almost lost her life which was only saved after two months of careful nursing and skin grafting at the hospital. Some patients come in with malignant malaria, or with longstanding typhoid, or swollen from starvation.

This hospital is a blessing to thousands of sick people who have no other possible chance of medical and hospital care. With the present rate of exchange, full hospital service including food, medicines, special diet and complete laboratory examinations, everything required, has cost for each patient less than a quarter of a dollar in American money a day. In twenty-two months the relief given has been as follows:

Number of in-patients treated free	8,280
Number of hospital days	176,110
Free prescriptions filled	125,333
Out-patients paying 1/10 cent US	144,104
Number of free laboratory exams	91,075

Last Spring the government decided to move its National Medical School from Shanghai into "free China" a thousand miles from here. Many students whose families did not wish them to leave home, tried to enter our school which is the only one for men and women remaining in this part of the country. As their requirements are lower than ours, these pupils had to drop back a year; this and the number of qualified students applying gave us a larger class than usual. Instead of twenty we had thirty, and as some of you know, having responded to my request, I was asked to increase the necessary equipment. The response from you was immediate and I believe will be adequate.

Our total enrollment is 102; of these sixteen are women. Our own daughter, Mary, was the first and only girl to have a medical degree from St. John's University. I celebrated last commencement, my twenty-fifth year in Shanghai, by giving her a hood. She is now Resident in Pediatrics in our hospital and hopes to go to America within a year for graduate work.

The less I write about the political situation, the better. The "perimeter" around Shanghai is completely closed and no one goes out or comes in without the consent of "our neighbors across the sea," plus cholera, typhoid and smallpox vaccination certificates. No foodstuffs can be brought in without toll to the conquerors. The prices of food in this city have risen from one to three hundred per cent for all necessities, not even luxuries. We have five hundred mouths to feed on that hospital compound and it is a real job keeping the larders supplied....

In the district where the hospital is located the streets are poorly policed by three different authorities: (1) the regular Settlement police; (2) the puppet government police under Japanese control; (3) the British "Tommies," this being the sector where they are on guard. Yet with all this, pedestrians and motor cars are held up on the streets in daylight; at night wise people stay out of the district.

I wish I could tell you some of the silly requirements for travellers but a few are not fit to print: People leaving trains are sprayed with what is supposed to be an antiseptic solution. Next they walk past large basins of Lysol and forty or fifty must wash their hands in the same basin, as they pass. One American woman refused to use the same basin as the crowd and demanded a fresh one. She really waited until it was brought but few take the time to make a fuss. A Chinese would not dare. Can you imagine such a performance in stations in America?

Our streets are full of policeman searching the crowds for weapons. They walk along, twelve abreast and all traffic is held up while every Chinese is searched. Tanks patrol the streets. Lorries full of police or soldiers ride around fingers on the triggers of their guns, ready to shoot. One fears these guns may go off accidentally, from a jolt on the poorly paved roadway. In spite of all these abnormal conditions our own lives go on as usual. We have just happened not to be there when shootings occur. Somehow, someday, this situation will be cleared up. Our boys at the front are doing their share though they are few compared to the need for doctors. We hope to keep on doing our part for a few more years to come.

Joe wrote on December 31, 1939 to his children:

I believe that I'd rather write you on this the last day of the year than do anything else.

We have had a very happy Christmas but not much like the last one or the days when we had a half dozen or more children at home. But we were made happy by the fact that we still have so many children and even though they are not with us, are themselves happy elsewhere and each of them is doing things and living such lives as should make any parent happy.

End of an Era (1939-1942)

This past week I received [a letter] from the Chairman of the Finance Committee of the China Child Welfare Committee of New York saying that they are sending me another grant of twenty-five thousand dollars local money for the next six months. Isn't that fine? A local relief committee has promised a thousand a month for six months so already I can see enough money to run the hospital through 1940.

The year 1940 was one of important family milestones, all missed by Helen and Joe in China. Joe, Jr. and Barbara, who had married September 17, 1938, had their first child, Josiah Calvin McCracken III, born January 14, 1940. Joe himself graduated from Medical School in June and started his internship in July at the Atlantic City Hospital. Margaret and Bill, who had married July 31, 1937, had their first child, Margaret Aileen, born May 21st. Ruth and Allen Cramer had a big wedding June 15, 1940 in Cleveland, and Mary who had returned to the States for a year of graduate work in Philadelphia, arrived in time so that all eight children were together. Elsie and "Hogy" (Hogeland Banes Barcalow, Jr.) were married July 1, 1940.

On January 28, 1940, Helen wrote:

We received with great joy the news of Josiah III. I hope that is really his name, for we had Mr. Powell to dinner and he put it in the paper. The message came during a Y meeting when Mr. Pettus was to tell of his trip to Chungking. He had just begun to speak when this cable came in. Daddy signed for it and then opened it slowly. I was bursting to know what it said. He looked up and nodded to me and his lips said, "Boy, O.K." I could have cried I was so pleased, but everyone was looking at me so I braced up. Now we shall be looking forward to Margy's....

For an old lady I think I have awfully interesting times; this week I played for my first wedding, a Chinese one. You all know how slow they usually are; Mrs. Lacy told them that I would not like to wait around for the bride. Believe it or not, that bride walked into the door precisely at four o'clock, and Dr. Caughey was hardly ready to come in with the groom.

I was petrified the night before and thought I could never do it but things went off quite well. There are two new bass stops on the organ and when one lets out the full power of the entire organ, it makes the building just shake with the sounds. When Mr. Dent plays the Mendelssohn *March* after the ceremony, he gives the full organ and I wanted to calm it down when I played. He said I must put on everything and I did. Maybe I don't enjoy that!

Mission to Shanghai

On February 9, Helen wrote:

I think of Baby Joe the second, so often. Mary will be so glad that she is to see him first.. I look at all babies with much more interest, having been off babies and small children for some time. The more I see of other small kids, the more I think you eight were pretty good. I did not have to fuss with you all the time about scratching, biting each other, crying over nothing, getting up and dressed on time for school, etc. I think over many, many happy times we had and things we always did together, taking drives on Sunday, singing about supper time, reading before bedtime. I am glad we had so much time together when you were small; you all grew up and left us so suddenly.

Last week we went to Rotary one day as guests of the Salvation Army who opened its drive for $60,000 that day. They had $53,000 the day they began besides the "Hot Rice Van" fund of $37,500 raised last week. That night I went out with the hot rice van with Mrs. (Brigadier) Morris, a friend of mine, who is the head of the Sally work here. First I picked her up at her home and we went to the big Tunsin Road camp where there are 15,000 refugees. This is the one that was built and supported by the entertainment tax and really has plenty of money. Under Chinese management it was not doing well. The Council asked the Salvation Army to take it and they did, on condition that the thirty-four camp managers were dismissed. The hot rice is cooked there and put into bags holding about a pound, and on top is a large piece of salted vegetable.

We rode down in a large marden van to a place on Avenue Edward the Seventh, and lined up on one side of the street were two rows of beggars or destitute people. They are rounded up by the Salvation Army scouts after six; they squat down in the two rows and are handed these bags of rice, a bag to a person. The third row of people is not given rice but it is not refused them. All they ask is that they go to the end of the line.

One would think the whole of Shanghai was there; quite a crowd come to look on. We gave out 900 bags or pounds there. Then we hopped back into the van and Mrs. Morris and I filled more bags for the next place. They try to have the bags filled but somehow that night had not completed the process and had six huge baskets of hot cooked rice. Filled, the bags are put into big wooden buckets and they do keep hot. I was surprised that they were hot and that the bags held together. In the van were their Chinese helpers, whom they call adjutants, and about eight refugees from the camp who go out and help. As fast as a bucket is emptied it is taken back to the van and another is there waiting by Brigadier Morris. I never saw such beggars in my life, wrapped in rags and tatters and matting and bags and papers over their shoulders. Of course the night I chose to go proved to be a rainy, cold, sleety night. I was quite warmly dressed and did not mind anything because I was so interested.

After this first place, we went to five more. Altogether we gave out 1500 bags. The last place was the worst; it was in a lane off Yu Ya Ching Road. Such a place; the holes and puddles were two and three inches deep. The men of the van had flashlights to take us in and find the people. Some of them sleep in the hu-tung all night right on the cobblestones. Mr. Morris told me there were a lot of places like that in Shanghai. I really loved going in the van as you probably suspect.

May 12th Helen wrote Helen, Jr. to urge her to go to Ruth's wedding:

Just because I cannot be there, and just because both Daddy and I have had warnings about our own health conditions and may not help to celebrate many more family affairs, we want you to join in this one. We want to feel that all of our children are together once more. I am just knocking off all activities for a month, under Dr. Fullerton's orders. If it were not for this wedding I would not tell you, for there is no use troubling people who are twelve thousand miles away. Daddy thinks it is just a question of rest and after three days on the bed, I have improved quite a lot. I am determined to rest enough to count, for it would be awfully hard on Daddy to have an invalid to look out for or to be left alone in Shanghai without one single offspring here. Don't tell all the rest for I do not want to spoil their wedding gaiety. I want it to be a happy family occasion.

Joe had succeeded in raising quite a lot of money for his hospital, Helen reported:

Yesterday he took Mrs. Hart around, the wife of the Admiral, and she gave him $20 gold which is about $400. The daughter gave him all she had in her pocketbook, $71 local. Red Cross money is gone now. The Baptist Mission has just given him $5000 local, and the Episcopalians $500 gold. The Association allotted him $1000 gold. It costs a thousand dollars a day to keep the hospital open. He has some of the Red

Cross money to help until January 1941 but hopes to keep it for the last part of the year....

Shanghai is interesting as always. What is to be done with the Germans in Frenchtown is a most interesting problem. It concerns us as the head of the Bayer (aspirin) has rented our house. Last summer it was decided that no aggressively unpleasant action should disturb the Germans, in that the white people should put up a more or less united front before the Japs. Yet the present Blitzkrieg is almost too much for the French to take. What a mixture of races and nations there are here!

We are sitting on a volcano; so far the Japanese have not thought it necessary for them to interfere; the English and Italian soldiers who are billeted next to each other have agreed to keep the peace.

The pressure was mounting that all Americans should be evacuated. In October Standard Oil recalled all their women and children, and mission boards began to make similar plans. Helen's letters begin to mention the new term which was being used: "evacuees".

Joe and Helen celebrated their thirty-fifth wedding anniversary with a dinner party and a showing of the movies of Ruth's wedding and film and pictures of Margaret's daughter and Joe's son. The strain of the hospital caused Joe to have a recurrence of his old trouble. He wrote to say that after six weeks of increasing discomfort and consultation with Dr. Tucker, they were planning to leave early in November.

Helen was experiencing mixed emotions: "All the time I am packing, I am divided between joy and disgust, joy at going home and seeing you all, disgust at having to leave at such an interesting time." But on October 21 Joe wrote of a change of plans in an airmail letter to Mary, describing why they would not be going to the U. S.:

> I have found that if I went on the *Coolidge* those left behind felt that they must now begin to close down the hospital, which also meant the closing of the medical school, for both will crumble together and very rapidly just as soon as a start is made.
>
> I feel that we cannot do that until we are forced to do so; no one can tell just when that may be. The mission has asked that all women and children leave Shanghai as soon as possible. That may be the first part of December or the last of November. If left alone, and we may be unless there is a definite break between U.S. and others, we can keep the Hospital and school going for months to come with the help of the Chinese. At least it is worth trying. My stomach is not much worse than

it has been, and with care I think it will carry one for two or three more months without too much trouble.

By November Joe was actually feeling much better and had again taken up clinical responsibility and the responsibility for both surgical services. "I am sure that you children know that Mother and I would love to be on the way home to see you for Christmas, and I am sure that each of you knows full well that there is not a thing in the world we would not be glad to do for you if it were within our power."

On December 1st he wrote his supporters:

Living in the Far East today is like watching a moving picture. day by day are changes which can hardly be foreseen. The signing of the Axis agreement with Japan, the embargo on Japan's purchases in America, the withdrawal of British troops from Shanghai, the evacuation of Americans from this part of the world, all these are steps in the current history of Shanghai. What comes next we do not know. There is always something new on the front page of our morning papers and the news is always interesting.

However, when one is trying to run a medical school and a hospital, he would prefer not to have quite such "moving" items on the agenda. Our school started off in September with 117 students. We had acceded to popular demand and taken in a large class of boys and girls, thirty-six in all. How far we are going to be able to keep them, remains to be seen. Our senior class is now doing extra work in order to finish lectures by the end of the term. For the other three classes the outlook is dubious. Some of our teachers are being forced to leave, and we may be unable to carry on. We shall if possible....

God working through many agencies has wonderfully provided funds for the maintenance of this free hospital for sick Chinese. Starting as a refugee hospital with a four months budget, we begin this month a fourth year. More than 14,000 patients have been treated as free in-patients who have received 275,000 days of free treatments. The out-patient department has given 240,000 treatments, no patient paying more than 1/10 of a cent. The hospital is always full. War makes trouble for the innocent by-standers, and men, women and children suffer in other ways than from bullets. Undernourishment causes all sorts of diseases. To close a hospital for these destitute people is heart-breaking. But the mission ruling that all American women must be evacuated, takes away our business manager, Miss Lamberton, and our head nurse, Miss Hurst.

Mrs. McCracken and I had planned to leave for furlough this fall; this emergency confronts us and we are postponing our departure until conditions either improve, or force us out.

After three and a quarter years of war, the Chinese are still unconquered. Just give these people a chance and they will find a way to make a living. A half mile from us there has grown up a squatter village; probably a thousand people live on that small piece of land, in matting sheds as close together as possible. There is always danger of fire in these huts and a month ago, fire burned out this entire district. The next morning the people were back, poling through the ashes to see what could be salvaged. In a day or so the matsheds were being put up again. During the building, the people spent the nights lying out on the ground, covered with newspapers, old rags, burlap sacks or dirty quilts, anything to keep out the cold, wind and rain. In this ability to endure and conquer hardship, lies the hope of China.

But China was gradually losing more and more of northern and eastern China, including the seacoast. Chiang Kai-shek and his government were forced out of Nanking, moved to Hankow and then set up the "free" China government in Chungking to which many people fled. At the same time, Chiang Kai-shek was fighting the expanding power and control of areas of China by Mao Tse-tung, who had led his group on the Long March west and finally set up a government at Yenan in Shensi Province. There was a tenuous partnership of the Two Chinas against the common enemy but the attitude of each government was primarily self-seeking, looking for the advantages to be taken in preparation for the peace which would come with the eventual defeat of the Axis Powers.

January 21, 1941, Joe wrote:

Yesterday I brought out thirteen thousand dollars to pay our monthly salaries before the Chinese New Year begins. This month we increase all salaries by fifty percent which makes a total of about one hundred percent in two years which is not too much when you consider how everything has increased in price. There have been so many payrolls stolen by robber gangs I went down to the bank early in the morning and had the money distributed before evening. It is now costing us over four dollars a day for every patient we admit. Fortunately we have gotten enough American Red Cross rice to last us about two months and hope for another shipment to come along by that time.

All examinations in the medical school for this term ended today. Now one of my disagreeable jobs next week is to determine which ones will have to be told they cannot continue in school. I am afraid five or six will have to go and about that number told that they will have to improve their standing next term if they are to be passed into the next class. It is only fair to the student to tell him as soon as we feel confidently that he is not going to carry the load and let him go into something else.

On January 30, Helen wrote:

You must be getting our letters for they are sent by American boats, but it is a long time since we have heard from any of you. The mail on the Taft, 85 bags, was taken off for censorship in Hongkong and has not been sent up from there. No boats have come directly from the U.S. and the consulate says that no mail leaves America now on Japanese boats.

Of course we have to look forward in the future to a time when we may be interned and we may have no letters going or coming. No one knows just what we face. But at least we shall have stuck it out together and stayed on the job as long as possible. I think you should make up your minds that we cannot see our way clear to leaving if the present stalemate goes on.

You all seem to be counting on our coming this spring. But so far as we can see there is no chance of it. Aside from the pleasure of seeing Martha's wedding [to be on June 21, 1941 to Calvin Dodd MacCracken, her third cousin and son of Henry Noble MacCracken], I have no regrets. Life here is interesting, Shanghai is home, and there are things to do. But of course we would love to see you all, and to see our grandchildren. You will just have some more on hand to show us how they behave when they are little.

On March 30, Joe wrote:

I thought that I might celebrate the Day and write to the finest bunch of kids on the other side of the Pacific and thank you one and all for my birthday good wishes and presents. It does not seem possible I am entering my sixty-eighth year. I do not know that I feel much older than I did ten years ago. So long as I keep fairly near to schedule so far as food goes, I get along pretty well. Mother and I had gone out to St. John's to preach at the six o-clock service and when we got back all the people in the apartment were in ours to wish me happy birthday and stay for supper.

In April Joe took on two more jobs: a position on the Red Cross Committee, a place which he had not taken before because he was such a heavy recipient of their gifts. This committee had charge of the distribution of rice, wheat and medicines now coming out to China. Bishop Roberts has also asked him to take over the "surgical supervision" of the two hospitals, St. Luke's No. 1 and St. Elizabeth's.

June 6th Helen wrote:

Yesterday was Commencement for the combined colleges. They have been getting together for four years now. There were 850 students and seats so scarce Daddy thought I might give up going. So I did but as I rode by on the bus I saw the procession marching in from the Foreign Y to the Grand Theater, quite an imposing sight.

Then on June 16th she added:

If we stay in China, as we shall probably have to do, in spite of plans and wishes to the contrary, be sure to send underwear for us--snuggies for me and a pair or two of those enormous full length cotton fleecy lined union suits for him.....He just has to have warm clothing, for this old car is a drafty affair and the rooms at the hospital are very cold. When coal is so scarce they only have fires until eight in the morning and after four at night.

I woke in the night last night and found Daddy awake. I asked him what he was doing and he said, "Oh, praying and thinking about our children." Many is the time I have spent an hour or two that way myself.

In a July 7 letter to Helen, Jr., Helen wrote:

I am glad Mary got down to see you. I wish you could have given more details about her. How on earth did you get her around? Just how does she get from Philadelphia to Lynchburg? It is a continual puzzle to me how she does what she does but no one ever mentions it. Daddy could use Mary very well but hesitates to have her come. He is afraid that if we did get a chance to go home for a visit that someone else would have to bear the burden of a handicapped woman in case of trouble. I do not think that worth mentioning! Daddy has written to the Christian Association that he did not think it advisable yet for Mary to come and she keeps sending Mailbag messages that she is sailing July 11.

End of an Era (1939-1942)

In the Spring of 1941 Joe received a note from a missionary who had often brought people to the out-patient department. It invited Helen and Joe to a tea at Fah Wha Village on Saturday afternoon at the Baptist church. The church was a simple building, the church on the first floor with wooden pews, upstairs classrooms and on the third floor a kindergarten room. Back of the church was another building. The McCrackens were asked to go upstairs and there found two tables, each set for ten people. Some of their staff arrived, three or four doctors, a member of the office staff and a nurse or two. There were ten at their table and at the other, ten from the T.B. Hospital. They were served with a regular Chinese dinner, many, many courses.

Helen and Joe had planned to stay only a few minutes but found it impossible to leave. After dinner, they were asked to go upstairs to the kindergarten room and see the view from the windows. Helen reported:

When we got there we found they wanted us to sit down. Some of the doctors were rather tall and had to stretch their legs out in front of them as they sat in the little chairs. More people joined them, until finally the church minister began to speak in Chinese; he said the people of the church were so grateful to the hospital that they wished to tell everyone all about it. One of their number had written a poem and sang it to a hymn tune, to the accompaniment of a baby organ. Then a little girl about ten years old came into the circle and put two small begonia plants in front of one of our doctors. She turned around and said, "I was born blind. I had never seen anything. But I went to this doctor and he did something to my eyes and now I am going to school and can learn to read." She was a child born with cataracts on her eyes and when these were removed, she could see. Then a woman stood up; she had a baby in her arms and her husband stood beside her holding the hand of a little girl of three. She said, "The first time I went to this hospital I was very much afraid. My little girl was born there and I learned to take care of her. Then I went two months ago and my son was born there. I am very grateful for the hospital." Then an old woman got up and said, "I too was blind and could see nothing but this doctor did something to my eyes and now I can tell day from night and see large objects and walk around by myself." Then a man rose and said he had been in great pain one night and was taken to the hospital; his wife was so afraid she would not sign the paper but he was in such pain he signed it himself and they operated on him and now he was well. He had had acute appendicitis. About twelve people testified, and then after singing a hymn they gave out framed paper tablets. The

193

first was given to Joe, for the whole hospital, and translated read:

> *To the Medical Staff: SKILLFUL HANDS TURN DEATH TO LIFE*
> *To the Nursing Staff: HEARTS OF MERCY*
> *We present this to the Nursing Staff of the American Hospital for Refugees in appreciation of their loving care and service rendered to the sick members of our church. These nurses are graceful in heart and active in service. They treat the sick as they would their own home folks. This is hardly to be found nowadays.*
> *To the business staff: A GREAT BLESSING TO MANKIND*
> *We present this tablet to the Business Staff in token of our appreciation for their charitable services rendered to the general public as well as to the members of our Church.*

In their thirty-five years in China the McCrackens had never had such an experience--an experience never to be forgotten.

Despite all of the war tensions, the indomitable Mary did manage to return to China. While she was finishing her work at Children's Hospital (completed July 1, 1941), the acting government had banished all women and useless men from China. Mary wrote and asked Joe's second cousin, Dr. Henry Noble MacCracken, President of Vassar College, to intervene with President Roosevelt (whom he knew) to get her passport approved. Through his intervention, she got her passport. Margaret had one day to get her off on the train, and numerous persons assisted her along the way. By August 5th Helen could report, "Mary came through with no hitches, and arrived yesterday afternoon about 2 o'clock. How she ever did it I do not see. She has gone to the hospital this morning....We just talk all the time trying to catch up on all the things we want to know about you all."

On August 25, Helen wrote:

> Daddy has been having "shingles" for about ten days. I always thought shingles was somewhat of a joke disease but I can think differently from now on. He had a fever and stayed in bed for twenty-four hours but has been on the job during the daytime all the rest of the time, and early to bed every night. Today I am glad to say he has felt like going to play golf for the first time in two weeks.

Joe wrote on August 31:

End of an Era (1939-1942)

To administer a hospital anywhere at any time is a pretty fair job but it would be a snap compared to running one out here in the "badlands" in this year of 1941 when political conditions change prices every hour and you cannot tell for sure which ones of your employees are "fifth column" adherents. If you fire a thief he hops right over to the other side and is likely to beat up the man who caused his dismissal. And for that reason many employees are afraid to report things to me for fear they may become involved. With half the population on starving wages or no wages at all, stealing becomes the order of the day and you can hardly blame them.

For my indoor sport this afternoon I emptied the fish tank and gave the sand and glass a thorough cleaning, very much needed not only for satisfaction of the fish but also Mother, who was beginning to threaten annihilation of not only the fish but me too if something was not done about the odor that came therefrom.

I suppose the political situation is a little more tense just now than anytime since war began. Japan cannot back down and out of China. America means business and will not back down on the proposition that status quo must continue in the Pacific. The question just now is will Japan or will she not allow that oil to go to Russia. Russia says she must or there will be trouble. America is likely to think likewise and so there you are. Will Japan dare run the danger of offending both the U.S. and Russia at the same time? A tight barbed wire fence is being put up all round Shanghai so that Shanghai will soon be a detention camp of some kind.

Notwithstanding all this, our lives are going along with very little hindrance or inconvenience. We have plenty to do, plenty to eat, plenty of rain, which has made this summer quite liveable. To be sure most of our friends are away but still there are some good ones left, so Mother and I and now that Mary is with us, are getting along in a fortunate way. We are proud of ever one of our children and only wish we could be seeing you more frequently. Here's hoping we can sometime next year.

Although the wish would come true, it would not occur as he expected.

The last letter from Helen before the Pearl Harbor attack was dated November 29, 1941.

Cold has struck Shanghai this past week, cold and rain, though today is clear enough. It means much suffering

195

among the poor. Last week 250 dead were picked up in the streets and seventy of these were small children. Daddy has not yet started the furnace in the hospital, and just has stoves in three places. He comes home stiff with cold every day because his office has no heat. You can see why the union suit was looking large in importance last summer.

Our apartment has heat from six to nine in the morning and from five to about eight-thirty at night. We are supposed to keep off three radiators so the average heat is not very high. Coal is $800 a ton, Mex. Still we are glad to have that much. We all wear sweaters and close off our bedrooms to raise the temperature elsewhere. We have on hand a few coal balls and if worst comes to worst we could use the grate on occasions. Perhaps Sunday afternoon we may splurge and have a grate fire.

The Marines left yesterday, bag and baggage. It remains to be seen what effect that has upon our daily lives. That plus the final results of the Washington Conference, may affect us adversely. The Japanese spokesman is still proclaiming that Japan must stick to her "immutable policy of co-prosperity in Asia" but how far they are prepared to go, no one knows.

I really thought we would get to America before this to see [your] darling babies. I am glad that there are two more coming along that we can perhaps see. Yet after these two American boats left, there are said to be no more evacuating ships left for anyone to take.

Knitting, refugee sewing, organ for me; hospital and medical school and a little golf for Daddy. Our life goes along in its accustomed way. The papers will doubtless tell you if we are put in concentration camps. Officers who were just about to leave volunteered the opinion that we would be registered, and restricted but allowed the freedom of the settlements, that no new supplies would come in from the U.S. and we would have to live off the country at high prices. I hope we can keep Daddy's milk supply at some price or other. For the rest I shall not worry.

The Japanese attack on Pearl Harbor on December 7, 1941 meant the end of any communication from Joe and Helen until their eventual return to the United States. On December 8th, the Japanese took over the American Consulate, the British Consulate, the American Club, the Army and Navy Y.M.C.A., sank the British gunboat because the crew would not surrender, and took the American gunboat which had a radio station for the government. In the succeeding days they took all banks, and one by one took over the large American and British institutions. Little by little they assumed control of the Municipal Council, police department and all departments, putting Japanese heads in the various ones.

Helen, Joe, and Mary were particularly fortunate to be living in their own apartment during these trying days. The foreigners brought into Shanghai were much more inconvenienced, suffered as refugees or evacuees, and could tell many different stories. And the first year after Pearl Harbor was not as difficult as the second, when there was internment of all foreigners.

Helen would remember that:

> We ourselves had no unfortunate experiences with the Japanese. I never saw any except when we went outside the French Concession and passed a few guards or when I saw patrols ride by in a motor lorry. At the hospital all negotiations were conducted in a dignified way with everything very polite. They told Daddy his hospital had a good reputation. We, none of us, were disturbed at home.

Later Joe wrote an article "Stricken Shanghai" for the October, 1942, issue of the *Pennsylvania Gazette* (alumni magazine of the University of Pennsylvania):

> We were able to keep the hundred bed American Hospital for Chinese refugees running full until December 8. After that date, going became especially tough and in three week's time we were ordered to close and be out by January 15. The puppet government wanted the hospital property to establish therein the Civic Centre or Administrative Headquarters of Greater Shanghai Municipality.
>
> Fortunately for us they did not wish to continue the hospital, so we were permitted to move all hospital equipment and supplies to a private residence loaned to us for hospital use. This property had a large yard. In two days' time the equipment and supplies of a three hundred bed hospital were moved a mile, mostly on two-wheel push carts, and dumped in the yard. Gasoline hardly exists in Shanghai today so that all trucking must be done by rice power (coolies).
>
> The next day after war was declared I told our flagman not to put up the flag. I did not wish to give the Japs the pleasure of tearing it down as they surely could and would do. I also felt that a Chinese representative of the hospital could negotiate with the Japanese better than could an American who had kept them off that valuable and desirable property for four long years. I resigned the superintendency of the hospital to the medical director, Dr. Hwang Ming Sing, a

graduate of our medical school and an alumnus of the Graduate School of Medicine of the University of Pennsylvania.

A sixty-bed hospital has been opened on a new site and I hope it may be able to continue for the duration and then be expanded as the University Hospital. The Medical school finished the year with its largest enrollment--one hundred and forty students. Plans were made before I left to open the school in August if still permitted to do so. The long vacation will be given in mid-winter. The cold weather makes satisfactory work in unheated laboratories almost impossible.

The Rockefeller Medical School in Peking was closed on a day's notice and the hospital turned into a military hospital. Many of their students have gone to Shanghai and applied for admission into our school. Twenty have already been admitted. In April it was thought best for the University if all Americans holding executive positions would resign. The chancellor of the University was taken by the Japanese and held for nearly five weeks. I turned over the deanship of the medical school to one of our oldest alumni and one of the first to come to Pennsylvania for graduate study. I feel that the school is left in excellent hands.

When the hospital was closed I was asked by the American Relief Committee to organize the medical relief and open an infirmary in the American School property, where plans were being made to accommodate five hundred stranded Americans. It was surprising how many unknown Americans turned up to be fed and housed. Some had lived in China for years and had never registered with the American consulate or had their passports renewed. Many were the Russian and Chinese wives or near wives of American Marines left behind when the Marines were removed elsewhere. One was a returned Marine who had been held in prison by the Japanese for eighty days. He had been released a week when I was called to see him and found him to be suffering from a severe attack of typhus fever. We brought him to the infirmary where he recovered. Another was an ex-sailor who had a Japanese wife with whom he was living when war was declared. He, too, had contracted typhus and recovered in the infirmary.

The Japanese had a list of all license numbers. Three men came to Helen one day with a French interpreter and asked for their car. Helen said, "Dr. McCracken has a license and is out in the car." They said, "Sorry," and bowed and left. Joe continued to use the car until they left, one of the very few men who did. All other cars were confiscated and shipped to Japan. Walking and bicycling, if you had a bike, were the order of the day. Business in Shanghai was dead.

End of an Era (1939-1942)

Joe's report continued:

Tens of thousands of Chinese are starving, and dying for want of food and medical care. In all my years in China I have seen nothing to compare with the suffering now being endured by the destitute Chinese. And next winter must be even worse. There is hardly a free hospital left in all Shanghai. Thousands of sick must just die where they happen to be and be put at the side of the street to be picked up by the municipal trust and taken to the country where piles of a hundred or more would be cremated at one time. Only desperate war conditions make cremation possible in China.

We were most thankful that we were permitted to be there and have a part in conducting a hospital for the poor....It was a grand opportunity to help make living and dying a little more bearable for a very small percentage of the thousands who were homeless, friendless and sick. It was hard enough living among such conditions when one was able to keep busy giving relief, but when forced to stop all such work, then life became almost unbearable.

Fortunately they were able to get out of China. The Consul-General for neutral Switzerland acted for the United States to engineer the repatriation of Americans, as well as other nationals. Because of their health problems Joe, Helen and Mary were given places on the *Conti Verdi*, an Italian ship which had been taken over by the Japanese. The *Conti Verdi* had 1600 passengers who would later be exchanged for the Japanese who were coming back on the Swedish *Gripsholm*. The first stop of the Conti Verdi was off shore at Singapore to pick up more Americans and Canadians, then down the coast of southeastern Asia, across the Indian Ocean to the Port of Laurenco Marques in the Portuguese Colony of Mozambique on the east coast of Africa.

At Laurenco Marques the Americans were happy to see the American flag and find government and civilian Americans eager to help them on their way. They were transferred to the Swedish *Gripsholm* which had brought the Japanese from Europe. As the Japanese marched off, the 1600 Americans and Britons marched on, passing each other in two lines. The *Gripsholm* then rounded the Cape of Good Hope and sailed across the Atlantic to Rio de Janeiro. Going north to New York, the boat swung out to the mid-Atlantic to avoid the submarines which were active along the Brazilian coast and in the Caribbean Sea.

On August 18th, aboard ship, the Doctors of Medicine on the *Gripsholm*, representing a variety of denominational support and stations in China, Korea, Hainan, Manchkuo, Thailand and Japan, discussed the situations of the hospitals in various parts of the Orient. Joe discussed the problem of medical education and he became a member of the committee assigned to draft a resolution later passed by the doctors and then by the nurses, who also endorsed the resolution:

August 18

Resolution passed: The Medical Missionaries on the repatriation ship *Gripsholm* recognize that with the expulsion of so many doctors and nurses, the closing of so many medical institutions, and the seizing of such large proportions of hospital and medical schools buildings and equipment in Japanese controlled territory, the medical mission program has reached a critical period. However, we wish to record our conviction of the continuing importance of medical missions including Christian medical education, and our desire to serve in any way possible. We wish to record also our deep appreciation of our Oriental Colleagues who have assumed responsibility for carrying on Medical work for their own people wherever permitted to do so by the Japanese military authorities.

At the present time we would urge our Boards and Churches while developing to the fullest extent the work in Free China, also to give prayerful consideration and encouragement to those who are bearing the burden in occupied areas.

There was an added sense of tragedy to this return trip. During the voyage Mary, who had evidenced some signs of illness before they left Shanghai, became bedridden. She had developed a disease which atrophied the cerebellum [meningitis] and lost all interest in life. Back in the States it became necessary to place her in a hospital.

This little known or understood disease, with its deteriorating effects, was not only a tragic end to Mary's remarkable life, but a prolonged tragedy for Joe and Helen to endure. In the fall of 1942 Helen wrote her oldest daughter:

The house is very quiet and empty today, even Daddy has been away. I have been dyeing some curtains, putting up others, and doing odd jobs around the house. By and by I am going to spend the night with the Silvers. I did not want to go, I wanted really to be alone and get hold of myself; but Daddy feels that if I were here alone he would worry about me.... I do like to have him concerned but wish he could see that sometimes one needs a bit of solitude, especially after the last few months. We were three in a cabin for eight weeks. I never came into the cabin without a blow, just as I could never take

Mary's condition in Shanghai....Bottled up inside of me it did things to me and I just must take time to think it out and adjust myself to it....Why this happened to her and to us, I cannot see. That is [why] I want time and quiet to adjust myself to. With all the rest of you happy with your homes and your babies it makes it harder to see through. I can work around the house and think it over and wonder about it by the hour.

Joe's grief was generally hidden, but Helen, Jr. remembers being in Philadelphia with him and going to Mary's hospital room in June of 1944; the tears streamed down his face as he tried to drive out of the hospital grounds after the visit. Joe wrote a brief account of her life which was used in a church daily inspirational booklet:

[In the fall of 1912] Mary came down with a severe attack of polio which left her completely paralyzed except for her diaphragm. It was fortunate that she could still breathe as there were no iron lungs in those days. Her father was a physician and her mother a graduate in physical education from Columbia University so they worked with the child tirelessly. For months she could not move, then she was able to move her hands and finally her intercostal [between the ribs] muscles came back. Her arms were exceedingly strong but she never regained the use of the muscles in her thumbs. This prevented her from using crutches to go up and down stairs although she could get along on the level....After graduation from Lake Erie College in 1931 she decided to specialize in biology at the University of Pennsylvania where she received the Master of Arts in Anatomy. The next year when her father came back to the U.S.A., she said, "Dad, if I do what I want to do, I'd study medicine." Her father invited her to study under him in China because he knew she could not get around in a medical school in the U.S. She entered the Women's Christian Medical College in Shanghai....Then she transferred to St. John's University, a larger Episcopal School, and in 1939 she graduated at the head of her class, the first foreigner to beat the Chinese. The other foreigners had been at the foot of their classes. After she had a year of internship there, she stayed on in the Pediatrics Department of the Refugee Hospital for another year....She went to Children's Hospital at the University of Pennsylvania to specialize in pediatrics. She was always a most independent person and never let anyone do anything for her that she could do herself. She finished her work at Children's Hospital July 1, 1941. At that time the [government] had banished all women and useless men from China. But Mary was determined to go back....At the Refugee Hospital which her

201

father was running she took charge of pediatrics....On December 8, 1941, the hospital was closed and Mary lost her job.

Mary died October 18, 1945; her gravestone is inscribed "Beloved Physician."

Mary McCracken, visiting in Ohio in June 1940

CHAPTER EIGHTEEN

JOE SERVES AT HOME
1942-1946

After thirty-seven years Helen and Joe were back in the United States to make their home and enjoy their six grandchildren, four of whom had been born since communications had stopped nine months earlier: Martha Ann Barcalow, born December 25, 1941; William Stewart Yates, born April 4, 1942; Helen McCracken Fulcher, born May 11, 1942, and Michael Calvin MacCracken, born May 20, 1942. Helen was sixty-four; Joe was sixty-eight.

Although they had been taken out of their alphabetical turn and were released from the *Gripsholm* a day earlier than scheduled, nevertheless, the McCrackens wondered why not one child was there to greet them. It was providential that, as they rode off in a taxi, planning to go to Philadelphia, they would see "baby Stewart" walking along the pier. He had left other family members in a borrowed apartment, gone to Philadelphia, and on the way back decided to go to the pier and visit with China friends, even though he knew his own family were not due off that day.

It was a happy reunion in the small apartment that night--only Ruth who was with her husband in service and Joe Jr. , his wife, and "Thirdy" [their nickname for their son], stationed in Washington, were missing.

Helen and Joe settled in Ventnor, N. J. and happily enjoyed the opportunity to spend time with their children and grandchildren. Helen also took pleasure in seeing old friends when she visited Martha and Elsie in the New York area, and attended the National Y.W.C.A.- Foreign Division conference in New York. Because of increasing problems with her high blood pressure and heart, she was frequently forced to be quiet and do very little for days and weeks at a time.

Joe immediately became busy professionally, making plans for his future and conferring with all the various organizations which dealt with the missionary and medical work in China and were trying to supply funds to those left out there and to preserve what could be saved under local Chinese leaders. There was an increasing scarcity of doctors for civilian medical services, so he began to do volunteer work at the Pennsylvania General Hospital where he had interned so many years before.

January 9, 1943, he wrote to his friends and supporters:

As has been my custom I write this annual letter of thanks to you for your continued interest in the Pennsylvania work in

China; also as an appreciation of thanks to God for His many blessings during the past years of uncertainty.

We were glad to leave Shanghai this time for powers over which we had no control made it impossible for us to continue our work. To live in a city where there is mass starvation and much sickness is not too bad so long as you have facilities and are busy helping to give relief, but when everything is taken away from you and you must simply ignore sickness and distress which is all about you and "walk by on the other side" then life becomes intolerable.

What have we for which to be thankful? A plenty!

(1) The Medical School during the first five years of war lost only two months of school time.

(2) The school has, notwithstanding war conditions, an ever increasing enrollment. Last year it was 140.

(3) During these years the school has been blessed with the use of increased laboratory equipment and clinical facilities so that our students, even though some of the faculty were absent, received better teaching than ever before.

(4) Of the four Christian Universities now in Shanghai, St. John's was the only one open when we left on June 29th [1942].

(5) For the privilege of being superintendent of the American Hospital for Chinese refugees where in four years we were able to admit free nearly twenty thousand patients--the sickest and poorest people ever seen anywhere. All this free work was made possible by the generous assistance from many local individuals and charitable organizations but the greater part of the support was generously supplied by the following three organizations:

> The American Red Cross--Surgical Dressings,
>   Drugs and Wheat
> United Church Committee in America--Money
> China Child Welfare Inc., New York--Support of
>   60 beds for children.

I am sure that tens of thousands of Chinese would wish me to extend their grateful thanks to all who have helped. Yes, the big hospital for Chinese Refugees was closed January 15th, but some members of the Chinese staff have been offered a large private residence and they have organized a sixty-bed hospital with an efficient out patient department and are there carrying on as capably as is now possible. We hope this hospital may continue for the duration and then grow again into a large teaching hospital.

Joe Serves at Home (1942-1946)

What of the future? "Pennsylvania in China" during these thirty-five years has helped to build up a medical school from an enrollment of fifteen to 140. Nearly three hundred   doctors have been trained in modern medicine and they have had and are having a leading part in helping to develop scientific medicine in China. [A list of graduates is included in the Appendix]. Many of our alumni have gone abroad for graduate study and are qualified to take up teaching positions previously held by American doctors. The Faculty and student body are well established but because of wars and rumors of wars, and for other reasons, the school plant and equipment are woefully inadequate. When this war is over the great need of the medical school will be a medical center beginning from the ground up. This center should include an administration unit, adequate laboratories for teaching and research and a teaching hospital of 150 to 300 beds. I hope to live long enough to see this center well established and I want an active part in helping to bring it about.

In March of 1943 Joe went to New York City to be given the William Guggenheim Honor Cup Award by the University of Pennsylvania Club of that city.

Commuting to Philadelphia, for volunteer work in the hospital, three times a week was difficult for Joe, who was still looking for a job. He tells of his decision in a letter written on October 12:

I have been asked if I would accept the position of Chief Medical Officer here at the Hospital. I would be responsible for arranging the work of 18 interns and some 8 or 9 resident physicians; the admission of all cases and contact with all doctors sending patients to the hospital. Some little job in itself. I already am the doctor to the nurses and assistant surgeon in the hospital and also have some teaching of the students from the Graduate School of the University, and the Compensation Clinic as well as the pay surgical clinic. The Chief Medical officer job, if I accept it, won't be before December 1st and maybe January 1st. I think I'll enjoy it but it will keep me pretty close to the hospital and to the telephone.

My 1901 Medical Class had a reunion last week with twenty out. They certainly looked like a set of old "duffers." Tomorrow I am going to University Club for lunch and to see movies of Penn's football game with Dartmouth. It was an exciting game--Stewart and I saw it. Tomorrow evening I am going to a meeting of the Chinese Club at the International House.

205

You kids have such interesting children but I guess no more so than you children were at that age. At the reunion I had by far the largest number of children and grandchildren than any one present--some accomplishment.

By 1944 they were settled into an old house close to the Hospital which made it so much easier for Joe. Stewart was living with them and they were looking forward to having Ruth and little Lan (Allan Miller Cramer, Jr., born July 31, 1943) move in with them when her husband went overseas. So Helen would soon have one grandchild to watch day by day in his development!
January 25, 1944 she wrote Helen, Jr.:

This ought to reach you nearer to your birthday than the book or the paper I ordered. I cannot believe you are thirty-six. When I was thirty-six we had just gone back to China with four children, you two little girls, Mary paralyzed and Joe [Jr.] not a year old. We took the slowest boat possible, one which went by way of Manila where we stopped for four days.

In March Joe had a difficult time with a carbuncle on the back of his neck. He finally went to the hospital for treatment and penicillin was used--then a new and scarce medication. He recovered in time to go to a Staten Island Hospital for a week's training given to those in the Medical Corps Reserve of the Army. When he first enlisted in 1943 (at age 69), he was part of the U.S. Public Health Reserves to deal with civilian emergencies. Now he and Dr. Silvers and others were under orders and received training for Army emergencies. An emergency might be a convoy of thousands of wounded being brought from Europe because of a big bombing or some kind of invasion. Joe had his uniforms and trained and later retired as a Major.
Helen suffered a stroke in June 1944 and was taken to the University of Pennsylvania Hospital and placed in an oxygen tent. In those days it meant to her that she might be an invalid, at which point she gave up the fight to recover. Around July first Helen wrote her oldest daughter that she must stay in bed for she had "done something to a valve in her heart." On August 11th Joe wrote that she had had another heart attack and been taken to the hospital.
Helen died late Sunday afternoon August 20, 1944, and a Memorial Service was held Wednesday, August 23rd, at the Chapel of the Second Presbyterian Church. Dr. Gordon Poteat, one of her favorite preachers from Shanghai days, was the speaker.
On Sunday afternoon September 10, 1944 Joe wrote his children:

Three weeks ago at this hour Mother was still with us and still able to speak but very weak and inside of two hours she was gone. It hardly yet seems possible that she is gone for good. Her going was very peaceful. I was glad that I was by her side although I was helpless to do anything for her. I think that everything that could have been done for her was done and I am glad that if she had to go she could go so peacefully and quickly without a long spell of suffering. It was such a comfort to me to have all you children who could come home and be here at the memorial service. I am sure that it was the kind of service Mother would have liked. I need not tell you children that you had a wonderful mother, so faithful, loyal, unselfish, energetic and wise. I thank God that I was allowed to have nearly thirty-eight happy years with her.

As I look back over those years I realize that she was not only the one who brought each of you into the world but it was also your Mother who made our home and trained you children and brought you up so that not one of you has ever done anything to make your parents ashamed. How thankful we have been for each one of you and how sorry Mother and I have often felt for the childless couple. How lonely must the one left behind [be] when the other member of the family is taken.

I have received so many letters from friends and acquaintances telling about some lovely, thoughtful thing Mother had done for them. I have already answered more than a hundred and more are coming in every mail.

Fortunately in some ways I have been unusually busy the past two weeks because the surgeon who is head of the service has been ill which makes me responsible as head and too, one of the younger surgeons has been on vacation. Yesterday was a record maker. We had seven operations scheduled for the morning beginning at 8. I was to let my young resident in surgery do three of the easier ones and I would do four. For one reason or another he failed to do one of his and I did not do one of mine. I got through mine at eleven thirty and went to the clinic for half an hour when I was called to see a very sick man who had just been brought in suffering from gall stones. I set the operation for two and went and had some lunch in the hospital and then laid down and read for nearly an hour. Just before starting that operation I was called to see a young woman who had just been brought in suffering from acute appendicitis. I decided to let the resident operate upon her while I stayed around to see if he might need me. Just about five when I said I was going home and call it a day, I was called to see a semi-private patient who had just been brought in. He was a man of sixty-one and apparently suffering from acute appendicitis. I set the operation for eight and went home for a short nap before supper and a little more rest before going back at seven-thirty. When I got back I found one of the nurses reported with a badly infected foot which had to be opened after the operation, which proved to be a gangrenous appendix, was finished. I got home a little before eleven tired and ready for bed but quite rested this morning. Please don't think that was a usual day's work!

It would look now as if we should just remain here in this apartment for the present. Ruth had decided before Mother's death that she would stay and help run the house and now she is even more needed. How long she will be able to stay no one can tell but at least until Allan is discharged from the Army. Stewart will need a home until next June when he should move into the hospital as an intern. That is about as long ahead as anyone can look at this time.

In addition to Lan, four more grandchildren were added from 1943 to 1945: Joe [Jr.] and Barbara's second child--Lawrence Lee McCracken, born April 17, 1943; Irene Stewart Fulcher, born December 23, 1943; Stewart Banes Barcalow, born October 8, 1944; and Joan Ellen MacCracken, born May 23, 1945. This made the eleven about whom Joe could then boast.

By 1945 Joe was once again thinking about how he might return to China. The Allies were winning in Europe and in the Pacific, although there would be much fighting before cessation of hostilities. After the atomic bombing Japan announced her surrender August 14, 1945; the end of Hitler had come early in May. The first written evidence of Joe's planning appears in a letter of February 24:

> I have been asked by representatives from Washington to help set up a medical program to be set up behind the army when and if they should clear the district in and up from the Shanghai area. It thrills me. I'd love to go in with the army or right behind them and help set up any plan that may be decided upon. It seems to me that I ought with my acquaintances, contacts and experience in this section to be of assistance. Possibly they will not send such an old bird. Anyway I am going to offer my services..
>
> It is now over six months since Mother passed away and I still miss her so. We were together nearly all of our married life and so happy together with all you children coming along at pretty regular intervals. You children certainly had a wonderful mother. She was so faithful, non-complaining and cheerful all the time. We were certainly proud of each of you and for very good reasons and I am still proud and so happy that you are happily married and have children of your own

coming along. It is wonderful to have Ruth and Stewart and Lan with me. They do everything possible to keep me from being lonesome and I am fortunate too to be busy at the hospital. I have so much for which to be thankful. And I am thankful to God the Giver of all good gifts.

On March 15th, he was given an Award of Merit by the University of Pennsylvania Varsity Club, recognizing his attainments in football and track:

Member of the Varsity Football Team	1897-1898-1899-1900
All American Half Back	1899
Varsity Track Team	1897-1898-1899-1900
Intercollegiate Champion Shot Put	1898-1899
Intercollegiate Champion Hammer Thrower	1898-1899
World's Champion Hammer thrower	1899
Member of U.S. Olympic Team at Paris	1900
World Record Hammer Thrower	1900
Third Place Olympic Hammer Thrower	1900
[Second] Place Olympic Shot Put	1900
President of his Class for Four Years	

September 29 Joe wrote:

The Bishop has written me wanting me to return to China as soon as possible. He thinks I should get my passport visaed and be ready to start soon after the invitation from the Chinese comes, which he thinks will arrive as soon as communications are open with Shanghai. I doubt if arrangements can be made for me to leave before the first of next year.

November 4 he wrote again to his children:

Some of you seem to feel that I should not try to return to China again. If the way opens up and I am asked to return by my Chinese colleagues to return to help them get started again, I feel that I might do more there for a short while than I might be able to do anywhere else. From the reports we are getting from Shanghai, conditions in and around the University are quite topsy turvy. The President of the University, whom I think has done a wonderful job under the most trying conditions, has had to resign the presidency. Some reports say that the acting dean of the medical school has been too friendly with the enemy. The faculty is evidently much split up and I may not receive any official invitation to return.

Bishop Roberts, who has already sailed, urged me to be ready to come on short notice. I have my passport and I am now taking my physical examination and will soon start all the required injections and will apply for tentative sailing some time after February 1st.

Nothing has been decided as to time of my stopping work in the hospital. I doubt if it will be before the end of January if then. Some doctors are returning so I hope soon there will be less for me to do. This Saturday I had four operations in the morning and then in the afternoon a desperate emergency case came in on which we had to operate at once to try to save his life; we failed. I was glad that I had not planned to go to the Army-Navy game.

Last Thursday night some eighty Old China Hands got together for dinner and I was relieved from the chairmanship. Dr. Bernard Read who had just gotten out and back from Shanghai was our speaker. The next night some two hundred members of past Olympic teams met for dinner and I had to make a little speech. Five of our 1900 team were present.

Tomorrow I take Stewart to the testimonial dinner for the Penn. football team at the Ben Franklin Hotel. On December 11 the Philadelphia International House of which I am a Trustee and the Chamber of Commerce are giving a dinner to all the foreign students in Philadelphia. They expect some 800 to a thousand out. I am an invited guest and will take some part.

It is wonderful to have Joe [Jr.] and Al back safe and sound. Stewart may get an extension of his internship so that he will not have to return to the Navy before July. It has been fun to have him as my assistant during the past two months. He is working very hard and is popular with his chief and with the patients. [Stewart had graduated from the Medical School of Temple University June 21, 1945.]

The early months of 1946 were crowded with activities as Joe made plans for returning to Shanghai. He was collecting medicines, supplies, equipment, books and journals to take with him. Suddenly it was time to return.

Joe Serves at Home (1942-1946)

Dr. Josiah C. McCracken (center) as a Major in the U. S. Public Health Reserves, flanked by Joe Jr.'s father-in-law Dr. Homer Silvers (left) and Joe, Jr.,(right), who served in the U. S. Army Medical Corps, rising to the rank of Major.

Joe enjoying visit with some of his grandchildren in the summer of 1945. He is holding Joan Ellen MacCracken. Others, from left, are: Stewart Banes Barcalow, Michael Calvin MacCracken, Martha Ann Barcalow, and Allan (Lan) Miller Cramer. Jr.

211

Joe with Dr. P. C. Nyi, new Dean of the Medical School of St. John's University (1947).

Graduation, 1947. Joe presents degree to V. C. (Wen Ching) Chang.

CHAPTER NINETEEN

REVIVING ST. JOHN'S MEDICAL SCHOOL
1946-1949

It was not easy for Joe, at the age of 72, to go, even though he wished to go. On April 17, Joe, with Ruth and little Lan, started off for Dearborn to pick up his new Ford, stopping by Cleveland to say goodbye to Margaret and her family and Elsie, who had come down to see him. He was to sail from Seattle on May 10. They stopped in Great Bend to see his brother and sister, who came up from Tulsa. They went over to Sterling for a reunion with old friends at the Wellman's home and then on to Twin Falls to see his brother Lee and his family. At Boise, Idaho, Ruth and Lan left to fly back to Cleveland. Ruth's letter described the rest of the trip:

> Daddy said he hated to say goodbye to the last of his relatives and that when he went back to the cabin he was afraid he shed a few tears. He had a good rest and then started out the next morning, drove 400 miles and then in to Seattle the next morning.

On July 16, 1946 Joe wrote that there was only about one free bed per each seven thousand of the population of the city. He and his colleagues felt as a minimum there should be one for every thousand.

> We had a nice Commencement [at St. John's] last Saturday held on the lawn. We graduated 28 doctors; a very nice class and the last I admitted before going home. They gave us a dinner afterwards at Dr. Pott's new house....A very pleasant evening except, as I told the class, that when I saw all the beautiful surroundings and realized that ex-President Sung, who with great sacrifice and danger for nine years had saved the University, and was now lingering in the Wards Road prison without trial as yet, I felt sick. And I did hope and pray that faculty, alumni and friends would have enough guts to fight until Sung was cleared, given a passport and allowed to leave for America for a much deserved rest. I am afraid he will lose his mind lingering down in that place unable to get in touch with anyone.
> Yesterday, I spent nearly all day showing around the Rockefeller Commission sent out to study the medical education conditions of China today. We had a very pleasant day and I think that we proved to them that St. John's has very little left to teach with but nevertheless is doing a good job con-

213

sidering the handicaps she is working under. Possibly someday in some way the Rockefeller Foundation may see its way
clear to extend a little help to our school, a thing they have
never done in the past.

I walked out to the University this morning through Sa Ka
Do and all of the crowds and filth! Now there seem to be no
police regulations so that the peddler, the vegetable shop or
the repair man not only squats all over the sidewalk but comes
out to nearly the middle of the street so that traffic is a jam.
This morning about every other vehicle was a two-wheeled
night soil push car, and when you get those bumping along
over a very rough road you, who were born in China, can well
imagine the condition of the atmosphere thereabouts but
when you see, as I did this morning, two carts trying to pass
each other and the wheels got locked together, well then neither you or anybody else can imagine. A skunk would be a
more welcome neighbor.

Joe's letter to his friends and supporters, dated November 15,
1946, gives us an general idea of what he found on his return:

Here I am back in Shanghai after four years absence and
what a change! During the first four Chinese war years I was
here, when there were refugees by the hundreds of thousands,
with want, suffering, and sickness everywhere. It was grand to
have backing, as I had, and to be kept busy helping those in
desperate need. During the last two years the war has been
won, the enemy sent home, the refugees have died or returned
to their native villages, the International Settlement and the
French Concession have been turned over to inexperienced
administrators and currency has become greatly inflated. All
of these have helped to create new and greater problems. It is
truly a day when faith, hope and charity, and time are needed.

My trip across the Pacific--my 21st--was uneventful. I
reached Shanghai June 13 [1946]. The reception given me by
Chinese and foreigners was cordial and warm--about 100 degrees in the shade. Since arriving I have been in the hospital
twice, the first time for eighteen days--diagnosis, cardiac
asthma--completely cured; the second time I was admitted for
gall bladder infection. I was scheduled to be operated upon
the next morning at nine; at eight-thirty a.m. three surgeons,
my own doctor and the patient all agreed that an immediate
operation was not necessary. I rapidly improved and left the
hospital on the eighth day. I am most thankful to God for
penicillin and for the earnest prayers of friends.

Reviving St. John's Medical School (1946-1949)

I found the Medical School ending a very successful year [1945-46] under most trying conditions. The last students whom I admitted before leaving for America were given their diplomas at Commencement this year. The graduating class gave me a reception that evening and insisted on a speech from the "Old Dean!" Two students--a boy and a girl--who were admitted only after special concessions on the part of the Dean, came up to thank me for making it possible for them to receive their medical training. I was glad, for they had done well. I found some of the faculty, who had gone through eight years of war, sadly in need of a vacation; others had been existing on less than a living wage and were showing the effects of such privation; but it was a great satisfaction to see how loyally they had stood by the School. Admitting a class each year, they carried on with no heat, little electricity, very few repairs, and supplies always more and more difficult to obtain.

Soon after my return I was asked to accept the Deanship again, which I had held for more than twenty-five years. I declined, feeling that the Chinese should now carry the responsibility. After two months, when I saw how much had to be done before the School could open in the fall, I accepted the appointment of Acting Dean. Since 1941 both the college and the Medical School have been compelled to use the old Medical School Building, because the Japanese had taken over the Science Building. Not until August first of this year could the Science Building be repaired and reoccupied. The old Medical School Building, which had been doing double duty for five years, then presented a most discouraging picture. What a mess! Every room required a complete going over. Doors were off their hinges, locks gone, electric wiring down, plaster broken, shelves, tables, desks missing. It looked almost hopeless. Only by engaging a gang of coolies, plumbers, masons and carpenters and spending millions of Chinese dollars were we able to open school on September 16. Repairing continued for some weeks thereafter and will be necessary frequently until a new Medical School is possible.

This Fall [1946] there were over sixty applicants for the first year class. By examination we chose our limit, 36, which makes a total enrollment 138. The tuition fee has been raised from $140,000 a year to $500,000 [Chinese]. About one-third of the students will be given whole or partial scholarships. No worthy student is refused because of lack of funds. The Medical Alumni have promised half a million a month (about US $150) to help meet emergencies; and the letter just received from Dana How, telling me of the special emergency grant recommended by the Medical Committee (Christian Associa-

215

tion's) is most encouraging. These two funds will be a great help and comfort.

Our faculty will almost equal prewar strength. We have just been able to engage a Chinese Ph.D. in Physiology from the University of Chicago, who has taught a number of years. Some of our own Alumni, with graduate degrees from American universities, would be glad to join our full time faculty IF our budget would permit.

PLANS
(a) For the present--conserve and make the best use of available facilities and personnel and add to both as rapidly as possible.
(b) For the future--make plans for building a new Medical School and Hospital, in one building, or at least on one site. Such a Medical Center is absolutely necessary if our school is to continue one of the leaders in medical education in China.

Yes, it will cost money--plenty of it--US$2,000,000 to $4,000,000 to begin with; but where else in the world can money be invested so as to bring in such large, vital income in an ever increasing amount?

A letter in November to Helen described a trip he took outside Shanghai:

I had a nice but cold trip to Soochow leaving here yesterday on 8:30 a.m. train and getting back at 4 today. By going first class I was able to reserve a seat. I was met by private rickshaw and got to the hospital at eleven. We made rounds, then had Chinese tiffin at the T's. They always have Chinese food at noon from the hospital kitchen as a matter of economy. Missionaries this winter are going to suffer for want of heat and some because of high cost of food. We in Shanghai are having and should have the food we need. We are getting quite a bit of army leftovers at very reasonable prices. In the afternoon I was in the operating room three hours watching Dr. T. operate. I am to make a report to the American Board of Surgery as he is trying for admission.

At 7 p.m. nine of our graduates who live in Soochow gave me a very nice Chinese dinner. Some of them I had not seen for many years. Soochow, noted for its beautiful women in olden days, is rather disappointing these days. I did see a few on the streets with painted checks, lips and fingernails!

"Peace" brought so many problems to the Chinese people and those foreigners returning to help. The Sino-Japanese War ended somewhat abruptly with the Japanese capitulation on August 14 and the Japanese troops in China formally surrendering September 9, 1945. The Nationalist China government moved back to Nanking for the tremendous tasks of reconstruction. The last few years of exile had brought   discouragement, a more dictatorial type of government and some corruption among the Nationalist leadership. This government returned from Free China to a large area of China which the Japanese had controlled for its own purposes and which for the most part had been left to the devastations of war. People were suspicious of each other's motives and recent activities. There were the "collaborators," who for both selfish and unselfish reasons had worked with the Japanese conquerors, trying to preserve something for the postwar era and just to live. It was easy to blame them for the eight years of suffering and hopelessness felt by the masses. Those returning from Free China could be criticized for having left and were supposed to be able to immediately improve the conditions of those who had been forced to stay under the Japanese.

During the war years the Chinese Communists had been less involved in the actual fighting against the common enemy, Japan, and freer to spread their control as well as their evolving Chinese communism and structure of government over large areas. They had also benefited from the Japanese surrender of supplies and ammunition by way of the Russians, who, as one of the Allies, accepted such material and turned it over to Mao Tse Tung rather than to Chiang Kai Shek. The struggle between the "Two Chinas" was more open and the world was more aware of what the struggle involved. The United States did try to bring about a better coalition in the hope of saving China as a united nation and world power.

From Joe's October 7 letter:

> Ruth's note saying that Stewart had phoned from [Mississippi] saying that in two weeks he would be starting to Shanghai is the most exciting news I have received since arriving in the Orient. Why he might now be in the air and here in a day or so; even if he comes by boat, he should be here in another ten days or two weeks.

> I have just gotten back from the Door of Hope. It is wonderful how that place came through the war. They now have three hundred and fifty girls. The place kept running all   the time and the Japs came nearly every day but did not molest them at all. Food and money came to them locally largely from their own girls who have during the years married and had families. The institution never sends out appeals to man, only to God and all their needs have been amply supplied.

217

Miss Deterlee, the only foreigner left to run the place, said early in the war she decided that they should give to less fortunate one-tenth of all they received and since that time there has been a plenty of everything coming in as needed. The place looks about as it did when I last saw it about ten years ago. I saw two rooms full of girls sewing and knitting and making cloth shoes and padded Chinese garments, etc. All appeared happy and busy. I am glad that we could make a small contribution to them, Elsie, receipt herewith enclosed.

Carrying on the McCracken tradition in Shanghai, Stewart was able to be stationed there by the Navy; he was able to share living quarters there for a short time.

On December 10th Joe moved down to live at the Foreign Y.M.C.A. where he would be more comfortable:

It has not been many days since I mailed a letter to you but in that letter I could not write much. For the last few days it has been so cold in my room I could not do anything even though I did have on extra clothing and a very heavy bathrobe. With the temp. around twenty-five to thirty outside, it's awful cold inside where there is no fire! The last two or three nights I was with the Tuckers; my nose was about the only thing uncovered. I thought it might freeze it felt so cold. It was the first time I ever realized the possible usefulness of a night cap. Here it is wonderful. I have a fair sized bedroom, a larger living room and a bathroom with a tub and running hot and cold water. The heat is only turned on for a while in the mornings and in the late evenings but the building is warm enough to be comfortable. Last month's daily cost of food was $9,998.45 which, at the present rate of exchange, is about two dollars [U.S. Currency--U.S.C.]. Here at the Y, I believe that I am to get board and room free for services rendered. I had not expected free board. Today's special lunch was $5,700.00.

The inflation in post-war China was almost unbelievable. For a dinner party in January of 1947 for twelve people at the Y.M.C.A. Joe paid a bill of $132,000. In May he wrote that the official rate was $12,000 for one (U.S.C.) but the black market rate was nearer $25,000 for one! In another letter he commented:

For some reason it is becoming harder and harder for a business man--Chinese or foreigner--to carry on a successful honest business. We won't pay "squeeze" so we are going to have to pay duty on this prefabricated hospital which we are putting up to take care of the sick and for teaching purposes and surely not to make money. The duty will be over four thousand U.S. currency. I pay a thousand dollars for a morning paper and another thousand for an evening paper. That's over eight cents apiece, so I glance over it at the breakfast table and if there is not anything I want to keep I give it back to the paper woman, get a smile from her and she sells it over again and makes 100% profit. Frequently I do that with the evening paper also. So it is not money entirely wasted. Even sitting right here it is hard to know what the U.S.A. should do to help the National Government here.

Joe celebrated his seventy-third birthday March 31, 1947 and Stewart surprised him with a party. For some time during March and April he was forced to restrict his activities and spend more time resting on the bed; but a change in his medication brought some improvement to his heart condition:

I have been off all medicine--digitalis--and am feeling better. It hardly seems possible that the very small amounts I was taking could bring on such sudden attacks of extreme weakness. So long as I stay out here and do a half day or more of work where I am very much needed I'd like to remain here. I doubt if I want to go through another winter here, especially where there is no heat, so I may be home before Christmas.

On May 17 he wrote:

Did I tell you some weeks ago that Mr. Luccock sent me a check for five hundred dollars to use as I wished, and also a check for $250 which was his honorarium for speaking at a District Rotary meeting? I gave the Rotary check to the local club. I had a wonderful time spending the first check, giving a million to the Salvation Army and to the Door of Hope and to St. Luke's for a free patient. And I received $10 from Cousin Mary. I am going to sell it for $300,000 and give it to the Door of Hope.

Every University in Shanghai excepting St. John's is having student strikes. The students of the National Universities are demanding more allowances for education, more food, better teachers, less school restrictions and some demand that their universities be moved to better locations. Two or three hundred of them commandeered a freight train and proposed to drive it themselves to Nanking. The R. R. took up a few rails just outside the city. After the mayor pleaded with them all night and furnished them free buses they were   taken back to the city. I am very glad to say that we at St. John's are so far going on peacefully about our own business. Never in my forty years in China have I seen such unrest, uncertainty, business at a standstill, streets crowded with parades, motor cars, etc.

Joe's letter of June 24 reported on his activities:

Friday at nine a.m. I was at the University for a meeting of the hospital committee going over the many problems regarding putting in of special utilities, rooms and what not and discussing staff and the taking over of the health care of the people and students on campus. The school doctor has gone to America. I am trying to get the Medical School Faculty and the hospital to take over the whole campus and everybody thereon, about two thousand involved, as a health problem and demonstrate what can and should be done to create satisfactory health precautions.

Yesterday was the big day of all the week. It has cleared up and was comparatively cool for June and Commencement Day. I took cap, gown and hood and walked across to the Theater at 9:40 in order to get placed in the academic line. It was 10:30 before the faculties of the three universities were able to march in and onto the platform. The whole service was in Chinese excepting what I said when presenting my class of 20 medical graduates.

On August 11 he wrote of continuing difficulties:

The greatest excitement around this place this week is the cutting off by the government of all supplies of crude oil for heating purposes. It means that now we have no hot water for bathing and soon none for the laundry and kitchen. We hope for some consideration of our needs before that time comes. It does not look very hopeful for the coming winter. It is not that there is a scarcity of oil but it is a matter of saving exchange. I am afraid that you will find me on my way home before the winter gets very far along.

On August 15 he reported on progress in getting the school year started:

Today I informed those who passed their entrance exams and those who did not. Quite a few disappointments but thank goodness none of them shed tears on my shoulders. I have admitted forty-five instead of forty, originally set as our maximum number.

On August 23, 1947 Joe wrote:

I believe the way things are shaping up I do not see why I should not be starting home in the early part of November. Stewart just stopped by a few minutes today on his way to the [British Officer Quarters] and left an old medicine bag I had loaned him. I am filling it with odds and ends of supplies and want to present it to one of the small Chinese hospitals which is run by six of our 1945 class. It is the same bag I used when I went out on the ambulance in 1903, 04, and 05--solid leather and almost as good as new.

At the Executive meeting of the Faculty this morning it was agreed that tuition should be five times what it was last term which means that tuition and laboratory and special fees will amount to about three million for one term and that is only about $75 U.S.C. Salaries are to be increased in about the same ratio. School opens on September 17 yet tuition fees are not yet really settled. I have admitted 45 in the first year med. school, the largest in the history of the school. Quite a number are applying for tuition assistance. The official rate for gold brought out from America has been moved up from $12,000 to $38,000 and as a consequence the price of everything has been raised. Business men are having a heck of a time.

Joe's letter of September 11 explained:

On Monday the President called a meeting which took a good part of my morning so I stayed out and had tiffin at the J. Potts and tried to finish up the morning job. This thing of personal relations and the unwillingness of people to cooperate or move when they have no longer a right to an apartment nearly drives the President and, in this case me, crazy. It seems to be getting "everybody for himself and the devil take the hindmost." If we cannot get this dispute settled satisfactorily we may lose our full time surgeon we have just taken on. He has six children and a mother and a wife. What a mess.

I think I got some very good heavy cloth which we need at the new hospital. The amount of stuff--hospital supplies, X-rays, clothing and even food stored in this city is appalling, as strange as that may sound. We just cannot get it distributed where it is most needed.

On September 19 he wrote about the opening of the school:

School opened Wednesday with an enrollment of 151, the largest in the history of the school I believe. There are so many things to be done I sometimes wonder if there will not still be much I could do even after Dr. Nyi returns and takes over the deanship.

His October 11 letter commented on the inflation:

Chinese dollar is depreciating rapidly. Today I believe the official rate has moved up to 65,000 while the black market has reached nearly ninety. Gas has been hiked from 13,000 to 25,500 per gallon. I do feel mighty sorry for those who have Chinese money. Monday I am planning to give full time staff $50.00 in U.S. money as a special gift.

Joe's October 26 letter was full of news:

It is almost church time. Stewart is supposed to play a round of tournament tennis this morning and this afternoon but it has started to rain and I expect to find him at church. He had a most exciting time last Sunday and another a couple days ago. No doubt he will write you the details but here is a sketch. Last Sunday he attended church at eleven, played second round of single tennis tournament at two at the French Club, rushed down to the Race Club and watched a football game fifteen or twenty minutes, rushed back to the French Club and played a round of mixed doubles and then is called to the sick bay where he delivered a baby and got back to the B. O. Q. for dinner! And then this Friday he helped marry a Marine to a Chinese girl at eleven o'clock and then delivered the bride of a baby before two of that day. Fast work!

Saturday afternoon the Bishop and Mrs. Roberts gave a big tea in honor of Dr. C. M. Lee and Mrs. Lee, who are leaving for America this week, and for Dr. Tsang and me who are leaving soon. The President wants to give me a farewell tea at the University but so far I have not set a date. There is plenty going on without another tea. As you children know very well, a person has to eat himself out of Shanghai.

Joe finally left Shanghai in November, 1947. He arrived on the west coast and then took the train across the U. S., stopping for visits with his family along the way, spending ten days in Cleveland with Ruth and Margaret and their families, and then leaving the 26th of December for Ventnor to stay with his son Joe and his family. Stewart was expected to be released from the Navy in the near future. Martha was living in Schenectady and Elsie in Easton. Helen Jr. was still in Amherst County, Virginia.

Joe's total of grandchildren grew to 13 with the births of Sarah Elizabeth McCracken, third child of Joe Jr. And Barbara born on June 29, 1947, and Mary Elizabeth Fulcher, third child of Helen and Tyler born on February 17, 1948.

Although he would be seventy-four in March of 1948, Joe did not relax in his efforts to assist both China and medical education. Reading his letters for that year one is impressed with all the travelling by train and bus he did for his work. Though Stewart came back from China early in 1948, it was not until summer that he was released from the Navy and could work out his plans to attend Graduate School at the University of Pennsylvania for a year and then take a several years' Residency at Temple University Hospital. Joe made his headquarters with young Joe through the hot summer, and in October he and Stewart rented an apartment in Philadelphia. One of his letters says, "Unless absolutely necessary I do not believe any relative should expect to settle in the midst of a young, growing family. I believe the parents should be left alone to train their children as they think best."

On January 31, 1948 he wrote:

On January 15th, I had a meeting of my Medical Committee of the Christian Association in Philadelphia and they want me to keep right on and not resign. They are ready to support me in any program that seems wise to try to carry out. I do hope that Penn. in China can still continue to function long after I am gone. They have asked me to write to our supporters telling of my trip to China.

His February 4 letter reported on his continued activities:

I expect to be in Philadelphia next week. Tuesday I attend a meeting at the International House. Wednesday evening a dinner meeting of the Board of Trustees of International House and on Friday evening the Philadelphia branch of the St. John's Alumni Association is giving a dinner in my honor.

Joe's March 5 letter described more activities in support of St. John's in China:

The New York Penn. Club had a very nice affair, black ties for all of us who were to receive something, others optional. This was the Guggenheim Award meeting. You may remember in 1943 I received the Award which meant that my name was inscribed on the big silver cup. This year they decided that they would give a scroll to each of us 16 who were still living since the awards began in 1911.

The following day I had lunch with the McMullens and heard a great deal about the doings of the United Board of Christian Colleges in China. McMullen has the main responsibility of raising $600,000 American money for the coming year and had most of it already raised and the rest in sight. That is the reason I had a phone call from Boston yesterday from the architects who have been given the job of laying out the building program of the new East China University--the union of Hangchow, Soochow and St. John's. They want to consult me about the medical department. I feel they need advice so I have promised to come to Boston. I should be signing and adding personal notes where I can to about five hundred copies of a letter I am sending out to contributors and friends.

The letter to his supporters was dated March 10, 1948:

Now that I am back in the States after sixteen months in Shanghai the most frequent question put to me is "Was it worth while?" My answer is "Yes, by all means." Let me tell you some of the reasons I think so.

In 1937 when the Japanese surrounded Shanghai the science department of St. John's University was forced to vacate its new science building across the creek and move back into the old science hall which already accommodated the School of Engineering and the dissecting laboratories of the Medical School. In that same year, I was able to rent from the Chinese Government a large experimental and research plant of eleven buildings located near the University. Into these buildings we moved the Medical School and opened a general hospital of 300 beds, and a T. B. hospital of 230 beds.

During these four war years (Dec. '37 to Dec. '41) the Medical School, under much protest from the Japanese, possessed and enjoyed by far the best teaching facilities in its history. When the Pearl Harbor incident happened the Japanese lost no time before they demanded that we close down the hospitals and vacate the property. The only thing then left to be done was to send the patients back to the cold camps, where many died, and to pile the hospital beds and equipment into an available Chinese residence and to move the Medical School laboratory equipment into the old, already over-crowded science building on the University campus. It was under these terribly crowded unheated conditions that the

Chinese faculty carried on so loyally and effectively for four years until the war was over.

It was then--June 1946--I reappeared on the grounds--and assumed the responsibility of reconditioning that old science building and getting it ready for the opening of school in September. Some job! Supplies and equipment ordered before I left America began to arrive. New textbooks from America were soon ordered. No new text books had been ordered since 1940. After giving entrance examinations to over sixty, thirty-six well-prepared students were admitted to the first year class. Then came the disappointing news that three of our American preclinical teachers were not returning. Fortunately we were able to find and engage a Chinese teacher who had received his Ph.D. in Physiology from the University of Chicago and had had experience teaching that subject. Later in the year we were able to engage Dr. Peter Ma, a Chinese born in Canada, who had his M. D. degree and M. S. degree in Biochemistry. Other preclinical teachers are sadly needed.

Few of us Americans realize the many problems skyrocketing inflation brings to a country. Tuition and laboratory fees for the term are not determined until two or three days before the opening of school. Even then the money collected with which your faculty is paid, may drop fifty to seventy percent in value before the end of the term and prices of every commodity they need may have more than doubled. Under these conditions what can a full time member of your faculty do? (1) He may leave your school and seek another job or (2) he may seek an additional job to increase his income as many of them in other departments have had to do or (3) in some schools (not ours, I am glad to say) a few teachers rather than let their children starve have been known to accept bills (money) from students for increased grades.

To forestall and make unnecessary any of the above our medical alumni decided to raise money and subsidize our full time teachers. In this way I was able to send to each staff member a check nearly equal to the monthly salary paid by the University. I was very glad to receive a special grant from the Christian Association which enabled me to add $2500 to this subsidy fund. If you have been a contributor to "Pennsylvania in China," you helped to make possible this grant. I hope that you are pleased. Today one of your dollars exchanges for about two hundred and fifty thousand Chinese dollars. China today is one of the easiest places in the world to become a millionaire!

225

This fall, before the new Chinese dean, Dr. P.C. Nyi, returned from America, I admitted forty new students, making our total enrollment in the five classes one hundred and fifty. Tuition and fees for one term were one million and eight hundred thousand dollars. About ten percent of the students received free tuition. So long as conditions remain as they are in China today no new building or expansion can be considered. The School authorities have decided that, for the present, we must carry on making the best possible use of the old buildings, personnel and money available, with the hope that in two or three years a new building program may be considered wise. These are very critical years and I do hope you will continue a vital interest in the future of this Christian Medical School.

The second most frequent question asked me is "Are you going back?" My only answer is, "God alone knows."

On April 28 Joe wrote:

On Friday morning I drove in to the C. A. [Christian Association] and at noon went downtown to have lunch at the University Club with Jack Minds, the Captain of my freshman football team at Penn. (1897) and Truxton Hare of that team and with whom I played for four years. We had a good time talking over things which happened a half century ago. From there I went back to the University to watch the preliminary day of the [Penn] Relays. I saw a man throw the hammer 172 feet. My record in '99 was 153 feet and eight inches. On Saturday I went in and had a chance to see a Negro athlete toss the shot 56 feet. He has put 58 feet, a world record, but was not able to reach that point Saturday. My intercollegiate record in '99 was only 43 feet eight inches. A half century has added much distance to all field events and lowered the time in all races.

On May 24 he raised the possibility of another trip to China:

A letter today came from the Foreign Y.M.C.A. in Shanghai urging me to return there and live in the building as I did before. So if I can't find a place to live in the U.S. there will be room waiting for me out there! I was just called on phone from New York to be asked if there is a brain surgeon in China. Yes, only one and he is in Peking.

In September he expressed his concern about conditions at St. John's:

226

Reports from the University are pretty bad and discouraging for it seems most of the faculty, foreigners and Chinese now wish to withdraw from the Union scheme which they agreed to go into some months ago. They appear to blame the union for all the troubles they had last spring. The trouble was they admitted far more students than they had accommodations for and some of the "guest" students were radicals and poor students, too. It will be unfortunate, for St. John's and especially the medical school if this union goes on the rocks.

On October 1st he moved into a new apartment which he shared with Stewart. His October 21 letter continued to indicate concern about what was happening at St. John's: "Word from China is not very encouraging but the medical school began the new term with 33 in the new class."

Joe's seventy-fifth birthday March 30 coincided with a luncheon meeting of the Philadelphia Rotary Club at which he was granted an honorary membership certificate. On April 10th he wrote about this:

Rotary conferred upon me a life honorary membership in the presence of over 600 Rotarians. I am the third ever to receive such a membership from Philadelphia Rotary. It was a grand meeting, but it was embarrassing to me, especially when the Chairman read the story of the Good Samaritan when introducing me. The certificate said: "In recognition of the distinguished service you have rendered as a medical missionary and as educator in China for forty-one years and your magnificent contribution in furtherance of the ideals of Rotary, the Rotary Club of Philadelphia is pleased to confer Honorary Membership for life upon you, Dr. Josiah Calvin McCracken. Your humanitarian service in behalf of a people far removed from your homeland, is a shining example of Rotary's motto "Service above Self" and marks you as a devoted servant of mankind and a great citizen of the world.

His annual letter to his friends was dated March 17, 1949.

China is going through one of the most distressing periods of her long history. And yet, the Medical School in which we have been affiliated for these thirty-five years as "Pennsylvania in China," has never closed its doors. It is the only School in all East China which did not close or move back to West China during the Japanese invasion. I had the privilege of serving this School as its Dean and Professor of Surgery for over thirty years. In that time, 392 doctors were graduated under the best Western standards of medicine. This was not accomplished over night; only 39 men were graduated in the first ten years, 69 in the next ten, 175 in the next ten and in the last four years, 1945 to 1948, 109.

At this writing the enrollment in the Medical School is 137. To appreciate the full significance of this accomplishment you must realize that in all China there are only about 12,000 doctors, for 450,000,000 people and of that 12,000, 75% at least are graduates of low standard medical schools or may even have taken only apprenticeship work in a hospital. The strategic importance of this contribution to modern medicine and public health can be understood when we realize that in this training of Chinese doctors we are helping to establish new medical schools, new hospitals and health centers throughout that vast country. Our graduates know English and all the teaching is done in that language. Many of them have come to America for graduate study. Over thirty have received their Master's Degrees from the University of Pennsylvania Graduate School of Medicine. Now the faculty of the Medical School consists largely of our own alumni who have taken graduate degrees abroad and nearly all of their teaching is a free gift to their Alma Mater. "Pennsylvania in China" has supplied personnel and dollars to this school, without which it could never have made such a record and probably could not have continued to exist.

During the past three years the situation has been extremely critical so that our Committee has felt it necessary to forward additional funds to supplement the salaries of the pre-clinical teachers whose regular stipends, because of inflation, have been entirely inadequate. I trust that you who have so loyally supported "Pennsylvania in China" will continue to do so, for I believe in so doing we are rendering a most vital service in a most efficient way to a worthy and appreciative people. China cannot achieve a modern civilization without a trained medical profession.

The most exciting event for this year was the lovely wedding of Stewart and Joan Adamson Fernley on June 11, 1949. Everyone managed to get to Philadelphia for varying lengths of time to enjoy the various events, including Joe's luncheon at the Cricket Club on Sunday for everyone. This was the only one of his children's weddings he was able to attend.

With Stewart leaving for his own home, Joe decided to continue alone in the apartment. It was so convenient to all his activities and friends and for his travelling to visit his children and New York. He also had the space to put up his children and grandchildren, who came frequently to visit.

In a letter dated June 19 he reviewed the occasion:

> While my dinner consisting of an orange, two poached eggs on toast and the balance of the Jell-O Ruth made when she was here is digesting, I'll write you all a note just to let you know I lived through the great day and also Alumni Day. It was certainly great to have everyone of you here, even though Joe could remain for only part of the day. However, even in that short time, with Michael's help, he became the hero of the crowd. [Joe, clad in his tuxedo, had had to jump into a small pond to rescue young Michael who had slipped into the water and was beginning to go under.]

On May 25, 1949, Shanghai was taken over by the Communists. Joe reported:

> I had a rather busy three days in New York, going over on Tuesday. That night we had an evening meeting from eight to nearly midnight of a part of the Medical Committee of the United Board of Christian Colleges in China. The four Christian Medical Schools each made a report telling what had been done to date and the plans and needs for the future providing the schools are allowed to continue under satisfactory conditions.
>
> The next day we reported to a larger committee. Of course no one can predict what may happen to any one or all of the schools but all are determined to continue as long as possible. I did learn that St. John's University had received from the UBCCC within the year $96,000 which was enough to pay the University's debts and carry them over the summer. I do not know yet how much of that the medical school received or will receive.
>
> Yesterday Penn had a big alumni day. I celebrated with my '99 College class our fiftieth. We had twenty-two of us at the University Club Friday night. Although I did not recognize many of them, they did recognize me for in those days I did play football. They insisted I tell them about China and my work out there which I was very glad to do. Yesterday since I was the biggest and strongest of the class I carried one of the two flags in the march to Franklin Field to the baseball game.

He was delighted to have a visit from the Sung family in late June. Dr. Sung had been the president of St. John's University and Joe had been so concerned because of his imprisonment when last he was in China.

His reports of conditions in Shanghai were not too optimistic. They have all of their family in the States now except two, a doctor to whom I gave a degree in 1947, and a sixteen-year old daughter who has T. B. They hope to find a way of getting them over here someday....

The Chinese [doctor] I got an internship for in Atlantic City arrived June 28th. I was afraid he would not be able to get out of Shanghai. He reports that before the term ended some of the St. John's students demanded that all teaching be in the Chinese language. What absurdity!

Joe's letter of July 26th tells of his elation that a classmate of his had decided to complete arrangements for a testimonial trust fund, the interest of which, amounting to about seven hundred and fifty dollars a year, was to be used to carry on Pennsylvania in China until "Gabriel blows his horn." At the same time the man became interested in International House, another one of Joe's projects, and made a gift of $1500.

In October 1949 he reported on the visit of a young American teacher who had just returned from China:

The report is that St. John's University is open and is allowed to run without too much interference but that many of the younger teachers and missionaries were returning to America and that many of the older ones were staying and having a hard time accepting the new administration.

On November 21 he attended a dinner meeting of the Board of Directors of the Christian Association. "Dana How, who had been Ex. Director of the C.A. for about twenty years, wants to call the C.A. building McCracken Hall, but I am opposed to it. Better keep the name Christian Association before the students."

Joe's letters of 1948 and 1949 give only hints about the tragic happenings in China, and particularly the dilemmas faced by those Chinese with close ties to foreigners. Chiang Kai-shek and the Nationalist Government had had their own experiences with the Chinese Communists, waged war with them, and fought in diplomatic circles to prevent a coalition which they did not believe would keep China a free world power. This had been done at the same time that China had fought the Japanese for four years before World War II started for other nations, and then four more long years. Others, both Chinese and foreigners, particularly part of the American military and Foreign Service, believed in and worked towards forcing a coalition of the two

Chinas. Many of these people looked upon the Chinese Communists as not actually Communists but as reformers who could, in an authoritarian way, bring much needed reforms to war-weary China more efficiently than the Nationalist government. Others, of course, both Chinese and foreigners, welcomed the Communist Chinese government's expansion because it was Communistic and the only real cure for China.

The United States, a long-time friend of the Chinese people, chose the policy of forcing coalition of the two Chinas and actually from the summer of 1946 to the summer of 1948 did not contribute military or other forms of assistance to the Nationalist government. Thus Chiang Kai-shek did not benefit from the same effort with supplies and leadership as was poured into Europe to revive it after the war ended.

During 1946 and 1947 it had appeared Nationalist China would be able to control the Communists and would have time for reconstruction. Noble efforts were made to bring financial reform, reconstruction, expansion of educational and health programs, and agricultural reform. But by 1948 there were signs of failure to control corruption and inflation, to satisfy the increasing demands of the common people (such as the farmers, students and factory workers) for quicker and specific relief, and to offset the insidious, constant propaganda from the Chinese Communists, who seemed to have all the answers for a better future. To put it very briefly and much too simply, eventually other world events began to demonstrate the menace of Communism in the world and the importance of aid to Nationalist China in order to save China and Asia from Communist takeovers. But by then it was too late and the assistance too little to "contain" the Chinese Communists who, with Russian assistance, had secured so much of the Japanese munitions and access to formerly Japanese controlled areas.

More and more Chinese turned away from the Nationalist Government, especially the intellectuals and soldiers and ardent patriots. The propaganda of the Chinese Communists skillfully made appeals that there could be a coalition of party members with other groups to bring in a new day for China, along with the promotion of anti-American feelings and a promise of religious freedom. On January 31, 1949, Peiping surrendered to the Communist army without any fighting--a signal that it would probably be impossible for the Nationalist Government to continue very long and a signal that the people themselves were passively withdrawing their support of Chiang Kai-shek. The Nationalist Government began the steps which led it to flee to Taiwan and continue the Chinese Republic there.

By October 1, 1949, enough of the big cities had come under Communist control, including Shanghai on May 25th, that the Chinese People's Republic was proclaimed. The next day the Soviet Union recognized the new government and for several years Communist

China had financial assistance and Soviet technicians to assist in the administrative organization and consolidation of power, the rebuilding of industry and communications facilities, land reform, and the ending of inflation.

Joe received a letter from the dean of the medical school in Shanghai written on December 20, 1949. The dean was still very enthusiastic about the new government and the way the medical school was carrying on. Based on the letter, Joe went to the Christian Association and requested that a check for $750.00 be sent to the dean's account. That meant a total of $3,000.00 he had had sent to them in the past twelve months. He hoped to keep that rate up for the next year.

In April of 1950 he wrote his family on the official stationary of the Chinese Christian Church and Center of Philadelphia, for he had consented to be General Chairman of a drive for $150,000 for a building fund. This church and its members became one of his favorite and continuing interests.

In late May he wrote:

> To you who are interested in China and especially to those who have so faithfully contributed to "Pennsylvania in China," I wish to report on what has occurred since my last letter to you dated March 17, 1949. Because of the increasing political tension in Shanghai the work of the Spring term, '49, in the Medical School was accelerated so that commencement was in the first week of May, instead of June. The National Government withdrew from Shanghai on May 25, 1949. No lives were lost on the campus, but considerable material damage was done when the retiring army blew up a railroad bridge 400 yards off the campus.
>
> Summer courses were allowed to continue without interference. During that summer many applications for admission to the Medical School were received and from these the dean admitted sixty; which number was fifty per cent larger than any previous entering class. When dean I had considered 40 the maximum number the laboratories and faculty could efficiently handle. The University Administration was soon completely reorganized, but the Medical School was not materially affected except more time and attention was to be given to the teaching of scientific medical technology.
>
> Inflation again made it impossible for many of the students to pay full tuition and laboratory fees. Many free scholarships were granted. The work of the fall term proceeded under considerable tension, especially when the city was being bombed by planes of the National Government. The dean reported that he had good cooperation from the faculty and

students. The attendance at the voluntary assembly had increased and the students were more seriously minded.

It was not until January 5, 1950, that what appeared to be a most serious interference with the work of the School occurred. The Dean wrote: "Since the fifth of this month all our 2nd, 3rd, and 4th year students and 19 doctors, 8 nurses and 7 technicians from St. Elizabeth's, St. Luke's, Lester Chinese and Margaret Williamson Hospitals have been sent to the country to combat *Schistomiasis Japonica.* This project may last two months. As a whole this group is doing a fine piece of work. They are divided into eight units carrying full laboratory and treatment supplies."

This left in school only the first year class of 60. Not until a letter received from the dean dated April 17, 1950, did we learn what had happened to those three classes. In that letter the dean reported as follows:

> Students returned from the country the 2nd of this month. All classes resumed on the 12th. Again a concentrated course has been worked out for the 4th year. 2nd and 3rd years will carry on per schedule to about the last part of August. We are glad that they had this experience with the liberation army and the people of the country. They are more earnest, frugal, and industrious. They have learned how to live as common people. And above all, they have learned the true spirit of service to mankind. Many of them will be better doctors and workers than we have ever had before.

Knowing the Chinese as I do, I appreciate what the dean reports relative to the value to students of this three months experience in serving through the army the poor people of that country; these students come, for the most part, from the non-laboring classes of China. So now all the medical students are on the campus working hard to make up for lost time somewhat similar to our medical students in America during the war when they attended school all the year to save time.

My last year's letter brought in the generous response of three thousand dollars. This entire sum was made available to the dean at periodic intervals during the year. He was most grateful and wished me to thank each of you. That additional fund enabled him to supplement the salary of the members of the faculty, each of whom received from the University only about forty dollars a month, with which to keep and feed his family at a time when the prices of everything were skyrocketing.

It is a satisfaction to know that there are nearly 300 doctors, that we have helped train, out there scattered over that great country doing everything they can to relieve pain and suffering and improve health conditions. As long as the dean and faculty are able to keep the School open and train doctors with satisfactory standards, I feel it to be a privilege to continue to give them every possible assistance with the hope, prayer and expectation that a better day will come, as has occurred many times after most distressing periods of uncertainty.

Joe with U. S. Navy nurses serving in Shanghai after the war.

CHAPTER TWENTY

THE DOOR TO CHINA CLOSES
1950-1952

Soon after the proclamation of the People's Republic of China October 1, 1949, Mao Tse Tung went to Moscow to conclude with Stalin a new Sino-Russian Treaty of Friendship, Alliance and Mutual Assistance. The United States' efforts to maintain relationships with and give recognition to the new government failed.

In the making of peace after World War II problems arose relating to Korea and to Formosa, where Chiang Kai-shek had fled to maintain Free China. North Korea, with supervision by the communists, had been designated to arrange surrender by the Japanese. South Korea, had been assigned to the United States and the United Nations for supervision of the Japanese surrender of this territory. It was expected that North and South Korea would then hold elections and become an independent nation.

As these plans faltered, the Korean War began and Communist China entered to assist the North Koreans. Truce talks began in July of 1951 and an armistice was finally agreed on in July of 1953, although there was some intermittent fighting during the truce. As a result of the Korean War, little was settled towards the goal of an undivided Korean nation and the division lines between North and South Korea remained much as they were at the beginning of the war.

But the Korean war helped unite China under its new government, which would now begin in earnest its job of "re-educating the masses" to understand Marxist philosophy and policies in the name of the "people's democratic dictatorship." This political program, as well as the economic programs to improve living conditions through agrarian and industrial changes, included a purging from power of many middle class and western-educated Chinese who had initially been attracted to and contributed their leadership and expertise to establishing the new government.

Joe had his 76th birthday in March of 1950; he would celebrate eleven more. His letters continue to demonstrate his concern for each child and grandchild. He took great pride in the grandchildren and enjoyed telling people how many children and grandchildren he had. Usually he topped everyone else but, to his dismay, the janitor of his apartment building had more. By the middle of 1950 he could boast of seventeen, for there were added Carolyn Ruth Yates, the third and last child in the Yates family, who was born February 20, 1949; Bruce Emerson McCracken, fourth and last child of Joe, Jr., who was born October 25, 1949; Judith Lynne Cramer, the second child in the Cramer family, who was born November 14, 1949; and Karen Lee

MacCracken, the third child in her family, who was born January 10, 1950.

Joe spent the summer with Joe, Jr. and Barbara. In addition to the pleasure of being with them, he enjoyed being a member of the Ventnor Shuffleboard Club in which he found many persons around his age and many Penn graduates. He tried to play two periods a day.

His July 20 letter indicated his continuing concern about conditions in China:

A letter from the Dean Nyi written on June 27th is not very encouraging, especially so far as standards of work is concerned. He had just returned from attending a conference on Higher Education held in Peking. He reports that the New Government is going to open many new medical schools and require only five years of study--above what I do not know, but probably not more than middle school if that. He thought St. John's would be required to admit larger classes and teach eventually in the Chinese language. All of which is very discouraging to me.

However it is their country and their job, and we can only be ready to help when and where we think wise.

His September 24 letter continued to describe his activities relating to China :

On Friday I had here for lunch with me downstairs Ned Wood and wife, H. H. Collins and wife, Dr. Geo. B. Wood and Dr. Fred Frayley. Those were the four men who have been on the Medical Committee of the C.A. for twenty-five or thirty years and have been responsible for keeping me in China. The oldest is eighty-four and the rest about my age. It was the first time all of us have been together for years. After lunch we had a meeting and they gave me authority to continue to send money to China as long as I thought it wise. I urged addition of young men to the committee so that this work in China will continue after we are gone. I raised the question of my resigning and they said, "No, no, keep on as long as you feel like it." So I am going on and I am going to find some younger people for the Medical Committee.

Joe's October 27 letter concerned both the past and the future:

To begin with, that "old greats" football dinner was a very delightful get together of some old friends whom I had not seen for forty or more years. Clark Williams, captain of the '95 team was there. He was the first Penn. man to write me about coming to Pennsylvania. Although I have once known him well I did not recognize him for I had not seen him for forty years even though he is an active eye specialist in Germantown. Jack Minds, my first year captain, sat next to me. T. Truxton Hare with whom I played for our years was at the game the next day when 11 of us were televised as we rode around Franklin Field in a stage coach pulled by two horses before a crowd of 40,000. We then lined up on the Field and were introduced to the crowd. It was quite an occasion--just fifty years after the last time I walked off Franklin Field....

Dr. Tseng is now Superintendent of St. Luke's on the campus of St. John's and wrote me an encouraging letter about the clinic there. He wrote that the hospital now has nearly 200 patients a day at the clinic and that no patient needing treatment was turned away because they had no money. The next day I sent $500 to the hospital and the same to the school.

In my daily reading I have just finished *The Epistle of James.* I have always liked James for I think it has a lot of down to earth advice which if more of us Christians would follow the church and the world would be better off. If you have not read the Epistle lately, read it and see if you do not agree with me.

As Joe was proud to describe, his "Chinese children" often sought his advice and assistance; they remained in touch with visits and letters and he helped in every way he could. An example was given in his November 27 letter:

There is a satisfaction in being able to do something for other people. For instance some ten days ago one of "my boys" now in New York wrote to me and said that he had applied for a residency in a hospital in Texas and asked me to write and certify that he was a graduate of St. John's and make a recommendation if possible. I wrote and got a letter back from the doctor saying that the application would be given every consideration. He also said that he almost knew me, for his father, a minister, had often spoken of my work in China. And yesterday I received a letter from my boy very much elated for he had received the appointment as resident in surgery which was for three years.

I was just now called to the phone at 3:33 and Mr. Houston, who built Houston Hall and was one of the three who offered to pay expenses of my first trip to China, was on the phone and said that one of his grandsons was not going to be able to go to a St. Andrews dinner tonight at the Bellevue

237

Stratford and his son-in-law, Dr. Brown, who has just returned from China, would be very happy if I at this late hour would come. Not having anything to do tonight I accepted with pleasure. Then Mr. Houston said "black ties." I do not often wear my tuxedo but I could hardly back out then. But I like to be dressed as other people, so I'll brush mine off and go along.

And so, at 76, Joe continued to reach out and take part in those organizations attempting to meet the social problems of the day, giving of his time to attend meetings and selective financial support. In February, he wrote of attending a luncheon meeting at the Negro YMCA, "of which I am a contributing member" to hear Bayard Rustin speak. He was well aware that his descendants would have to resolve the country's racial problems. Another day in February, he wrote of attending a World Affairs luncheon meeting at the University Museum to hear Dean Rusk, then Assistant Secretary of State for Foreign Affairs. He also continued to be active on the Board of Trustees of the International House.

Joe's February 28 letter reported on fund-raising:

A letter from Dr. McMullen said that the United Board of Christian Colleges in China had offered to send to the ten Christian Colleges in China $76,000 a month, but not one college responded so he realized that they were not allowed to receive money from this imperialistic source. Since it has become impossible for me to send any more money to China, I have asked the Christian Association to give from the China Fund two thousand dollars to the Church and they have individually consented.

In February, Joe was elected an Elder of his Church, First Presbyterian, and was inducted on March 4. At first he hesitated to accept such an honor, but he found great satisfaction during the years he served and was faithful in doing all he was able to do.

The April 18 letter reported on his continuing close association with the University of Pennsylvania:

I, as a guest of President Stassen, attended the biggest money raising rally I ever attended. What a crowd, 1000, and what a lot of money pledged to complete a $2,000,000 drive to build a new Wharton School of Finance Building....You know I attended that School for one year before taking up Medicine. See what I might have done had I not studied medicine, but had gone on in the Wharton School and had become

238

a Philadelphia politician as Mike Murphy, my trainer, said I should do instead of going to China as a medical missionary!! Even though I do not have the money to burn, I do not for a minute regret my choice.

Throughout this period, Joe kept very active. He was elected chairman of the Friends of China, was made an honorary member of the Sphinx Senior Society of the University of Pennsylvania, spoke at the 75th Diamond Jubilee Dinned of the Intercollegiate Association of Amateur Athletes of America (representing the first quarter century), and was visited by his sister Daisy and older brother Gib.

Sometime in 1951 Joe wrote Dr. F. S. Tang about his discouragement about conditions in China:

> I had heard a little about each of the plans for extending the hospital and school facilities but nothing of details. Now that all such opportunities are passed, I think that we had better decide that since God did not answer our prayers these were not the ways He wished the School and Hospital to develop, but keep on working and praying for His guidance that his will be done at all times. When we have done all we can do, then we must leave the results to God and not worry if things do not turn out as we had thought best.

Joe accepted an invitation to attend a conference to organize "Social Action," to be held at Howard University in Washington, D.C. At Howard he met such leaders as Reinhold Niebuhr, Kenneth Underwood, Marquis Childs and Davis Burgess. He was quite impressed with the University and with the students he met while staying in a dormitory.

His letter of October 21 described his continuing church participation:

> We had communion in our church this morning and I suppose your churches had it, too, for it was a "world-wide" communion and I think it was supported in all denominations. There was such a big turnout at our church there were not enough cups of wine to go around. I do not know when that has ever happened before. It was quite an impressive service. I hope you children were in church attendance somewhere. Too many of us Protestants let very little keep us from attending church....If America is going to represent the workings of a democratic government to the world it's high time we live up to our Constitution and the teachings of our Christian religion.

239

On November 14th Joe spoke at a dinner meeting of the Philadelphia chapter of the National Sojourners Club, which is a club made up of Masons who are or have been officers in the Army, Navy, or Marines. Of course his subject was China. He described the last few years of the medical school and reported on some of the government regulations since the People's Government took over, saying:

> I hope we'll be patient and not get our own soldiers into a helpless battle there. If Russia folds, the present situation may have been good, especially if we are patient and give them a chance to find some way out themselves.
> It is amazing how the Communist movement has covered such a large area as China and their propaganda is excellent, but many people are beginning to think they are worse off than before.

He also discussed some of the People's Government regulations in the past two years against American-supported missions and schools such as St. John's. He said many of the restrictions were aimed at so-called "American imperialism" through churches, U.S. action in Korea and aid to Western Europe. He mentioned a recent Communist proclamation banning any expression against the government's code of three selves--self-support, self-government and self-propagation.

In April 1952, he again wrote to his friends and supporters:

> This is just a personal report to you on what "Pennsylvania in China" is doing outside of China. As you know from the daily papers the China doors are closed and no longer can any assistance of any kind be sent from America to any institution within China, not even to Leprosoriums, Blind Schools or Orphanages. Very few letters were received from China during 1951. The last one, dated in August, indicated that the St. John's University and Medical School and Hospital were now fully under the control of the Red Government. The entrance requirements of the Medical School were immediately reduced and last fall sixty students were admitted without examinations, supposedly on the old standards, and one hundred and twenty were admitted on the new standards, which require no college preparation. Students were admitted from schools which might be equal to an American Junior High School. They may qualify for the M. D. degree after five years study. The Chinese language is to be used as much as possible. All this means increased numbers with lowered standards.

The Door to China Closes (1950-1952)

With the doors to China tightly closed our China Medical Committee began to explore conditions outside of China where there might be a need and an opportunity to help. For a number of years the Baptists and Methodists have been carrying on Christian work among Chinese living in and around Chinatown in Philadelphia. These denominations with the addition of the Evangelical and Reformed and Presbyterians decided in the Spring of 1950 to unite and form one church and put on a drive to raise $150,000 to build in Chinatown, a Chinese Christian Church and Center. I was asked to be the General Chairman of the drive. The undertaking appealed to me because it was for the Chinese, interdenominational and something which could be done at once. Our Medical Committee recommended that the Christian Association make a contribution of $2,000 from the Pennsylvania in China Fund to help build this much needed church. The Association did make this grant and on January 27, 1952, sod was broken to begin the erection of this church.

For this year the Christian Association Board, on the recommendation of the Medical Committee, has decided to make a grant of $5,000 from the China Fund to help the splendid work of Dr. Victor C. Rambo in India. Dr. Rambo graduated from the University of Pennsylvania Medical School in 1921 and has worked in India for nearly thirty years, building up a Christian hospital specializing in eye diseases. In that section of India cataract, causing blindness, is very prevalent. By a delicate operation these blind can be made to see again. Victor has not only brought physical sight to these patients, but also spiritual sight to a large percentage of them. His one hundred-bed hospital is crowded to overflowing. During rush seasons as many as one hundred patients may be sleeping on the floor, on the veranda, or even under the shade of trees in the yard. He reports that as many as one hundred and twenty-five cataract cases are operated on in a week. This grant is made to enlarge and equip the bed capacity of the Ophthalmology Department of the hospital. Dr. Rambo reports that it costs $10 gold to bring sight to a blind person. I am glad we can, with our gifts, have a share in this great enterprise.

The Christian Association has upon the recommendation of the Medical Committee also made a grant of $2,000 to the Christian Children's Fund, Inc. of Richmond, Virginia, formerly called China's Children Fund. Many of you already know what a grand work this organization, for more than twenty-five years, has been doing for orphans around the world. Until recently they were helping to support forty-two orphanages within China. They have nineteen orphanages for

Chinese children outside of China. It is this group of homeless Chinese children which our appropriation will serve.

Much of my time is now spent meeting or corresponding with the more than sixty graduates of the St. John's Medical School now in America. They are studying in graduate medical schools or working as residents in hospitals. At present all of them are busy in one way or another, but during the year many changes must be made and that is where my assistance comes in. It is a very pleasant and worthwhile job. Many of these doctors are already well trained and are anxious for conditions in China to so change as will permit them to return home.

In May of 1952 Joe visited a number of relatives, including his three daughters now in Cleveland, his sister Daisy in Tulsa, and his brother Gib in Great Bend, Kansas. They drove over to the Wellmans home in Sterling and visited the family graves, and Joe decided to sell the old McCracken farm. He reported to his children:

Now that there is no hope of getting oil in that neighborhood I had no idea what I might expect to get for the place. I had less than fourteen hundred invested in it and I decided that if Ed would offer me $3,000 I would take it but would leave the amount entirely up to Ed. To my surprise he said that he would give me a check for four thousand and we drove at once to the county seat and settled the transfer without a bit of trouble.

For a number of years I have hoped that someday in appreciation for what Cooper College, now Sterling College, did for me and has been doing for other young people since then, I might make a contribution to the college fund. Last year I sent them a check for a thousand dollars and when this sale was made I sent the College a check for three thousand for its endowment fund. So the income on these four thousand dollars should bring in an annual income of at least two hundred dollars as long as the college exists.

CHAPTER TWENTY-ONE

THE WORK GOES ON
1953-1962

Joe's annual letter to friends and supporters was mailed out in
May, 1953:

A year has passed since I last sent you my warm greetings.
Again I must report that I have had no direct contact with our
mutual interests, medical education and hospital service, in
Shanghai. However, we have not been inactive. The China
Medical Committee continues its interest in Chinese, wherever
they challenge our concern. We do know that last fall the
School of Medicine of St. John's University had been completely taken over by the Communist government and had
been united with a French and a Chinese Medical School and
the three called The Second Shanghai Medical College located
on the French campus. I am glad that they dropped the name
St. John's.

Encouraging reports have come of the splendid work
[that] the Christian Children's Fund, Inc., to which the Christian Association contributed last year, is doing for Chinese orphans outside of China. Also the Christian Children's Fund
reported the awful conditions of orphans in Korea where war
conditions have existed many months. As you may know,
many of the intellectual class of Chinese escaped from the
Communists and are now in Hongkong. Many are now in
need and living on the streets without sufficient food or
clothing. Representative (Congress) Dr. Walter Judd, who for
many years was a medical missionary in China, has organized
a Committee to raise funds to help move some of these families to Formosa and other countries where they can again become useful citizens. Dr. Victor Rambo also reported that, because of the increased cost of building in India, the $5,000
contributed to him last year was not sufficient to complete the
100 bed addition to the hospital. After careful study of these
reports the China Medical Committee recommended that the
Christian Association, from current China Medical Funds,
make the following contributions for 1952-53:

A. Christian Children's Fund, Inc.
    1. For Chinese orphans $2,000
    2. For Korean orphans $1,000
B. An additional grant to Dr. Rambo's
    work in India $2,000

C. Aid to Refugee Intellectuals, Ins. $1,000

Such donations as these could not now be made had not so many friends of "Pennsylvania in China" given generously to make possible the hospital and medical educational work which has been carried on by the Christian Association for these past forty-five years. We pray God that this grand work may not only continue now for Chinese outside China, but may soon again be operative inside.

The sixty or more graduates of the School of Medicine of St. John's University now in USA are all busy in some capacity or other, earning a living and preparing themselves to give better service in China when they return. Fourteen of them have already formed a medical faculty, each member preparing himself for teaching that subject assigned to him in that medical school which they propose to organize when they return home. The conditions in China today do not discourage them. One of them wrote me, "In fact we are more assured that the devil is daily digging his own grave and we trust that the day of liberation will be nearer than if they had not been so wicked."

The Chinese Christian Church here in Philadelphia, toward the erection of which the Christian Association contributed $2,000 is now completed and was dedicated last month. The Rev. T. K. Chiu is a highly educated, devout and most active minister. We feel that this interdenominational church, though small, will grow and be a great inspiration to the Chinese in and around Philadelphia.

In February I went to the old Pennsylvania Hospital for three weeks and had a radical operation such as many old men must undergo. Operation was a complete success and the patient lived! Going to the hospital where I took my two years internship a half century ago and where I spent three years in 1943-46 as surgeon and chief of the resident medical staff was almost like going home again.

Much of my time is still happily spent doing something for and with the Chinese doctors now in America and those outside of China who wish to come to our beloved Country.

In a letter in August Joe described going to see Bishop Tsu and his family in one of the missionary cottages and finding Jimmy Yen and his wife, a sister of Mrs. Tsu, visiting:

Yen is the man who started the movement to simplify the Chinese written language (also the leader in the mass adult education programs to reduce illiteracy and encourage mod-

244

ern farming methods). While I knew much about what he was doing I could not remember of ever having met him. To my great surprise they informed me that I had brought their first two children into this world! What a memory. I do not recall one thing about these jobs but they said I did so I guess I must have.

Later in 1953, he wrote a general reference letter, understated as was his style, for use by his many students in the United States:

When the alumni of the medical School can go abroad and in a foreign tongue gain the respect, confidence, and the highest praise of their ability as physicians, as do the alumni of the School of Medicine of St. John's University, it does not seem to me that any state offering to them the privilege of taking the examination for a license to practice can be running any serious risk of lowering the standards of profession in America....These doctors are friends of America and should be treated as such and given every possible opportunity to increase their usefulness while here and when they return home.

At seventy-nine years of age Joe continued to maintain an inquiring mind, open to new adventures. His September 17th, 1953, letter tells of having dinner with Mr. and Mrs. E. C. Wood of the Christian Association and Dr. Harvey Howards, formerly of Canton, and then joining six or seven others for a seance:

We collected in the living room with all the doors and windows closed; fortunately it was a cool evening. Ned Wood played the piano and we all sung a hymn and then he led us in prayer. The light was then turned off so that there was perfect darkness. Then another hymn was sung while the medium was going into a trance. Almost immediately a strong voice came in. It was Barbara Hutchins who frequently comes from the spirit world and who is well known to Ned. She began to talk to different people there and they asked her questions.

Her first to me was, "Two ladies wish to come through to speak to Dr. McCracken." I asked her who they were and she said, "One is your wife." I expressed great pleasure and asked that she be brought on. Your Mother's voice was so weak that I could not understand what she was trying to say. I asked her if she was happy up there and they giggled at the idea of being up there and not being happy. Your mother said that she was very happy and told me to take care of myself and enjoy this world as much as I could. Then I asked if Mary was there and if she could come through. She did and said that she was with Mother frequently. I asked her if she still used her crutches and she said, "No, never up here." The other lady with your mother proved to be the first wife of Dr. Howard. They had a few words back and forward and then she said that she was glad he had found such a nice lady to live with him and that they were so happy together.

In 1954 Joe celebrated his eightieth birthday. He continued to write every two weeks to his family. He enjoyed reading social action pamphlets, religious books, novels--a variety of printed matter and his letters include comments on his current reading:

I just finished "The Healing Light," by Agnes White Sandford, daughter of missionary parents and wife of a missionary at Changshu, now living in New Jersey. She does not rule out the doctor or surgeon but proves that prayer can often help the doctor and patients often go on to a perfect cure after the doctors have given up all hope of recovery. I have read two or three other small books on divine or spiritual healing; I believe the medical profession, or some of them at least, are beginning to realize that spiritual and mental conditions have much to do with the physical condition of the patient. I believe doctors will go further along that line.

In June he wrote a last letter to his friends and supporters:

If you have seen, as I have, the distressing, hopeless conditions of Orphans in a war riddled Asiatic country, you will be glad, as I am, that the Christian Association has decided again to give substantially of its expendable China Fund, to the support of these children. You may recall that the Association's original gift to this work was made through the Christian Children's Fund, Inc. in Richmond, Virginia. After reading the report of this organization we are convinced that our $3,000 contribution was well made.

My "boys and girls," graduates of the School of Medicine, St. John's University, Shanghai, China, who are now in America are gradually solving some of the problems a foreign doctor must solve before he can practice medicine on his own in America. I find deep satisfaction in giving a good portion of my time now to helping my former students with these problems. It is a real joy to render them every assistance possible, for they are not only a credit to the medical profession but also to China and the medical school from which they graduated, The School of Medicine, St. John's University, Shanghai, China.

The Work Goes On (1953-1962)

A highlight of the fall was:

The show of all shows on a Wednesday night. The Olympian Association gave a banquet at the Ben Franklin Hotel to raise money to help support the U.S. Olympic teams. Over eighteen hundred were there and twenty-five dollars was the cost of the ordinary place but I, being one of the oldest Olympians there, was an honored guest, as were the other two 1900 Olympics team present. We were all from Penn. We were seated at the speaker's table and when our names were called, had to rise and bow to the clapping audience.

Christmas of 1954 he spent with Joe and Barbara. He had had a dizzy spell early in December and it was felt he should not fly to Cleveland as usual. In January of 1955 he returned to his apartment feeling "quite recuperated".

In February of 1955 he attended a Rotary meeting, reporting:

I do not go every week but yesterday we were celebrating our Golden Anniversary 1905-1955. It was a grand meeting with over 400 present. In fifty years that club now has about 8000 clubs scattered in 89 countries and regions with a membership of about 400,000. It is said that now there is a Rotary lunch being served somewhere in the world every hour every weekday of the year. It is certainly a great honor to be an honorary member of such an organization.

The summer passed quickly in Ventnor and so did the fall, especially since Ruth and Al were now close by and he could visit them and talk on the phone. The number of grandchildren had changed now to twenty-one for Timothy McCracken Cramer was born May 6, 1952, Mark Mitchell MacCracken born March 21, 1954, Ellen Clute McCracken, daughter of Stewart and Joan, born July 15, 1954, and Stewart McCracken, Jr. born August 20, 1955. Joe liked to surprise people with that number and I think only once did he find someone with more--the janitor of the apartment house. He would finally have two more some years later: Mary Newpher McCracken, born June 1, 1957 and James Christopher McCracken born September 20, 1961, both children of Stewart and Joan, making a total of 23.

One letter remarks that he has an official list of all graduates from 1901 until 1950 from the Medical School of St. John's University so that he can make official reports as necessary [included in updated form in the Appendix]. He was especially proud that St. John's University Medical School was the only one in East China supported by foreign nations that did not close or move back to "Free China" during the Japanese invasion and World War II.

Another letter commented on his fortunate physical condition:

[On a Thursday in October he hosted a] luncheon for Jack Minds, captain of my first year Penn football team fifty-nine years ago, 1897, and T. Truxton Hare, one of the greatest football players of all time and with whom I played my four years, and John Mahoney who was in college at that time and a reporter of athletics at Penn. What a time we had talking over them "good old days," when we won nearly every game during those four years. Minds walks with a cane and Hare, too. Both are lawyers. I appear to be in much better physical condition than either of them.

There is a lovely Christmas poem and greetings for him from Dr. Shao Chang Lee, living at that time at Michigan State University in East Lansing, Michigan. There is the Chinese writing in the form of an eight-line poem, each line consisting of seven ideographs or characters and then the translation as follows:

TO DOCTOR JOSIAH CALVIN McCRACKEN: AN APPRECIATION
by Shao Chang Lee

I love my teacher, Doctor J. C. McCracken
Few could match him in human-heartedness and kind deeds.
For four decades he was in Cathay; he returned to his
homeland.
He has trained his followers to be great physicians;
He has freed the innocent ones from the double bondage of
superstition and disease
Daily he still goes about doing good; me thinks the older he is
the more spiritual strength he possess.
Throughout the four seasons he is the light that shines like the
Spring sun.

In its issue of December 31, 1955 *Pfizer Spectrum,* a medical journal, featured an article on the All American Football Squad, 25 players and a coach, all of whom are physicians and who had once been All-American. Joe's picture had the caption: "halfback, Pennsylvania 1899. He served for many years as a medical missionary to China." Joe was also mentioned as one of two who were also outstanding all-round athletes and Olympic track stars. This recognition caused Joe to note wryly, "I'm the only physician still living who played in the last century!"

Joe was hospitalized for three weeks by a heart attack in late January of 1956. This was followed by visits for recuperation with Stewart and Ruth. At his own pace, he continued his work for his Chinese boys and girls:

> I have had and am going to have more notarizing to do for them. So many have decided they should try to get American citizenship and a license to practice in one or two states. All that requires a lot of notarized papers of one sort or another and since I am the last resort from which they can obtain such documents, some would like to have one or two extra in case this source of supplies might cease to exist.
>
> I am glad I am here to help them for they are all busy and most grateful and I have every reason to be proud of each one of them. I have my filing cabinet set up and to date have most of my Chinese letters filed and what a job. Some times the last name is the first name and again the first name is the last and often spelled in a different way and under which name will I file all the letters from that person! The next job will be to have a card for each one showing names, year of graduation, address and changes as they are made, what Boards passed, etc.

In April he met with Dr. Cornell, secretary of the Medical Class of 1901. It fell to Joe, as president since 1897, and the secretary to make plans for the 55th class reunion on Alumni Day in June.

On May 23, 1956, The Pennsylvania Track Club held a dinner announcing the organization of a Track Hall of Fame. Joe was included as one of the first thirteen to be put on the list of Pennsylvania athletes. The next morning the *Philadelphia (Morning) Inquirer* reported[1]:

PENN NAMES 13 FOR ITS
HALL OF FAME IN TRACK

> Thirteen outstanding Penn trackmen were selected to the Pennsylvania Track Hall of Fame by the University Track Club last night at the annual dinner for the track and field squad in Houston Hall.
>
> The chosen group--all world record holders or Olympic champions--and first to be picked for the newly organized memorial, included...Dr. Josiah C. McCracken, Sr....[and] Horace Lee [who] was the first man in the world to run the 100 in ten seconds flat on May 26, 1877....
>
> Dr. McCracken, a Walter Camp all-American selection at guard in 1899, was the intercollegiate

shotput and hammer thrower champion in 1898-99. He also set a world record in the latter event in the 1900 Olympics.

Joe participated in the Rotary International meeting held in Philadelphia in June. One morning he approached three Chinese to introduce himself. Only one spoke English; when he saw Joe's card he exclaimed, "Oh, Dr. McCracken of St. Luke's Hospital, why you took out my appendix when I was a student at St. John's."

"Quite a pleasant surprise for us both," Joe wrote. "He had a camera and insisted on taking my picture to show our many mutual friends in Formosa."

With the help of the Christian Association staff he had sent questionnaires to some 87 of his former students. He enjoyed the answers coming in and was pleased to find that all had passed State Boards for license to practice and were doing more research and holding more assistant professorships than he had been aware of.

Also that fall he completed a project he had spent much time in planning--he gave each grandchild a $2000 fully paid up life insurance policy. December 19th he wrote the following Christmas note to his children:

This is just another wish and prayer that you all may have a very happy Christmas. I wish you all were going to be coming here to have Christmas with me. Since that cannot be possible I wish I could be in seven different places at the same time and since that is not possible I write you this letter to tell you all, 7 plus 21, how proud I am of each one and how thankful I am to God that he gave me your mother for a happy thirty-eight years together and permitted seven of you to give me twenty-one grandchildren each one of whom has already made a grand start and I expect with God's help each one will continue each day. To live a real Christian life is not easy. We need God's help so let us read our Bible daily and seek guidance from Him. God has blessed America and we Americans as no other nation are blessed. Let us not only be merry this week but let us also be most thankful to God for the Christ whose birthday we are celebrating.

On March 28th, 1957, the Alumni Varsity Club paid homage to the former Penn greats who represented the United States in Olympic Games, with a dinner at the Racquet Club with 250 diners present. About the same time he met with Fred Weede, Bruce Byall and George Benn--all four having known each other for over 65 years.

May 21st, taking Stewart and Joan with him, he accepted an invitation to all Olympians to be special guests to see "Wee Georgie," a fascinating movie of a little boy who decided he was going to be a strong man and how he grew up and developed until he was a hammer thrower at the Melbourne Olympics:

> When we were leaving I was asked to wait a minute for they wanted to take a picture and who did they bring out and line up with me but Karen Anderson, a javelin thrower in the 1956 Olympics in Australia. I had never met her and sorry to say knew nothing about her record. They took a very good picture of both of us headed "New and Old," Karen Anderson, 1956, and Josiah McCracken 1900. If I can get some of the photos, I'll send each of you one to show you what company I am keeping these days!

Summer with Joe and Barbara was as pleasant as usual except Joe felt there were not enough shuffleboard players so he might play as much as he desired, and he managed to force himself to say "no" to the tempting food and thus keep his weight down to 200 pounds.

Back in Philadelphia the four old friends from Kansas got together again:

> As I think you know, George Benn was the man from Sterling who came to Penn in 1894 and talked so much about me as a football player I came in 1896 and I talked so much about Fred Weed I got him to come in '97. He tells me that he landed in Philadelphia with about 21 dollars and that I got him into my boarding house and that when he went to register at Penn he was asked for ten dollars and did not have it, so he said he would go out and get it and came and borrowed the ten from me and said he paid it back as I am sure he must have although I did not remember loaning it to him. We four had much to talk about.

Joe's November 15th letter gives further expression to his interest in the life hereafter:

> Tomorrow I am expecting Ned and Anna Wood over to have lunch with me. Ned does not get around very much but he keeps busy circulating messages and experiences he has with those who have passed on to the next world. They with others have convinced me that there is contact with departed spirits and that those spirits know what we are doing here and influence and guide us more than we think. I too can believe that there is no death but immediately the spirit leaves the body and very soon is up there on a certain plane determined by what the person has done here while on earth.

While your mother was alive there was nothing we would not do for her but when her spirit left her, her lifeless body meant nothing to me and we had it cremated as I expect to be when my spirit leaves my body. It is a joy to know that there is no death and that the spirit immediately passes on to a place where it may be busy and happy beyond all earthly imagination. It is an exciting study and I believe an important revelation of God's way of doing things. If any of you are interested and wish to study the matter I'll be glad to assist in having information on the subject sent to you. Keep an open mind and do not be afraid for there are a lot of people who still think this is all bosh. More and more people are believing it is God's revelation.

For Christmas his children gave him his first TV set:

First of all I want to thank you each one of you for this wonderful Christmas present brought to me last week. You are most generous, kind and thoughtful. What a surprise! I never thought I would own one.

In May, at the age of 84, and after much "thinking and praying" he decided to fly out to visit his sister Daisy and his brother Gib, joining in the visit by his brother Lee's four daughters. The family reunion was held first in Tulsa where most of Daisy's children lived. The Lee's daughters took Daisy and Joe to stay at the Wellmans in Sterling to visit the family graves, Sterling College and friends. After a trip to Great Bend to see Gib, the nieces took their aunt and uncle to Kansas City to Daisy's daughter, Roberta's home, for another reunion. This was a happy experience for him.

At the June Board of Directors meeting of the Christian Association, it was announced that the Christian Association had just received from the estate of an old doctor friend of Joe's, a check for "Joe McCracken or his successor for the continuance of his work in China. The amount of the check was $36,650.18. Joe was speechless, but not for long. That brought the total China Fund up to over $80,000, and Joe exulted, "The China Committee will get busy and see where and how best at least the income can now be given for relief."

The night before Thanksgiving he wrote the family:

This being the day before Thanksgiving it seems to be quite in order to write you all and tell you how thankful I am to God for each one of my children and grandchildren. Seven children and all with their spouses and a total of 22 grandchildren [later 23] with no deformities or incurable diseases, and all doing well and active in a church of their choice for which

252

I am most thankful to God. We all here in America have so much for which to be thankful. I believe that America is the only country which has an official Thanksgiving Day. Let us not only be thankful tomorrow but every day and pray God daily for peace.

Joe remained active on the Board of Directors of the Christian Association. Much of the time at meetings was spent on discussing what should be done with all the accumulated China Medical funds. The Executive Secretary had recommended that some of the income be used to pay off several thousand dollars of the Christian Association's debts. Joe strongly opposed such a move; he could not help but believe that all the China fund during many years had been given for human relief, and the money should be used for that purpose somewhere in the Orient. Dr. T. R. Talbot, chairman of the large Institute for Cancer Research, was elected chairman of the Board and moved that there be further study of the problem.

Joe wrote:

There are now hundreds of foreign students in the University and the number is increasing very rapidly. We may decide to let the C.A. use some of the income of the China fund to extend its work among these students.

On June 16th he was invited to a luncheon meeting of the Executive Committee of the Christian Association to study further the use of the China Medical Fund. They came in with a different recommendation from the one they made at the last Board meeting. They now asked that amount be used for increasing the C.A. work with and for the rapidly increasing number of foreign students in the University. They pointed out that this fund was given to Joe to train leaders and now that conditions have changed and so many foreign students are at the University training to become leaders when they return home it was important to train them as Christian leaders. Joe heartily agreed and "all were happy," he reported.

Joe continued to live independently through the winter. On February 22, 1960 the family gathered at Stewart's to celebrate Joe's 86th birthday. Soon afterward, however, he suffered a severe stroke while getting ready to go to church one Sunday morning. Thus, his actual birthday, March 30th, was celebrated in the hospital with Martha and Margaret joining Ruth and Stewart there.

Before long he was able to move to Rest Haven to live. This nursing home, was chosen so the grandchildren could visit. It was so close that Stewart and Joan and Ruth and Al could drop in easily to see him.

He slipped from this world February 15, 1962, having built bridges that, through his students and family, will last for generations.

253

Joe's sons and daughters with him at his 86th birthday party in 1960. Seated next to him are Helen and Martha. Standing from left are: Ruth, Margaret, Joe, Stewart, and Elsie.

Joe and Helen's seven surviving children and their spouses, pictured in 1962. From the left: Allan and Ruth Cramer, Bill and Margaret Yates, Tyler and Helen Fulcher, Hogeland and Elsie Barcalow, Stewart and Joan McCracken, Calvin and Martha MacCracken, and Joe and Barbara McCracken.

CHAPTER TWENTY-TWO

REMEMBERING JOSIAH C. McCRACKEN

The Memorial Service for Dr. Josiah Calvin McCracken was held February 17, 1962 at 3 p.m. at the First Presbyterian Church in Philadelphia with Dr. J. Ernest Somerville presiding. Bishop William Roberts of the Episcopal Church, a friend for many years, gave the prayer. The address was given by Bishop Y. Y. Tsu and is quoted here in full:

We are gathered here together in God's House to pay our respect for a great medical missionary and friend of the Chinese people, and an outstanding alumnus of the University of Pennsylvania. It is my privilege, in behalf of our people, to express our deep-felt gratitude for the life and work of Dr. McCracken in China. He invested all the working years of his long and fruitful life for the advancement of medical education among our people. Literally he threw his lot with our people during one of the most crucial, tumultuous and, let us hope, ultimately creative periods in the nation's history.

When Dr. McCracken first went to Canton, South China in 1907, the country was passing through the throes of the closing years of the 300-year old imperial Manchu Dynasty that was soon to end in dissolution. When he finally retired from China in 1948, the Red Armies were sweeping down from the north, soon to seize the rein of government in the land. Between these two terminal dates, we went through the Revolution of 1911, led by Dr. Sun Yat-sen, who ushered in the Republic of China. This was followed by World War I which began in 1914, and followed by the Japanese invasion in 1937 and by World War II in 1941.

It was my privilege to have known Dr. McCracken and his work ever since his arrival in Shanghai in 1914. He had spent seven years in Canton as representative of the University of Pennsylvania Christian Association to found as their missionary project in China, a medical school. Soon he found his work handicapped by the scarcity of Chinese students adequately trained in the use of the English language so that they might be benefitted by the medical textbooks and medical journals available to them in the English language.

And so he cast his eyes for "greener fields" farther north. He decided that Shanghai was a more propitious site for the projected medical school. For even in those days, Shanghai had become an international metropolis, and English had become the prevailing "lingua franca." Besides around Shanghai was a cluster of high standard Christian colleges, like Nanking University, University of Shanghai, Hangchow Christian College, Soochow University and St. John's University, whence could be expected to come qualified candidates for the medical school. With the invitation of St. John's University and the support of the University of Pennsylvania constituency, "a marriage" was arranged, and the result was that the medical school of St. John's University became the "Pennsylvania Medical School" of St. John's University with Dr. McCracken as the first Dean of the School.

St. John's University had from very early days provided medical training, and there had come from the U.S.A. a succession of medical missionary personnel through the years. In 1880 came Dr. Henry Boone, brother of the first missionary for China, and he started regular medical classes for training medical personnel for the mission's hospital work. Dr. Boone retired in 1910. In 1899 came C. S. F. Lincoln, now in his nineties and still living and active. In 1900 Dr. William Jeffreys came to join the medical missionary staff in Shanghai. On his retirement from China, Dr. Jeffreys served as a voluntary city missioner of the Episcopal Church in Philadelphia; and his son, Rev. William H. Jeffreys, Jr., is now rector of St. Martin's Church, Radnor, Pa. There followed Dr. Augustine W. Tucker, in 1906, Dr. Ellen C. Fullerton in 1908, and Dr. Harold H. Morris of Philadelphia in 1911.

Dr. McCracken's deanship and the amalgamation of the resources of St. John's University and the supporters of the University of Pennsylvania Christian Association resulted in the raising of the standard of the medical school, so that in his 1918-1919 report, Dr. McCracken was able to report that the medical curriculum had become the full standard five year course, with the fifth year for internship. In his 1931 annual report, he was able to state that eight of the medical graduates of "Pennsylvania Medical School" were taking graduate work at the University of Pennsylvania; that to date 111 physicians had graduated, more than half of whom were working in mission hospitals, "enabling those hospitals to do a higher grade of work than otherwise possible." He mentioned two of the alumni who were deans of medical schools. One was Dr. F. C. Yen who after serving many years as dean of the Yale-in-China Medical School in Changsha, Hunan, had become the dean of the largest Chinese Government Medical School in the suburbs of Shanghai. The same Dr. Yen, now in his eighties, is still actively serving as superintendent of the famed Chung-shan Hospital of the Government in Shanghai. Another alumnus, Dr. Edgar T. H. Tsen, was head of the National Epidemic

Prevention Bureau in Peking, which prepared serums and vaccines for epidemic prevention in China and other Southeast Asian lands. Another alumnus, Dr. Voonping Yiu had done more than anyone else in building up a scientific terminology in the Chinese language. In the 1931 report, he added significantly, "A large percentage of our men before graduation became Christians. Many of them are staunch supporters of the Church and we believe that this adds to their contribution, as they reflect in their lives the influence of Christian love and service to their fellowmen."

When the Sino-Japanese War erupted in 1937, western residents, including Americans in Shanghai, were able to carry on as before except for wartime restrictions as they were neutrals before Pearl Harbor. So it was that the opportunity arose for Dr. McCracken and his colleagues to organize a refugee hospital to minister to the tens of thousands of refugees that had flocked into the International Settlement from the countryside around Shanghai and from inland towns and cities. As many as 300 in-patients were accommodated. The nursing staff came from evacuated mission hospitals and nursing schools of inland cities; the beds and equipment came from a mission school nearby that had to close down its dormitory. Food and medical supplies came from the American Red Cross. Dr. McCracken had made such a reputation for himself in Shanghai for honest and honorable dealings that he found a ready response in the pleas for financial aid. Dr. McCracken became the superintendent of the hospital and the chief physician, and his "right-hand man" was Miss Anne Lamberton as business manager of the hospital.

When it was found that it was necessary to provide accommodation for the 3rd and 4th year medical students in the refugee hospital, Dr. McCracken had added on him the duties of dean for the students, and on Miss Lamberton the duties of the school registrar. They were a devoted and efficient team running the hospital and the school in those turbulent war years. In spite of the difficulties of the situation, there was an unusual compensation. Those teaching in the wards found unequalled opportunities for practical demonstrations in that one hospital for the refugees furnished them with almost every kind of disease known in China. The medical students of those years had therefore a better training in diagnosis than those in any other years.

After Pearl Harbor, exchange of civilian war prisoners was arranged between America and Japan, and the McCrackens were returned to America in 1942. Right after the close of World War II, Dr. McCracken was again induced to return to

China on the pleading of his former colleagues and students to assist in the work in an advisory capacity. Even though he was no longer young and was not in good health. It was an advantage to the medical school simply to have Dr. McCracken in the city as his prestige was so great not only among the medical profession but also throughout the whole community. His health broke down, however, which necessitated his retiring altogether from the field. Before his departure he was nearly killed again (by kindness) by the dinners and feasts with which all his friends feted him.

He has however by no means withdrawn from the work for the Chinese. He has been the chief instrument in helping many of his former students to get to America in order to take up graduate study, and in aiding those who are staying in this country, often against their will, to obtain permission to take examinations which will enable them to practice here. A number of Chinese graduates of St. John's are now in positions of responsibility in hospitals in various sections of America. He had kept up until his last illness personal correspondence with over one hundred of his former students in America. Dr. McCracken also took an active interest in the work of the Chinese Christian church and Center in Philadelphia, of which he was for a number of years trustee and of which the minister was an old friend of Canton days, Dr. Yam-tong Hoh.

Recalling the wonderful record of Dr. McCracken's service in China for a people not his own and his dedication to the cause of medical education [that] he felt he was called to serve, one would want to know the motivation of his life, or to use the language of the street, what made Dr. McCracken tick? The answer must be his Christian faith, the rich heritage that had been passed on to him by his parents, Isaac and Ellen McCracken, in years of youth spent on the wide plains of Kansas. This verse in the beautiful hymn may well describe the faith that had activated his whole life:

> *Master, work beside me*
> *In the shining sun*
> *Gently guide Thy servant*
> *Till the work be done.*

When he felt the end of his journey near, it must have been a source of great satisfaction to realize that he had spent the years of his life unselfishly for the well being of his fellow man and that his labors had borne fruit in the lives of his many students who had come under his instruction and the influence of his personality. As he quietly slipped away and passed on into the Beyond, we could almost hear him humming the closing stanza of the hymn:

Birds are winging homeward,
Sun and shadow cease;
Saviour, take my spirit
To Thy perfect peace.

The printed program for the Annual Meeting of the University Settlements conference on May 14, 1962, included a dedication by Mr. Dana G. How, Secretary:

Dedicated to Dr. Josiah C. McCracken, who for over sixty years intimately identified with the Christian Association of the University of Pennsylvania, moved into life's new adventure on Thursday, February 15,1962 at the age of 87 years. His rich, creative living began immediately with his enrollment at the University in 1896. Not only was he a member of the All-American Football Teams of 1899 and 1900 and captain and star hammer thrower of the Track Team, but he was also elected President of the Christian Association in his senior year.

One afternoon at the close of team practice, he and a teammate walked across South Street Bridge and found the boys "building forts in preparation for the Spanish-American War." He returned to the Christian Association and told Tom Evans, then general Secretary, that "something must be done for those lads; everything is against them." As a result of Joe McCracken's deep concern, the Christian Association rented a property in the 26th and Lombard Street area, where University men provided a volunteer program out of which came in 1907 the establishment of University Settlement House at 26th and Lombard Streets. This service project, instigated in its initial stage by Joe McCracken, gradually expanded until the Christian Association was operating two other settlements and two summer camps for disadvantaged youth of Philadelphia.

Following Dr. McCracken's graduation from the Medical School of the University in 1901 and upon completion of his internship, the Christian Association urged him to survey the medical needs of China in 1906. This general missionary assignment introduced Dr. McCracken to his over forty years of medical service; for the first few years in Canton and then in Shanghai were he helped to organize at St. John's University, a Department of Medicine which he served as Dean and Professor of Surgery. Over 300 Chinese learned Western medicine from this well equipped and devoted teacher. With the intrusion of the Communists in 1948, Dr. McCracken had to leave China, hopeful that some of the men he trained would carry on. In the recent years he has maintained a significant relationship with many of his Chinese doctors who settled in this country.

This limited record of an unlimited life presents the story of what happened to a Pennsylvania man whose life was spent under the leadership of his Heavenly Father in expressing to his utmost his love for his fellow   man.

The Board of Directors of the Christian Association adopted the following Resolution at its meeting May 29th:

> WHEREAS, Almighty God, by His grace, has called to Himself, Josiah Calvin McCracken, who has perfectly   symbolized the mission of the Christian Association by his life of service; who was three times President of the Association; cofounder of the Association's Settlement work; was a representative of "Pennsylvania in China" as surgeon, professor and administrator of University Medical School of Canton and Pennsylvania Medical School of St. John's University in Shanghai; and who, throughout his work brought honor to the University and the Christian Association as a dedicated physician and active churchman; who became friend of the Chinese people, a constant witness to his Lord Jesus Christ, and the inspiration of young students for Christian service:
>
> THEREFORE, be it RESOLVED by the Board of Directors of the Christian Association of the University, that we bear testimony to his exceptional ability, his faithful service and his deep Christian commitment; and to offer to his family our sincere sympathy;
>
> BE IT FURTHER RESOLVED, that a copy of this RESOLUTION be presented to the family of our former colleague, and to the Trustees of the University of Pennsylvania, and that it be   entered upon the Minutes of this Association.

There were many letters of condolence, but perhaps this one from Ah Hin (formally, Fung Hin Lin Wang), the young Chinese woman whom Joe and Helen had helped go to America for college soon after they went to Canton, says it best. It was addressed to Stewart:

> Mrs. Y. Y. Tsu has just written me about your wonderful father's passing and the fine memorial service you had for him. I am very sorry I did not know of it in time to attend it. He and your mother were certainly two of the greatest missionaries of that generation. Hundreds of men and women of

260

China had received help and inspiration from them. I was one of those. I was helped by them in Canton, China at the Canton Christian College in 1905-1908. Their interest and help followed me to this country and Wellesley. We were friends for the rest of our lives....

His contribution to the training of Chinese doctors will go down in history as an unusual record and his and your mother's inspiration to us Chinese men and women has great and lasting influence. As a recipient of this wonderful help and inspiration I want to take this opportunity to make it known to you and your brother and sisters.

May God bless you all abundantly.

Joe with one of his "Chinese grandchildren," the grand-daughter of one of his St. John's students

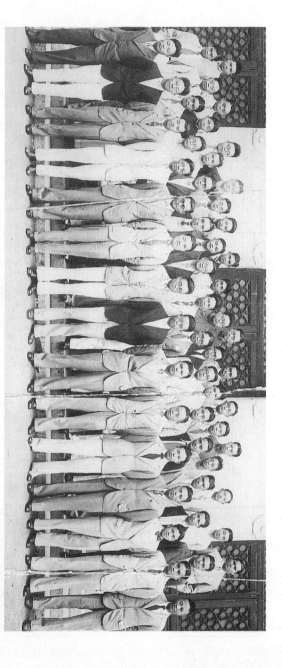

Group picture of the classes of 1940 to 1943 of the Medical School of St. John's University (taken in mid-1940). From left to right:
Back row: Luke Tsai, Chi Tai Wei, Chi Nai Ping, Wu Tuh Ping, Paul Lee, Huang Tse Keh, Lin Kang Chuan, Kao Yu, Lew Heng Ming, Chen Sui Heng, Jui Hong Lih, Liao Yung Lien, Chang Kwang Han, Tseu Kia Wei, Han Sing Ying, Nyi Zung Ching, Yang Wei Sing, Kuh Ming Wei, Chow Lien Ji, Lee Shing Loh, Ho Shang Chi, Chen Hsi Sheng.
Middle row: Chen Ching Hsiang, Chow Siao Dah, Tong Yong Hsi, Yui Ching Nien, Lin Ping Chuan, Wang Zau Ung, Ling Chun Chieh, Daung Sung Yuan, Doo Kyi Yoong, Fan Chi Chun, Voong Zoo Moo, Jui Hong Jih, Ho Loh Tsi, Chu Ruh I, Ho Chu Huan, Chen Yen Yu, King K Ting, Tong Yam Sam, Tsai Poh Ioen, Chang Suan, Chen Cheng, Tung Fong Chung.
Front row: Chen Liang Hsiang, Ho Yong Chao, Hwang Kao Hsi, Chien Tien Fu, Liang Ching Hua, Kwang Lung Hsun, Tsu Yu Mien, Chai Hsiang Chien, Tsang Lien Kwei, C. C. Morris II, Yu Kan Tsou, Tai Kwei Yoong, Hu Yuin Sien, Kwoh Hsai, Chang Hui Tseng, Tsang Tuh Hsing, Chow Ping Ling, Liu Shuan Yuen.

GRADUATES OF THE MEDICAL SCHOOL OF ST. JOHN'S UNIVERSITY[1,2] 1901-1950[3]

Class of 1901

Kyoong, M. U.
Siao, T. I. M.
Tso, K. S. Peter
Woo, N. Z.

Class of 1903

Day, Eli
Tyau, E. S.
Yen, F. C.
Yang, Z. L.

Class of 1907

Dzau, S. Y.
Li, T. M.
New, W. L.
Yui, C. V.

Class of 1909

Chen, H. C.
Hyui, S. Z. (Hyui Soong
  Zien)
Koo, U. K.
Wong, P. C.
Woo, T. H.

Class of 1911

Chen, Y. N.
Li, T. L.
Wong, F. S.

Class of 1914

Char, George Y.

Kau, Edward Y.
Shen, S. J.
Tsen, Edgar T. H.
Woo, C. Y.

Class of 1916

Liau, C. C.
Woo, L. S.

Class of 1919

Han, L. C. Owen
Hsu, W. Imin
Ling, C. Y.
Toong, S. K. (F. S. K.
  Toong)
Toong, Zee Zau
Yui, K. T.
Zung, C. H.

Class of 1920

Chen, Ji
Voong, K. K.
Yau, Shou Gin (S. Y. Yau
  or Bernard S. G. Yau)
Young, Kenneth B.
Zau, I. Y.
Zee, Harvey N.

Class of 1922

Chen, H. T.
Hsu, J. C.
Hsu, K. L.
Ling, L. C.
Ling, S. M.
Loh, C. C.

263

Sung, K. S.
Sung, L. K.
Tai, J. T.
Ting, S. K.
Tseng, S. W.
Wong, S. D.
Zau, F. D.

Class of 1923

Chiang, S. F.
Feng, Nelson B. H.
Nyi, Z. Z.
Wong, Amos I. H.
Wong, V. Y.
Zung, Z. B.

Class of 1924

Faung, K. S.
Kau, L. S.
Tsang, M. L. (M. L.
    Chang)
Tyau, C. H.
Wong, I. K.

Class of 1926

Chen, P. T.
Chen, T. M.
Cheng, C. C.
Foong, Z. U.
Liu, D. P.
Lieu, John K. W.
Sun, P. S.
Tsoong, P. T.
Wong, C. L.

Class of 1928

Chang, L. C.
Chen, Teh
Chen Hsi Teh
Chow Chen
Khoong, Hsien Jih
Li, She Hsun

Liu, Teh Chi
Soong, Te En (C. A. Sung)
Tan, K. L.
Tansinsin, Manuel
Ting, Winston K.
Wen, Kan Chen
Yui, C. H.

Class of 1929

Chen, Jui Yung (Joseph Y.
    Cheng)
Chen, Wen Ching
Ch'i, Ta Chih
Chiang, Wei Lung
Chin, Nai Yi
Ho, Wayne
Kau, Z. M.
Kwan, Chien An
Ling, Z. Z. (O. S. Ling)
Moo, J. F.
Po, Chuan I
Su, Yen Chen
Tsang, Foh Sing
Tsha, Joong Zu (C. Chay
    Vizcaera)

Class of 1930

Chang, Louis W. S.
Chen, Hsiang Chung
Cheng, Chien Shih
Hsu, Piao Nan
Ing, Edmund T. K.
Jen, Yen Yung
Kam, Thoo Kwe (Kam Teh
    Ming or Edwin T. K.
    Kam)
Kwan, Li ng Wei
Kiu, S. H.
Sun, Chih Jung (C. Jung
    Sun)
Waung, Tsung Teh
Yang, Ming Ting
Yang, Pao An
Zung, Sing Yen

Class of 1931

Bousfield, Cyril

Class of 1932

Chung, P. M.

Class of 1934

Chen, Vesin (Vincent V. Chen)
Chiu, Shao Ling
Howe, Yah Ming
Hsia, G. Tshaung
Hsu, Jen Hui
Huang, Ming Sing
Kwei, No Tsung
Lieu, Vi Tuh (Vi-Tuh Lieu)
Pan, Joseph
Shan, Chin Yen
Ting, Zau Sing
Tsu, Pao Lieu (Arthur P. L. Tsu)
Tyau, Yu Dau (Christie Tyau)
Waung, Kyuin Kaung
Wu, Chien
Zee, Zoong Ung
Zung, Tsoong Ben

Class of 1935

Chang, Yu Shih
Chen, Hsiao Ren
Ho, Si Hwei
Hwang, Ming Nie
Kwan, Yoh Loo
Kwauk, Dick
Lim, Yang Tsze
Siao, Peh Suang
Tsao, Foh Kong
Tsao, Yu Feng
Woo, Lih Tuh (David Woo)

Yang, Yu Wen (Clifford Yang)
Yung, Yau Lung

Class of 1936

Ching, George
Chow, Zong Kong
Dao, Chin
Lao, Siang Bing
Li, Tien Hsiang (Lewis Loo-Yi Li)
Ling Tsung Liang
Ling, Wong (Lum Ding Wong)
Ting, Sui Tong
Wong, Richard

Class of 1937

Chan, Bean Chye
Chao, Jung
Chen, Shih Chang
Hung, Henry
Lee, Edmund
Li, Loo Yi
Li, Yung Seng
Ma, An Chuen
Mao, Chun Yeu
Pan, Tsu Ying
Shen, Shu Chu
Tien, Shueh Ping
Tsou, Szu Tai
Wang, Chi Ming
Wong, Gien Yu
Yap, Raymond

Class of 1938

Chen, Pang Hui
Chen, Paung Hsien
Hsu, Lung Chang
Kuo, Pei Teh (Peter Kuo)
Lee, Frank Shin
Lee, Otis Jr.

Lieu, S. Jang
Loh, Ping Kaung
Tsai, Toong Faung
Waung, Yoong Kwaung
Yui, Tsing Kyi

Class of 1939

Chang, Shih Jung
Chen, Cheng
Chen, Samuel
Chien, Chun Shun
Davis, Richard
Ho, Chi Hung
Hsu, Tseng Kwang
Li, Hsien Peng
Li, Kya Kung
McCracken, Mary
Miao, Chi Yan (Chi-Hsien
    Miao)
Tai, Shih Ming
Tan, Pia Chu
Toong, Dau Tseu
Tsai, Shih Shuan
Tyau, Henry
Woo, Khoo Hyung
Yuan, Sung Ling

Class of 1940

Chai, Hsiang Chien
Chen, Hsi Shen
Chen, Yen Yu
Chien, Tien Fu
Chow, Ping Ling
Chu, Ruh I
Ho, Loh Tze
Ho, Yong Chao
Huang, Kao Hsi
Jui, Hong Jih
Lin, Ping Chuan
Nyi, Zung Ching
Tsang, Lien Kwei (John L.
    K. Tsang)
Tyau, Steven
Woong, Stephen S. M.

Woo, Zung-Pah
Yu, Ching Nien

Class of 1941

Chang, Suan
Cheng, Chung (Lawrence
    C. Chen)
Chow, Lien Ji
Han, Sing Ying
Ho, Chu Huan
Ho, Shang Chih (S. Z. Ho)
Kao, Yu
King, K Ting
Kuh, Ming Wei
Kwang, Lun Hsun
Lin, Kang Chuan (Francis
    Lum)
Liu, Shwen Yuen
Tong, Yan Sum
Tsai, Poh Ioen
Tung, Fong Chung
Yang, Wei Sing (Vincent
    Yang)

Class of 1942

Chen, Liang Hsiang
    (Andrew Chen)
Chow, Sio Dah
Chee, Nai Ping (Chester
    Zee)
Daung, Sung Yuan
    (Samuel S. Daun)
Doo, Kyi Yoong (Gerald
    K. Doo)
Fan, Chi Chen (Quincey C.
    Fan)
Hu, Ku Jien
Huang, Tsu Ke (Paul
    Huang)
Lee, Shing Loh
Lew, Heng Ming
Liang, Ching Hua
Ling, Ji Toong
Tong, Yung Hsi

Tsai, Shu Ling (Luke Tsai)
Tseu, Kya Wei
Tsu, Yu Mien
Wong, Edward
Wu, Tuh Ping
Yu, Kan Tseu

Class of 1943

Chang, Hwei Chen
Chang, Kwang Han
    (Ronald K. H. Chang)
Chang, Teh Hsing
Chen, Ching Hsiang
    (Calvin H. Chen)
Chi, Tai Wei (David T. W.
    Chi)
Chung, Yung Ken
Feng, Pao Ch'un
Hsia, Kwoh
Hu, Yuin Sien (Y. S. Irene
    Chang)
Jui, Hong Lih
Koo, Siang Hua (Tass S.
    Koo)
Kwok, Shew Nan (Francis
    Kwok)
Lee, Paul
Liao, Yung Lien
Ling, Tsun Chieh
Sun, Keh Ming
Tai, Kwe Yoong
Waung, Zau Ung (Thomas
    C. H. Huang)
Young, Cheong Ken (C. K.
    Yang)

Class of 1944

Chang, Chu Huai
Chang, Ju Wen
Chang, Li Chu
Chang, Pei Chu
Chen, Chin
Chen, Ping Mei
Chu, Philip

Feng, Tseng You
Howe, Mo Lin
Hu, Yu Ming (yu Min
    Pien)
Huang, David Hong Jen
Huang, Ming Zai
Jea, Shwu Miin
Kao, Wei Zu
Lee, Tien Hsi
Li, Kuo Pan
Li, Kuo Wei
Li, Tsung Ying
Lin, Shun Hua
Liu, Chen Nan
Lu, Te Chuan (Abraham T.
    C. Lu)
Ma, Lien Sheng
Nicolsky-Dronnikoff, Alla
Sun, Chin Yun (Lucille
    Sun)
Tang, Ti
Wu, Hsien Chen
Wu, Shuenn Jeou
Yue, Wen Yao

Class of 1945

Chang, Chi (Charles C.
    Chang)
Chang, Ming
Chang, Siang Yuin
Chao, Jen Hung (John Jen-
    Hung Chao)
Chen, Tso Wu
Chiang, Shao Chi
Chiang, Yun Ling
Chou, Hsi Keng (C. K.
    Chou)
Chow, Shu Liang (Mildred
    S. L. Chow)
Chu, Chin Sheng (johnson
    J. Chu)
Dao, Ling Yuan (Thomas
    L. Y. Dao)
Hsiang, Ning Hsuan
Hsu, Chang Te

267

Hu, Siu Yuan
Huang, Liang Chuan
Kao, Wei Yu (Eugene W. Y. Kao)
Katznelson, Daniel
Kuh, Sing Zung
Kuo, Pang Fu (Paul P. F. Kuo)
Li, Fook Kuen
Li, Sing Hsiang
Li, Tsi Yuen
Lin, Cheng Shan
Ling, Li Lih (Lilie L. Ling)
Ling, Tak Hong (David Ling)
Liu, Shu Fang
Loh, Tse Lan
Lu, Ching Shen
Ma, Ming Chio
May, Chin Liang
Shen, Tseng Yung (Jerome Tseng-Yung Shen)
Sun, Chuan Han
Teng, Hsi Ching
Tung, Yung Chiao
Wang, I Shan (Stephen I. S. Wang)
Wang, Yueh Chin
Wong, Swee Chee
Yang, Chuan Ying (Dorothy C. Y. Yang)
Yang, Shao Te
Yang, Te Fang
Yu, Shih To

Class of 1946

Chang, Nan
Chang, Shih Man (Robert Chang)
Chao, Wei Jen (Wayland Chao)
Chen, Hsi Sun
Chen, Mai Pu (Mabel M. P. Chen)
Chen, Peter

Chen, Wei Hsiu
Chiang, Hung Yu
Chin, Yun Tsung
Chou, Chia Lin
Chou, Hsiang Sheng (Johnson H. Chow)
Chow, Sophie
Chu, Jen Chu (John Jen-Chu Chu)
Han, Kai Tai (David Han)
Hsieh, Chia Lu
Katznelson, Alexander
Kuo, Chih Te (John C. Kuo)
Lee, Zu Gno
Lin, Mao Chih
Ouyang, Hsiao Chen
Sun, Chen Hwa (David C. H. Sun)
Sun, Chen Tung
Tyau, Yu Kung (Victor T. K. Tyau)
Waung, Hwei Kwaung
Wong, Helen (Mrs. Ling)
Wu, Chien Fen
Wu, Shou I

Class of 1947 (January)

Throop, Edward

Class of 1947

Chang, Fu Chieh (Francis F. C. Chang)
Chang, Nai Cheng
Chang, Wen Ching (Emilie Chung)
Chi, I Ken
Chiu, Fu Hsi
Chou, En Hung
Chou, Shan Man
Chung, Hsin Sun
Fu, Fu Yan
Huang, Ku Liang
Kwong, Yao Ling

Lee, Chan Hoo
Li, Chuan Hsiang (Chuan-Hsiang Lee)
Ling, Charles L. S.[4]
Liu, Chien[4]
Pu, Pin Hsiu
Shen, Chia Chi (George Shen)
Shen, Hsun Ling (Mary Anna Sung Hsi)
Wang, Chiao Chi (George Wang)
Wu, Wen Yen
Yao, Chuan Wen
Yuan, Hsun Piao (Robert H. P. Yuan)

Class of 1948

Chao, Chih I
Chen, Jen Ti (John T. Chen)
Cheng, Chi Hsuan
Cheng, San Hsi (Samuel H. Cheng)
Chien, Ho Ying (Sophia Ho-Ying Chang)
Chiu, Chu Ping (Susan C. P. Chiu)
Chou, Chia Hsiu
Chou, Te Chuan (Theodore T. C. Chou)
Chuang, Hsin I
Chuang, I Sheng
Fan, Tu
Hsiao, Yung Wei
Hsu, Te Lung
Hsu, Yu (Irene Hsu)
Hua, Yu
Li, Chi Hao (Edwin Chi-Hao Lee)
Li, Kan Lin
Lu, Cheng Wei
Lu, Chi Hsin
Mih, Alexander W. S.
Pan, Yen Jo

Shao, Hung Hsun
Teng, Wen Man
Wang, Chung Heng (Herbert Chung-Heng Wang)
Wang, Nien Tsu (Samuel Nien-Tsu Wang)
Wu, Mang Chiung
Yao, Hao (William H. Yao)
Yeh, Chia Fu
Yuan, Li Lu (Lilu Yuen)

Class of 1949

Chai, Pen Fu
Chi, Pei Fen
Chou, Shelley N.
Fang, Chao Hung (Harry Fang)
Feng, Cho Jung
Hou, Chi Shou
Hsiao, Pi Lien
Hsu, Hsiao Hsi
Hsueh, Pei
Hua, Chia Tseng
Hu, Rou Chen
Ko, Chun Yun
Liang, Shao Fu (Daniel S. Liang)
Liu, Ti Lin
Pan, Chia Hsiang
Pan, Shui Peng
Shen, Pao Lo
Tang, Liang Chih
Tang, Yen (Rosie Y. Pan)
Tsai, Nai Chen (Nai Shun Choy)
Wang, Mei Hsien
Wang, Sheng Wu
Wang, Shih Kan (John Shih-Kan Wang)
Wu, En Hsien
Yiu, Kuo Shui
Yu, Yen I

Class of 1950

Chen, Hsun
Cheng, Tsung O
Chi, Wei Liang
Chien, Chao E
Chien, I Chien
Chou, Chih Lung
Chou, Kuang Yu (Guang-
    Yu Zhou)
Han, Mei Ling
Hsia, Szu Yu
Hsu, Chia Yu
Ku, Chen Sheng
Kuo, Te Wen
Li, Kung Sung
Li, Te Hsing
Lin, Pao Min (Paul M. Lin)
Lu, Kuo Hua (Lincoln K.
    W. Luke)
Lu, Pei Chung (Henry Bei-
    Chung Low)
Shen, Tsung Jen
Shen, Yu
Wang, Hsiu Nan
Wang, Tao Hsin
Yang, Pei Chen (Betty B.
    C. Yang)
Yang, Tsun Hsing
Yen, Chun Hsiu
Yu, Chung Kang

Notes

Chapter 1

1. Through the research of Constable MacCracken, the son of a second cousin of Joe's, much is known of Joe's family history [See *The Descendants of John McCracken, Gateway Press, Inc., Baltimore, 1979; Library of Congress 79-91257*]. John McCracken, Joe's great grandfather, was the son of Henry McCracken and Abigail Black. (This may well be the same Henry McCracken who signed the Pine Creek Declaration of Independence on July 4, 1776 and, while serving in the Northumberland Militia, was later killed by Indians on September 24, 1780.) Little is known of John until he became a landowner in Liberty (Union) Township, Butler County, Ohio, in 1805, by which time he had married Martha Wilson and had three children, including Samuel Wilson (Joe's grandfather), who was born March 14, 1801 near Cincinnati, Ohio.

In 1822-23, John traded his land for unimproved land belonging to a Judge Burnet in Greene County. So John McCracken with his three sons, Samuel Wilson, John Steele and James Black, hewed a home out of the wilderness in Beaver Creek Township just west of Xenia, Ohio. John McCracken deeded a quarter-section to each of his sons. After considering their situation, John Steele and Samuel Wilson left these quarter-sections to get their education at Miami University: "My older brother (Samuel Wilson), and I (John Steele) sat there upon a fence which we had builded and debated whether we could not then afford to leave farming, begin to prepare ourselves for the college course of four years and the Theological Seminary in order to be ministers according to the ordinary Presbyterian requirements. We then and there declared to one another that we would make the attempt."

According to the alumni records of the University of Miami, Ohio, Joe's grandfather, Samuel, graduated with distinction with the Class of 1831. Upon graduation, he accepted an appointment as Professor of Mathematics at Maryville College in Tennessee before returning to Miami University with a similar appointment in 1832. There he received his Master's Degree in 1836 and went on to also serve as Professor of Ancient Languages from 1835 to 1837. However, other interests were drawing him. For the school year 1833-34 he took leave to study theology at Allegheny Seminary in Allegheny, Pennsylvania. While continuing as Professor at the University of Miami, he was licensed by the First Presbytery of Ohio on April 21, 1835 and ordained by the same group April 30, 1836. He was instrumental in the formation of the Associate Reformed (Presbyterian) Church at Oxford and held the pastorate there from 1835 to 1840. In 1840, he resigned his professorship and moved six miles north of Oxford to Morning Sun, Ohio, where he served as pastor of the Hopewell Church until his death on September 10, 1859.

Samuel's first wife was Catherine E. Monfort, daughter of Rev. Peter Monfort, who married them on October 13, 1830. Before her death of cholera on July 17, 1849, they had five children:

1. John Calvin, who was born January 19, 1833, and was variously a

teacher, merchant, and farmer in Oxford and Urbana, until his
death in 1922.

2. Isaac Lawrence, who was born July 18, 1836, and was the father of
Joe McCracken. He died in 1908 in Sterling, Kansas.

3. Catherine E., who died as a child on January 10, 1844.

4. Samuel Monfort who was born in 1842 and died in August 1864 of
wounds inflicted while serving in General Sherman's march
through Georgia.

5. Charlotte, who was born in 1844, graduated from Oxford (Ohio)
College, and married William J. Craig, a Scottish immigrant, in
May of 1870. They lived in Oxford and had four children before
her death in 1893.

Two years after Catherine's death, Samuel married Mary Leech on June 24,
1851 in Dunlapsville, Indiana, and they had three children (Joseph, Mary, and
Laura) before he died of typhoid fever September 10, 1859. The family continued to live in Morning Sun until twenty years after Samuel's death, when they
moved to Alabama.

On October 29, 1857, Joe's father, Isaac, married Ellen Watson Stewart,
who had been born December 9, 1835. They lived briefly in Spring Grove, Il-
linois where their first child, Alla Mary, was born October 27, 1858, before
they returned to Morning Sun, Ohio. Here Frank was born December 3, 1860.
On August 18, 1862, at the age of 26, Isaac enlisted and was mustered into the
93rd Ohio Voluntary Infantry at Dayton, Ohio. On August 22, 1862, he departed for service, leaving behind his pregnant wife, a four-year old daughter
and their baby son, who died only a month before daughter Myrta Catherine
was born March 27, 1863.

Reports of Isaac's service reveal that he became sick after several months
and spent the rest of the time as patient and then nurse in hospitals. He was
transferred to the Veterans Reserve Corps on August 31, 1863; however, he
was not mustered out until June of 1865. He had given his occupation as
butcher on the enlistment papers, but family records also speak of him as a
merchant, miller, farmer, and bricklayer.

After his return to Morning Sun, the couple had three more children:
Charles Samuel on April 27, 1866, Lee Stewart on January 10, 1869, and Gilbert Gordon October 19, 1871. Isaac and his wife moved south in 1872 to near
Fayetteville in Lincoln County, Tennessee. There Josiah Calvin (Joe) was
born March 30, 1874 and Daisy Ellen on November 21, 1878. For part of
these years, Joe's mother taught school in the first schoolhouse in the south
with glass windows; Isaac operated a grist mill. There also, Isaac and Ellen's
eldest daughter, Alla Mary, married David Ramsey August 15, 1878.

Chapter 2

1. For a more detailed story of Penn football, see *Fight on Pennsylvania: A Century of Red and Blue Football* prepared by Dan Rottenberg in 1985 for the
Trustees of the University of Pennsylvania.

Notes

2. In *Quest for Gold: The Encyclopedia of American Olympians* by Bill Mallon and Ian Buchanan with Jeffrey Tishman [Leisure Press (now Human Kinetics Publishers), 597 Fifth Avenue, New York, NY 10017, 1984] the citation reads:

> B. 30 MAR 1874. D. 15 FEB 1962 Chestnut Hill, PA. Silver: 1900 Shot Put; Bronze: 1900 Hammer Throw. Josiah McCracken was a useful all-round performer in the weight events, taking the shot/hammer double at the IC4A championships in 1898 and 1899. By international standards he was perhaps a better performer in the hammer and his career best of 153'-8" in 1898 ranked him second in the world that year.
>
> Despite his Olympic successes, track & field was only a secondary sport for McCracken as, at Penn, he was better known as a footballer and was on Walter Camp's All-American team in 1899. The silver medalist in the 1900 Olympic hammer throw, Truxton Hare, was also an All-American football player at Penn and in was only the Irish immigrant John Flanagan who prevented the two Penn footballers from taking top Olympic honors at Paris.
>
> McCracken earned an M.D. degree from Penn and later served as a medical missionary in China for 50 years.

Chapter 3

1. Helen's mother was the daughter of Ephraim Delano Briggs and Elizabeth Doan Pelton. The Peltons and Doans held original grants in the Western Reserve.

2. There are many relatives of the Newphers in the Lancaster area of Pennsylvania.

3. A picture of Helen Briggs as a young woman indicates she conducted the chorus in the Old Morley Chapel at Lake Erie College. She published a book *Sacred Songs for Little Singers* for use in primary Sabbath schools with many hymns and adaptations of music. This book, published in 1883, has a frontispiece etching of her two nieces and nephew.

4. Sophia Strong Taylor was a friend of the Newphers and of Helen Briggs. She was a generous financial supporter for many years. At one point she promised to shoe Helen's children. Twice a year while in China, Helen drew outlines around her children's feet, sent the drawings off to Ohio, and two pairs of shoes for each of the eight children arrived back in Shanghai. Mrs. Taylor's photograph had a place of honor on the mantelpiece in China.

Chapter 6

1. A book, *The Seed of the Church in China*, written by his granddaughter, Muriel Boone, tells of the life and mission of Dr. Henry Boone.

2. For more information on Dr. Henry Noble MacCracken, Joe's second cousin, founder of the American Junior Red Cross, and president of Vassar College, see *Bridges to the World: Henry Noble MacCracken and Vassar College* by Elizabeth A. Douglas, College Avenue Press (SAN: 298-2838), Clinton Corners, New York, 1994 (Library of Congress Catalog Card Number 94-31965).

Chapter 8

1. Helen's mother died November 4, 1921, soon after sending Helen the check.

Chapter 10

1. Helen had selected black pongee material to make bloomers and middy blouses with white ties for the girls so that the need to do laundry would be cut down.

Chapter 11

1. Helen, Jr. and Margaret had secured jobs for the summer of 1927 at Pocono Lake Preserve. Cousin Lawrence Ramsey, in Stroudsburg, Pennsylvania, helped the girls purchase a 1914 Model Ford to use in getting back to college. Margaret could and did drive, and Helen, Jr. cranked it up!

Chapter 21

1. Reprinted with permission from *The Philadelphia Inquirer.*

Appendix

1. For consistency and where information is available, the names are given using English notation, with last names followed by a comma, and ordered alphabetically. For those for whom last name cannot be identified, the names are left as they were on a class listing from about 1950. Where known, names used after graduation are also given. Our apologies for any errors.

2. For information on the medical graduates of St. John's University, please contact the St. John's Medical Alumni Association: Dr. Jen-Hung Chao, 279 W. Van Buren St., Elmhurst IL 60126 is the current president (spring 1995). This alumni association was founded in 1959. For information on other graduates of St. John's, contact the St. John's University (Shanghai) Alumni Association in North America. In the eastern United States, they may be contacted at 12A Seabro Avenue, N. Amityville NY 11701, Tel. (516) 842-1907.

Notes

3. In 1950, the Medical School of St. John's was taken over by the Communist government. The medical school was combined with two other medical schools and named the No. 2 Medical College. Some of the students at St. John's in 1950 graduated from this combined medical college. For information on graduates after 1950, contact the St. John's Alumni Association of North America; see note 2.

4. These graduates were transfers from Western Union Medical School in Chengtu, Szechwan, China.

Picture Credits

1. The Day Missions Library and Special Collections section of the Divinity School Library of Yale University (Martha L. Smalley, curator) provided the pictures of the University Medical School (page 22), the McCracken family (page 30), St. John's University (pages 48 and 212), the reception with U. S. Navy nurses (page 234), and the classes of 1940-43 at St. John's (page 262).

2. The University of Pennsylvania Archives and Record Center (Kaiyi Chen; Mark Frazier Lloyd, director) provided the picture of the awarding of the honorary degree (page 98).

3. R. M. Vanderberg provided the picture of the attack on Shanghai (page 148).

4. Other pictures are from the family collections and albums.

Information for Ordering

Mission to Shanghai is available from:

Tiffin Press
P. O. Box 1786
New London, NH 03257
United States of America

In your order, please indicate:

Number of copies of **Mission to Shanghai** desired: _____

Name: _____

Address: _____

City: _____

State: _____ Mail Code: _____

Country: _____

Telephone (for express mail delivery): _____

Please include a check or money order for $12.95 in U. S. currency for each book ordered; credit card orders cannot be accepted. New Hampshire has no sales tax to be added to the cost of the book.

Please add $2.00 for postage and handling for each book ordered for addresses within North America and for surface mail overseas; for express mail in the United States or for air shipment overseas, please include $10.00 for each book ordered.